The volume fairly vibrates with erudition and esprit. In his prose, as in his poetry, Shapiro enchants.
—Ange Mlinko, winner of the Randall Jarrell Award in Criticism

The prose assembled in You Are The You, an invaluable complement to David's poetry, is a master class in the aesthetics of the New York School and the Avant Garde in general.
—from the Foreword by David Lehman

"Poetry is magic after Rimbaud," Shapiro writes at 17 in the prescient piece that opens the volume—then goes on in the works that follow to disseminate the magic. His bent is artistic and pluralistic; a sui generis mix of lightness and depth, of wide-minded, many-angled, improvisatory verve and great freshness of thought and language. Sympathetic insight into the aesthetic processes of others is his forte. He invokes William James: love discerns more than "blinding objectivity." He relates the discontinuities of John Ashbery to the Uncertainty Principle and notes that Frank Lima's use of "the disjunctive poetics of the New York School" is an art of "welding disparate worlds" together. It's an art innate to Shapiro's prose, where voices and ideas from multiple perspectives combine to shed light on a work, amplify a discussion, deepen a context. Likewise, the interviews are riveting partly because of the candor and camaraderie with which he brings the words and views of other thinkers into his replies ... As for the New York School, thanks in part to David Shapiro's remarkable elucidations, it's a movement that has expanded the sayable for innumerable poets and readers and remains a liberating, poetry-wide force.
—from the Editor's Note by Kate Farrell

All of David Shapiro's writing is simultaneously earnest and explosive.
—Joanna Fuhrman, author of Data Mind and co-editor of Hanging Loose Press

You Are The You

Writings and Interviews on Poetry, Art, and the New York School

You Are The You

Writings and Interviews on Poetry, Art, and the New York School

David Shapiro
Edited by Kate Farrell
Foreword by David Lehman

MadHat Press
Cheshire, Massachusetts

MadHat Press
MadHat Incorporated
PO Box 422, Cheshire, MA 01225

Copyright © 2025 David Shapiro
All rights reserved

The Library of Congress has assigned
this edition a Control Number of
2025930023

ISBN 978-1-952335-91-4 (paperback)

Cover design by F. J. Bergmann
Cover image: detail of *David and Lindsay Shapiro*
by Fairfield Porter, oil on canvas, 1972
by permission of the Fairfield Porter Estate and Lindsay Shapiro
Photo by Matt Flynn
Book design by MadHat Press

www.madhat-press.com

First Printing
Printed in the United States of America

In memory of Kenneth Koch

Table of Contents

Foreword: The Perishing Beauty of Light Snow by David Lehman	xi
Editor's Note by Kate Farrell	xxi
Words in A State of Sparkle	1
Urgent Masks: An Introduction to John Ashbery's Poetry	7
Imago Mundi	21
Transcendental Meditations: Review of *The Crystal Lithium* by James Schuyler	31
In Conversation with John Tranter	35
Falling Upwards	47
Toward Stevens: The Will to Poetry	49
On a Villanelle by Elizabeth Bishop	65
Review of *Days and Nights* by Kenneth Koch	73
Proverbs	77
Review of *The Complete Poems* by Edwin Denby	97
Review of *The Happy Man* by Donald Hall	101
After the New York School: Interview by Joseph Lease	105
Walter Benjamin: A Lost Poem	112
Six Books of Poetry: A Maximalist Manifesto	111
Review of *Operation Memory* by David Lehman	145
A Night Painting of Ron Padgett	149
Poetry and Architecture, Architecture and Poetry	159
The Funeral of Jan Palach	159
Denise Levertov: Among the Keys	163
Living Things: The Poetry of Anne Porter	171
Van Gogh, Heidegger, Schapiro, Derrida: The Truth in Criticism	175
Pluralist Music: An Interview by Joanna Fuhrman	193
I Loved You Once by Pushkin	204
The Story of the Tower of Babel	205
Conversation with Michael Goldberg	213
Frank Lima: The Poetry of Everyday Life and the Tradition of American Darkness	229
Some Notes Toward Twombly: A Man Without a Boat, or A Boat for Everybody	235

Table of Contents

A Book of Glass	251
New York Quarterly Craft Interview by Malachi Black	253
A Birthday Notebook for JA: *The Vermont Notebook*	291
The Painting that Took the Place of a Mountain: Letters to Tsibi	303
The Joy of Influence	315
You Are The You	328
Acknowledgments	329
Biographies	331

Foreword: The Perishing Beauty of Light Snow
by David Lehman

"You write naturally in sentences," Gertrude Stein told Scott Fitzgerald. David Shapiro spoke naturally in poems. David was a master of table talk, and a great pleasure of his new book is that it contains several compelling interviews with him. Listening to his freewheeling discourse, you get a strong idea of the associative logic that makes his writing so unusual and enriching.

The prose assembled in *You Are The You*, an invaluable complement to David's poetry, is a master class in the aesthetics of the New York School and the Avant Garde in general. It is also an introduction to his enthusiasms and a wondrous cabinet of casually tossed-off insights. "The Bible is an anthology," he tells Joanna Fuhrman in an interview in *Rain Taxi*. In *Pataphysics* magazine, he describes Marianne Moore to Joseph Lease as a "kind of collage poet" who was interested in collage as "a principle of continuity." And surprisingly, tells Malachi Black in the *New York Quarterly*: "Some people seem to think that I have a Catherine Deneuve complex, that I'm looking for an aesthetic of easy symmetry."

My friendship with David goes back more than five decades to our undergraduate days at Columbia University. From the start, I admired his *sui generis* discourse, whether expressed in formal writing and interviews or in our private conversations and correspondence. In the hope of capturing the spirit of his discourse, I've organized what follows according to some of the tropes that recur in David's mosaic of talk and imagination.

1.) Snow

When Malachi Black playfully notes in *A New York Quarterly Interview* that it's "not uncommon for snow to appear in a David Shapiro poem, or hands, or different colors, even violins," David runs with the riff. "I sometimes feel that it's terrible to have so much snow in my work. Now that global warming is becoming a reality, however, maybe it will have a political aspect."

The subject of snow stretches in David's mind from Wallace Stevens' "The Snow Man" to a book called *The Economic Significance of Snow* and from there to snow as a holiday from school. He recalls admirable lines from John Wheelwright's "Why Must You Know?" in which a frozen bird falls on the snow. And from James Schuyler come these lines depicting "night / and snow and the threads of life / for once seen as they are / in ropes like roots." David reveals that his own "Einstein poem, 'Snow at Night,' was a collage of footnotes of idiotic things that a biographer or two had put down."

Snow also enters David's mind when he writes "A Letter" dated May 28, 2008, in verse to an old college friend (me) after I told him about my visit to Mongolia and what the poets there were up to:

> It's three o'clock. The Mongolians should be asleep.
> Mayakovsky sleeps and Josef Brodsky
> used my book as a door stop
> a few minutes after I gave it to him.
> The Inner and Outer Mongolia sleep.
> And David sleeps with Stacey in Mongolia
> and David's eyes rapid as a sparrow
> or a starling in snow sees something
> in the bookshelf: an old book sleeps
> like bats in the rafters like bats out of mind.
> I will try to find some poems in the snow
> Or little lashed poets all in a row.
> It is late now, later than a monkey.
> I look in the mirror and am just like a gibbon.
> Same voice box, same genitalia, same pride.
> Who has placed us in this zoo of worlds?
> He who has a strong bell and shepherd's arrows.
> Let us take as they say arrows of our enemy
> And use them in our fight as if they were our own.
> O photo of myself I hope to find you
> the one that doesn't cause disgust in Baudelaire
> the one I saw on the island of love in mistranslation
> never knowing whether we had landed or
> were taking off. The island had little snow.
> The loudest sound was some flirtation.
> I sent you my virtual collage. You sent me Mongolia.

The occasion is simply hello and goodbye—a quotidian occasion that is a hallmark of New York style. A casual erudition is another. The poem begins with an allusion to Mayakovsky's suicide poem and ends in an exchange of gifts, a statement of friendship. The pivot occurs when "David's eyes rapid as a sparrow / or a starling in snow sees something / in the bookshelf" and in those lines I like to think that "David" stands for both author and recipient.

In the *New York Quarterly* interview, snow makes it onto David's list of indispensables:

A friend of mine once said in college, "It's hard for a leper to have a hypochondriac as a friend." I said, "That's a defense of why we need Kafka. Lepers should listen to other lepers. That is, if we're all damaged in particularly interesting ways, we need each other as compensation. I find it very hard to believe in life without Mozart, chocolate, snow, or James Joyce."

In the dialectic of David Shapiro's imagination, snow stood at the opposite end of fire, as in this "self-cento" he composed under the title of "Haiku of Two Towers and for Rudy Burckhardt" in 2007:

and so the snow fell
and covered up poetry
and so the snow fell

and so the fire fell
and covered up our friends.

2) *The Joys of Influence and Affinity*

When the late Australian poet John Tranter asks about the New York School in an interview in *Meanjin* magazine, David airs a general dissatisfaction with academic labels, which he likens to "false can-openers." He tries out analogies ("Kenneth [Koch] is like our Claus Oldenburg, and John Ashbery is like Rauschenberg and Johns put together"). But it is precisely the inclusiveness of the New York School—its anti-programmatic program— that makes it hard to summarize. You can enjoy the music of Elliott Carter and learn a lot from John Cage, too, and the differences between them are more interesting than the similarities. The same is true of the writers on whom the New York School has had a beneficent influence.

In the Tranter interview, David discusses the New York aesthetic as one that embraces "speed recollected in tranquility," the joys of influence from diverse sources, and the idea of poetry as an escape from the confessional personality ("purple, melodramatic, encrusted") in vogue when Robert Lowell was considered our most distinguished poet. On the value of spontaneity, David quotes Ted Berrigan: "My poems really are written in the present," which may be the single pithiest way to state the originality of Frank O'Hara's *Lunch Poems*.

David's loyalty to the aesthetics of the New York School goes back to his emergence as a teenage prodigy both as a violinist and as a poet. He discovered Frank O'Hara's poems in Donald Allen's important anthology, *The New*

American Poetry. In pursuit of O'Hara's spirit, David met Kenneth Koch, who championed his work. As an undergraduate at Columbia, David was Koch's favorite student. Kenneth handed David a typescript of "The Skaters," Ashbery's masterpiece, which affected us in the mid-1960s the way *The Waste Land* affected its first readers forty years earlier. In an issue of *Conjunctions* in honor of Ashbery's 80th birthday, David describes that moment: "I read forty pages with the sensation a young violinist has listening to Heifetz play with Piatigorsky and Feuermann the late Mozart *Divertimento*."

In an essay on Ashbery in *Field #5*, David discusses *Three Poems*, the title of which has a particular significance given that the book is written in prose. David acknowledges the Auden of *The Orators*, among other literary precedents, but grows most excited when he turns to metaphor and simile. "Ashbery's intense employment [of prose] is an adventure, as interesting as the day Jasper Johns remembers dreaming of painting the American flag." Even the useless simile has its uses: Ashbery favors "an extravagance of connection that leads nowhere, as in Koch's 'as useless as a ski in a barge.'"

David remarks in the *NYQ* interview that Koch loved "similes as in Pasternak, that are drawn from everyday life. 'It was hot as the top level of a Turkish bath.'" Why is Koch's work under-valued? In "Words in a State of Sparkle," an early piece that appeared in the *Columbia Spectator*, David writes: "A fair response to Koch's work seems almost never in the coming: his humor has steel wires inside it, as does Mozart's." And a review of Koch's *Days and Nights* in the *Poetry Project Newsletter* suggests that it is not only because the comic is confused with the non-serious but also because Koch has been misunderstood. "Like [the paintings of] the late Fairfield Porter, who abhorred abstract antinomies, Koch's poetry is always at once abstract and realistic, always concerned with process but never careless, always embodied with the light of the particular."

Praising Ron Padgett's ambitious prose poem "Light as Air" in a *Talisman* review of Padgett's *The Big Something*, David evokes the melancholy of Cézanne's poker players to modify the poem's buoyancy. "The poet of optimism turns out to be the master of a fairly ambivalent misery; the theme of light, as in the impressionism of much of the poem, is made into something melancholy through self-consciousness." And to clinch the deal: "In Japanese, the phrase for 'light snow' means 'perishing beauty.'" By means of such associative logic, David arrives at a succinctly stated conclusion: "Padgett's burden has indeed been evanescence, how to make of New York School impressionism something solid as the poems of the tradition."

David has illuminating things to say about Ashbery's sources (Gertrude Stein "furnishes a specimen source for the opacities" of "Europe" in *The Tennis Court Oath*); about Edwin Denby's sonnets ("In Denby, precision and energetic flair replace Romantic atmospherics. He is the Balanchine of poetry"), and about Walter Benjamin: "there's been a mistake made about Benjamin, where he's either treated as a Marxist or treated as a supernaturalist. There's another way, which is to treat him as a poet." In the *American Poetry Review*, David considers Frank Lima's "journey from the poems of prison, drug-addiction, and the frenzy of sexuality to his new poems and autobiographical narratives." The verdict: "a triumph of what Erik Ericson used to speak of as the antinomy of wisdom and bitterness." I don't pretend to understand what it means to say, as David does in the *Poetry Mailing List*, that Wallace Stevens is "the central Lucretian explanatory poet in his minimal explanatory mode." But of Stevens' crucial presence in David Shapiro's aesthetic, there can be no doubt.

Ever wonder what became of the painter Mike Goldberg, a central figure in some of Frank O'Hara's most memorable poems (such as "Why I Am Not a Painter")? Here, from David's lively conversation with him, is Goldberg on the subject of Pop Art: "I thought very little of Andy [Warhol], but at the same time, Andy forced all of us to look at art in a different way and that's not given to many people to do. And I always thought that Andy was the purest disciple of Duchamp or an inheritor of Duchamp."

Of exceptional interest is "The Story of the Tower of Babel," in which David discusses his Judaic heritage and identity. Here is an excerpt from his brilliant reading of the tale.

> All the commentaries agree to disagree. The story must be placed next to destroyed contemporaries. Noah's generation was butchered in a stormy allegory for its disunity in murderous internecine corruption. Meanwhile, the Babel Tower was built with urbane or imperial unity. A unity that was only punishable by multiplicity, of course. Even the modern Hebrew poet Bialik speaks of the two essential movements of the Jewish people as dispersal and homecoming. And further, the Babel story speaks of the essential concentrate of 'civilization' as either a profound mistake or monstrous excess. A Blakean reading, for instance, will permit the Tower always to be more interesting than the sin of building it. After the covenant, we hardly expect a rainbow behind this Ziggurat, but we are compelled to see the story as

a uniquely horrifying addendum to the Rainbow. A covenant of peace with man is immediately followed by a story of immense penology.

3) *The Spontaneous Aria*

David was a master of the spontaneous aria. During a phone conversation in 2009, I wrote down his words: "O imagine Donne reading Donne. I would be undone. If a poet bores you, just wake up and look for another voice. Lovers know that the voice is a sexual organ (see Jewish law). If your lover's voice doesn't please you, you are already divorced. If an architect's drawings are better than his house, you have made an ontological mistake."

4) *Advice*

In praise of memory: David has read widely and seems to have committed to memory much of what he has read. In a piece aptly called "The Joy of Influence," his imperative is to read everything, with a strict allegiance to nothing, and to integrate the greatest lines of poetry into your own discourse:

> Memorize something every day, and then even when you are waiting for a bus, you will be able to play 'Silence' by Cage or the poem you love. Like Buson's 'The sound of the bell / as it leaves the bell.' Or: 'one candle lights another candle / evening twilight.' Thousands of memorized poems, and you will endure all the glut and exile of the world.

5) *Collaboration*

When we were undergraduates at Columbia (he a junior, I a freshman), David took me under his wing and gave me advice on whom to read and what to listen to ("less Debussy and more German and radio music"). He criticized my poems severely (one of them was "too farfetched, hackneyed, or vulgar") excusing his candor by saying that my work "shows talent." David had already published his amazing first book *January*.

At a *Columbia Review* meeting he read aloud his four submissions for the next issue. First, he read a pantoum, "Master Canterel at Locus Solus," then "For the Princess Hello," in each case explaining the title's esoteric references. I remember the unforced laughter, a blend of astonishment and delight, when he said, "the next two poems have less difficult titles." They were "Ode" and "Elegy for Sports," and all four are as fresh today as when the twenty-year-old poet presented them to us.

Foreword

In college I shamelessly imitated his style. He and the poet Larry Wieder liked collaborating on midnight poems (one began: "Good morning, morning that I never see"), and they sometimes let me play along. A great collaborator, David likes corresponding by verse, and the miracle of e-mail allowed him and me to correspond in poetry in 2003 and 2007. On New Year's Day 2003 when we began, he suggested we exchange haiku in January, couplets in February, aphorisms in March. At first, I thought we should limit ourselves to one or two haiku a day. He replied "I agree: some days / are more inspiring: snow / city sparrows, friends. // But mostly, compact /as cell phones, haikus need / a whole day to grow—"

But when either of us got on a roll, there was no stopping him, as when the subject was snow. On January 17th, David wrote "Links of Snow":

> Snow to me, I say,
> Is what bananas are to
> Gabriel Marquez!
>
> I thought snow useless
> Until I saw a book sez:
> Economic Snow.
>
> A physicist cried:
> Wake up, David, you never
> Thought snow was useful!?
>
> No, no, no, never
> Have I ever thought that snow
> Was useful! To skis,
>
> trees, warming flowers,
> giving symbolists white hours—
> SNOW IS NOT MONEY!
>
> A snowman blinks, War.
> Time of the empire, fat whore!
> On the lawn, new snow!

In February 2003, we corresponded in couplets. On the thirteenth, David wrote:

Foreword

> A couplet comes down on you like death's storm.
> Afterwards, Dave, you're never quite so warm.
>
> A couplet edges downwards like black snow.
> But so dramatic! like snow in a Noh.

In March 2003, when we wrote aphorisms David continually surprised me with his deployment of the aphorism as a form consisting of an epigram plus commentary. Consider:

> A realist told me not to say, "If I die" but "When I die." I resented it. I also resent a friend who thinks he is my reality principle. I also hate women who think they are beyond the pleasure principle. I also hate poets who think hatred among poets is not shameful. It is real, but it is shameful (Freud's "Narcissism of small differences.")

And:

> Ron [Padgett] I call the Henry Fonda of poetry. When Frank O'Hara screamed at me at a party for being too prying, Ron saw me weeping and said, 'It's time for the straight men to leave,' I was sixteen and thought he was referring to comedy's straight men.

And:

> Speech is my medium. Have you ever really been charmed by a poet who spoke little? The shy poet, the wordless poet. George Plimpton tried to strangle me for talking too much, but he is also a great talker. I notice this. Kenneth Koch said to me at a party without resentment: This party is too small for our egos, David. John Ashbery is shy, but after a time, he is speedily cracking jokes as if he were a whole theater of comedians.

During our aphorism exchanges, David produced a terrific poem, one of his best from that period, when he took his point of departure from Kant's "Out of the crooked timber of humanity, no straight thing was ever made."

In fall 2007 we resumed the practice of daily exchanges by haiku. David defined the form for us:

> What's a haiku? sonnet
> condensed to even smaller
> nuns than Wordsworth.

Foreword

On the tenth of September, David composed this vision of Bashō, the great Japanese master of the haiku form:

> In wartime, Bashō
> saw dreams in the grass soldiers'
> dreams in soldiers' grass
>
> And near death, dying
> he saw his illness fly past
> perilously fast
>
> In a like autumn
> Basho said he was alone
> In the dingy night

David conjoins the minimalism of the Japanese haiku with the world of astrophysics in his poem "The Cherry-Blossom Proof":

> The Milky Way is shrinking
> So the cherry-blossoms are growing
> Larger. You write me longish letters.
> Therefore, God exists.

(*In Memory of an Angel*, City Lights, 2017)

You, reader, are the you in "You write me longer letters."

One of the benefits of collaborating with David on a daily basis was that you learned to express yourself in the required form, and I would like to conclude this little preface to David's new book of prose with the haiku sequence I wrote on 9/27/07. David's *New and Selected Poems* had just appeared:

> David Shapiro,
> let me congratulate you
> on the great reviews
>
> you should be getting.
> You deserve no less. Does each
> get what he deserves?

Foreword

>Maybe not, but you
>have written poems that will
>live on for decades
>
>and win new readers
>and inspire the poets
>of our future so
>
>mysterious and
>so strange to us who welcomed
>you when we were young.

Editor's Note
by Kate Farrell

You Are The You originated in the summer of 2017 in an email conversation with David Lehman. Thinking Lehman was still the general editor of the University of Michigan's *Poets on Poetry* series, I asked if they had considered publishing a volume of David Shapiro's prose. Lehman replied that if he were indeed still the editor—which he wasn't—he'd snap up the book. In the ensuing exchange, we speculated about the contents, agreeing it would ideally include some of Shapiro's interviews and poems on poetics. At a certain point, Lehman suggested that if I would edit the collection, he'd write a foreword. All hesitations on my part were quashed by the enthusiasm of Shapiro himself, soon my assiduous guide in tracking down the materials. Finding way too much for one volume, we set our sights on a compellingly various selection and left the rest for future collections.

Seven years later, not long after the completion of the manuscript, David Shapiro died of complications from Parkinson's disease. The tremendous outpouring of emotion that followed reinforced the notion that his legendary friendliness and generosity were synonymous with the open-hearted pluralism that buoyed and invigorated his thought and writing.

Prose was, for Shapiro, a prolific second calling, the prodigious other half of his writing. The author of monographs on John Ashbery, Jasper Johns, Piet Mondrian and Jim Dine, Shapiro had also produced numerous book chapters and forewords, columns for *ARTnews*, catalog essays for galleries and museums, and other sorts of articles and reviews. All while composing eleven books of poetry and teaching literature, art history, cinema and interdisciplinary courses at Columbia University, William Patterson University and the Irwin S. Chanin School of Architecture at the Cooper Union.

The book is largely organized in the chronological order that close to five decades of work seemed to call for. Details about the previous publication of a piece are noted on its first page, and interviews and poems about poetics are interspersed throughout. The volume opens with "Words in a State of Sparkle," a delightful review Shapiro wrote for the *Columbia Spectator* as a 17-year-old undergraduate. From here, the tone and style vary quite a lot— from the scholarly precision of an essay on van Gogh, to an exuberant riff on the wonders of reading, to singularly insightful pieces on figures like Elizabeth Bishop, John Ashbery, Barbara Guest, Jasper Johns and Denise Levertov. The

Editor's Note

mix of erudition and artistry in essays like "The Story of the Tower of Babel" and "Some Notes on Twombly" almost amounts to a new genre. The book's title *You Are The You*—with its Buberesque capital T—is taken from one of Shapiro's poems.

By age ten, David Shapiro, a violin and literary prodigy, had decided to be a poet. Every day, he checked out armloads of books, in a plan to read every poetry collection in the Newark Public Library. He kept "falling in love," he reported, with new poets without giving up the earlier ones. "A different poet," he tells the poet Joanna Fuhrman in an interview here, "would be a different universe." At 12 or 13, he discovered the poetic universes later known as the New York School and, at 15, met two of them—Frank O'Hara and Kenneth Koch—at the Wagner Poetry Conference. Soon after, he received a fan letter from John Ashbery. "I simply can't 'digest,'" wrote Ashbery, "the fact you are only fifteen." At 16, he enrolled at Columbia University, where he studied with Koch and the art historian Meyer Schapiro, both of whom became lasting friends and important mentors—the latter's "radiant pluralism," a north star for Shapiro's prose.

From the first, Shapiro was exceptionally attuned to the enthusiasms and concerns of the poets of the New York School, of which he would with time be regarded as a leading poet, exponent and scribe. He shared their fascination with collaboration and the mutually illuminating connections between the arts—and possessed the pair of traits whose "rare mixture" Mark Ford considers a prime characteristic of the group: "high seriousness leavened with a sense of humor" and "faith in the acrobatic capabilities of language." Shapiro insisted, however, that his greatest influence was "being born a violinist." He speaks of the discipline of long practice—and of the urge to write poetry as multiple as a chamber work by Beethoven or Bartok. Having come up with the term "the joy of influence" to counter Harold Bloom's "anxiety of influence," he says that, for him, one influence does not supplant another. He quotes Swedenborg: "The more angels, the more room," and in articles and interviews lists hosts of influences, from, say, Kafka, Stevens, Wittgenstein and Lady Murasaki to Martin Luther King, Pasternak, Maya Lin and the prophet Isaiah.

In an interview by Joseph Lease in *Pataphysics Magazine*, Shapiro's politics comes up—and the photo in *Life* magazine that made Shapiro's face the face of the Columbia Uprising. "I was part of the generation of '68," he says, "who thought they could do something"—then cites Lionel Abel's remark that we either overestimate that we can do everything or underestimate that we can do nothing. Asked about the title of his book *House (Blown Apart)*, he replies that while America is the "house blown apart," the title also refers to a poem by the 8th-century Chinese poet Tu Fu, in which a storm blows the poet's thatched roof off. Whereupon Tu Fu begins to dream (as the rain pours down and the village kids make fun of him) of a house with thousands of windows and doors that could "shelter all the poor scholars of the world." A "public dream," as Shapiro puts it elsewhere, "of shared and secret space." And it's not a stretch to see his prose—much of it composed at a time when the New York School was routinely deprecated and misunderstood—as a sheltering, multi-windowed house for the poets and artists he writes about.

"Poetry is magic after Rimbaud," writes Shapiro at 17 in the prescient piece that opens this volume—then goes on in the works that follow to disseminate the magic. His bent is artistic and pluralistic; a *sui generis* mix of lightness and depth, of wide-minded, many-angled, improvisatory verve and great freshness of thought and language. Sympathetic insight into the aesthetic processes of others is his forte. He invokes William James: love discerns more than "blinding objectivity." He links the discontinuities of John Ashbery to the Uncertainty Principle and notes that Frank Lima's use of "the disjunctive poetics of the New York School" is an art of "welding disparate worlds" together. It is an art innate to Shapiro's prose, where voices and ideas from multiple perspectives combine to shed light on a work, amplify a discussion, deepen a context. Likewise, the interviews are riveting partly because of the candor and camaraderie with which he brings the words and views of other thinkers into his replies.

As for the New York School, over the years spanned in these pages, it has come to stand for an era that, in retrospect, seems as salutary as it was exciting—as well as for the multi-minded, humor-leavened poetics whose "restless unities" and shifting perspectives seem ever more relevant to our wildly uncertain world. Thanks in part to Shapiro's remarkable elucidations, it's a movement that has expanded the sayable for innumerable poets and readers and remains a liberating, eye-opening poetry-wide force.

"You Are The You," the poem that closes the volume, encapsulates, in a sense, Shapiro's open-armed, New-York-School-inflected pluralist aesthetics. It starts as a simple love poem—"You are the you in this poem, / Mon amour"—

Editor's Note

then shifts to the bleak precarity of the world: "Harrisburg, mon amour. Boats break." A literary scuffle ensues, in which "So-and-so" (presumably a critic) asks the poet to whom "the you" in the poem refers. The poet protests—"Are you feeling well, So-and-so"—then states the obvious: "It's the beloved, So-and-so." "Oh is that all," shrugs the interloper. "Well ... she wouldn't think / It was so little," replies the poet, who once again addresses the beloved "you" directly, this time disclosing the vast expanses of her all-but-transcendent status: "To look up into your face / Is like looking into the devastated stars." A status lofty and ravaged as that of poetry itself ... Then characteristically brings in the rest of us:

> Lights of all kinds I traced,
> You and you and you and you.
> You are the you of this poem, mon amour.
> Boats break.

L to R: Gerard Malanga, Amiri Baraka, David Shapiro, Bill Berkson, Frank Lima, Frank O'Hara. Photo by William T. Wood. The 1962 Writing Conference at Wagner College at which the 15-year-old Shapiro initiated his association with the New York School.

Words in A State of Sparkle

Wallace Stevens writes somewhere that, although it is regarded as quite normal for politicians to study politics, for a poet to regard language as his concern makes him a "fribble and something less than a man of reason." An example of the outcome of language contemplating itself can be seen regularly in the contents of "C," *A Journal of Poetry*, edited by Ted Berrigan, and available throughout New York. Concentration on freshening up words, and rendering them into a state of sparkle, seems to be the united goal of the artists represented therein, many of New York orientation: Kenneth Koch, John Ashbery, Frank O'Hara, Allen Ginsberg.

With the mention of the latter, the aesthetic questions start rolling, since Ginsberg has consistently avowed a love-and-social-reform approach to poetry, and his influence seems moral as much or more than poetical. Berrigan, however, as editor, seems simpatico to both the surreal technical innovations of Ashbery and the Whitmanesque breadth of Ginsberg, the superb and shocking prose of William Burroughs (portions appearing in "C"), and the very talented poetry—though perhaps not as fulfilled or developed—of younger poets: Joseph Ceravolo, Ron Padgett, Frank Lima. For this catholicity, which seems sometimes to border on sloppiness or a mad friendliness, Ted Berrigan is rather to be commended than despised.

The Columbia Daily Spectator (The Supplement), Volume VI, No.2, edited by Robert Caserio (November 24, 1964). A review of a legendary issue of "C," *A Journal of Poetry*, Vol. 1, Number 9, edited by Ted Berrigan, published by Lorenz Gude (Summer, 1964). Written when Shapiro was a 17-year-old undergraduate at Columbia University.

To give an example of the plenitude of a single issue, one may take the current fall issue as an exemplar. Featured in the issue were a group of short poems by Koch and some animal-plays by him also. Most striking for an efficient view of the fantastic, the stars of the plays are giraffes and elephants, walruses and hippos. The result is a dreamlike theatricality which should be a good antidote for the present miserable state of New York theater, in which used-up and dead language are being purveyed as "avant-garde."

Another attraction of the issue is a long love poem by Joseph Ceravolo, entitled: "What Is That Flying Away?" Ceravolo employs a flat-surface technique of extremely simple statements. These strokes, however, are charged and result in a new music:

> What's the name of this
> sea level? I can't
> get up
> It's so diligent to
> shine.

Frank O'Hara's long poem "For the Chinese New Year and for Bill Berkson" and Allen Ginsberg's "The Change" are two masterworks also offered in this issue. O'Hara moves from almost unbearable cynicisms ("A wart / something dumb & despicable that I love") to grand lyrical statement ("it seems that breath could easily fill a balloon and drift away"). He accomplishes all this with a casual manner never seen before, as if his poetic energy were as natural as puffing a cigarette.

This is not the case, of course, with Ginsberg, who makes any reader aware of the terrific anxieties and fears pressed upon him in his prophetic role. It's the Kierkegaardian world of the poet bleeding in front of his audience: "Oh how wounded, how wounded, I murder the beautiful Chinese women." Allen Ginsberg determines here to establish a love relationship with his readers; he is of the few who offers more than he asks and offers to give us himself "before preaching or law."

Ginsberg has been defining his prophetic role for over fifteen years. His first book, *Howl*, besides being a superb personal lamentation for a group of his friends, outlined the conduct, gestures, and legend of a generation of war-wrecked young men, drifting between Frisco and

New York. In his second book, *Kaddish*, Ginsberg published some even more frankly political poetry, namely "Death to Van Gogh's Ear," in which attention is not mainly to the melodic beauties of line-forms, but to the accusations against American civilization in general, and against Hoover, Congress, narcotic laws, movies, etc., in particular. His last book, *Reality Sandwiches*, strikes a more lyric personal note throughout, but like Mayakovsky to the Russian Revolution, Ginsberg is one of the rare American poets whose most personal gestures become publicly didactic. He represents a poignant cry for a free press, pacifism, and creativity. Often, however, he is aware that his prophetic role is comical: at such points the need for a "true" statement becomes even more agonizing and crucial.

The graceful and fresh work of a younger poet, Ron Padgett, is also represented here. Padgett (Columbia College '64), a sometime editor of "C" and the *White Dove Review*, creates with an exciting silence around his work and a spare and "delicious" music. I am not qualified to talk of the work of William Burroughs, but he must be read, and bears an interesting relationship with the work of the poets published here, a relationship of method.

Many of the poets in "C" are taking American poetry on a trip it has never gone on before. Frank O'Hara's transformation of New Yorkese, gossip and the world of art, is something grand to witness. A fair response to Koch's work seems almost never in the coming: his humor has steel wires inside it, as does Mozart's.

Koch's poetry represents the outcome of a certain aesthetic, that is, that poetry bears only one relationship to discursive prose—poetry contains words. In Koch's poetry, flat statement is utilized as one more color, as are fact, description, metaphysical questions, etc. This does not mean that Koch isn't concerned with producing real emotional effects: this is his prime concern, but he realizes that his only weapons and tickle-instruments are new combinations of words, not an attitude or mood. And the words no longer have the easy one-to-one relationship with the external world they might have had for poets in 1870. Poetry is magic, after Rimbaud, the successful completion of an intellectual, musical illusion. As John Ashbery wrote me in a letter: "The subject matter of our poetry is the way things happen." Many readers, in search of content that appears absent in the new poetry, may now understand that occurrence and repetition of seemingly arbitrary events is dramatic content.

Koch, Ashbery, and O'Hara all utilize chain-association and breakdown of "logical" connection, in ways that can be nothing short of humiliating for a whole generation of American writers (Wilbur, Tate, Nemerov) who seem to have retired with the publication of Archibald MacLeish's "Ars Poetica." The fault with the New Yorkers is often a preciosity or a certain tedium of the non-consequential: perhaps due to the very refinement and facility which give the good poems value.

At any rate, the saintly Ginsberg is usually present for those who like extraordinary mixed bags. Where else can one find his work and these other poets? A bonus is the startling cover-work of artist Joe Brainard. Read this magazine for what is in the air in poetry.

David Shapiro at President Kirk's desk during the six-day campus uprising and protest at Columbia University, New York. Photo by Gerald Upham

When Shapiro died in May 2024, both the *Washington Post* and the *New York Times* included the above photo in their obituaries. After the photo appeared in *Life* magazine in May 1968, it came to represent, as the *Post* put it, "the era's revolutionary zeal." Shapiro was an avid participant in the antiwar protests, but as both articles note, not a leader of break-ins. Gerald Upham, a fellow student, handed him the cigar and snapped the picture. Shapiro discusses the photo and the relation between poetry and politics in an interview on p. 105 by Joseph Lease.

Urgent Masks: An Introduction to John Ashbery's Poetry

Some movement is reversed and the urgent masks
Speed toward a totally unexpected end
Like clocks out of control. Is this the gesture
That was meant, long ago, the curving in

Of frustrated denials ...

—"Song," *The Double Dream of Spring*

... But there was no statement
At the beginning. There was only a breathless waste,
A dumb cry shaping everything in projected
After-effects orphaned by playing the part intended for them,
Though one must not forget that the nature of this
Emptiness, these previsions
Was that it could only happen here, on this page held
Too close to be legible, sprouting erasures, except that they
Ended everything in the transparent sphere of what was
Intended only a moment ago, spiraling further out its
Gesture finally dissolving in the weather.

—"Clepsydra," *Rivers and Mountains*

Note: Observations in quotes are from Shapiro's extensive conversations with Ashbery, 1964–71.

David Shapiro

John Ashbery once took a course of lectures in music by Henry Cowell at the New School. Cowell remarked that the intervals in music [the distance between the pitches of two sequential notes] became wider as music grew more sophisticated. "For instance, if you compare 'The Volga Boatmen' and the 'Love Duet' from *Tristan und Isolde*, you see how vastly wide the intervals have become; and the ear seemingly becomes accustomed to unaccustomed intervals 'as time goes by.'" Chromaticism is also apparent in the tone clusters of Cowell himself, analogous to the striking juxtapositions of Ashbery, but one can deny expectations with a much wider palette of possibilities. One cannot really anticipate the next note in many serial pieces, and this sort of suspense is a fine quality of Ashbery's own work, and a theme:

> These decibels
> Are a kind of flagellation, an entity of sound
> Into which being enters, and is apart.
> Their colors on a warm February day
> Make for masses of inertia, and hips
> Prod out of the violet-seeming into a new kind
> Of demand that stumps the absolute because not new
> In the sense of the next one in an infinite series
> But, as it were, pre-existing or pre-seeming in
> Such a way as to contrast funnily with the unexpectedness
> And somehow push us all into perdition.

("The Skaters," *Rivers and Mountains*)

When Ashbery interviewed Henri Michaux for *Art News*, the French fabricator of imaginary communities spoke of surrealism as *une grande permission*, in the sense of an army leave. Surrealism tends to be used and abused; for example, Robert Bly tends to exaggerate certain overblown qualities of Spanish surrealism. Ashbery's surrealism is subtler. Raymond Roussel's flat, bland, and objective style, typified by Michel Leiris as "French as one is taught to write it by manuals in lycées,"

Field #5, edited by David Young and Stuart Friebert (Fall 1971). Reprinted in *A Field Guide to Contemporary Poetry and Poetics*, edited by Stuart Friebert, David Walker and David Young (Oberlin College Press, 1997).

a French that can comically be compared to Larousse, has been a minor if decided influence. Ashbery was a connoisseur of Roussel and began a doctoral dissertation on him, but decided not to go through with it, although characteristically he collected many minute particulars about the eccentric. One associates the modulated parodies of narration in *Rivers and Mountains* with the labyrinthine parentheses of Roussel's poems and novels—a contagion of the parodistic tone that seems to lead structurally to a "Chinese box" or play-within-a-play. Apart from this parenthetical mania, other idiosyncrasies of the author of *Locus Solus* did not impinge on the early work of Ashbery, who did not read him thoroughly until the 1950s, which he spent in France. Later Ashbery wittily employs another device of Roussel—the specious simile, "the kind that tells one less than you would know if the thing were stated flatly." In place of the organic and necessary simile, Ashbery learned from the French master an extravagance of connection that leads nowhere, as in Koch's "as useless as a ski in a barge," though this example is perhaps still too suggestive. "As useless as a ski" would be Ashbery's paradigmatic revision. Ashbery is also a master of the false summation, the illogical conclusion couched in the jargon of logic, reminding one of the false but rich scholarship of Borges:

> We hold these truths to be self-evident:
> That ostracism, both political and moral, has
> Its place in the twentieth-century scheme of things;
> That urban chaos is the problem we have been seeing into and
>   seeing into,
> For the factory, deadpanned by its very existence into a
> Descending code of values, has moved right across the road from
>   total financial upheaval
> And caught regression head on....
> ....
> To sum up: We are fond of plotting itineraries
> And our pyramiding memories, alert as dandelion fuzz....
>
> ("Decoy," *The Double Dream of Spring*)

> The rise of capitalism parallels the advance of romanticism
> And the individual is dominant until the close of the nineteenth century.
> In our own time, mass practices have sought to submerge the personality
> By ignoring it, which has caused it to branch out in all directions.
> ....
> And yet it results in a downward motion, or rather a floating one
>
> ("Definition of Blue," *The Double Dream of Spring*)

Ashbery has properly been called a "business-like and rather peculiar" child of the muse of Rimbaud. Auden also places him, in the rather distant tones of the Introduction to *Some Trees*, within the tradition of Rimbaud's *dérèglement de tous les sens*. Contrary to expectation, Ashbery denies French poetry as a major influence. He does, however, acknowledge the influence of Pierre Reverdy, whom he read as a "simple poet" accessible to a student with limited French; he later translated some cubist concoctions. He admires "the completely relaxed, oxygen-like quality" of Reverdy, whose cadences he likens to "breathing in big gulps of fresh air."

Roussel, of course, is a very "prosy" poet and Ashbery too is interested in the poetic possibilities of conventional prose, the prose of newspaper articles. His recent poems in particular function by proceeding from cliché to cliché, in a "seamless web" of banality transformed, by dint of combination and deformation, into a Schwitters-like composition in which the refuse of a degraded quotidian is fused into a new freshness:

> It is never too late to mend. When one is in one's late thirties, ordinary things—like a pebble or a glass of water—take on an expressive sheen. One wants to know more about them, and one is in turn lived by them. Young people might not envy this kind of situation, perhaps rightly so, yet there is now interleaving the pages of suffering and indifference to suffering a prismatic space that cannot be seen, only felt as the result of an angularity that must have existed from earliest times and is only now succeeding in making its presence felt through the mists of helpless acceptance

of everything else projected on our miserable, dank span of days....
The pain that drained the blood from your cheek when you were
young and turned you into a whitened spectre before your time is
converted back into a source of energy that peoples this world of
perceived phenomena with wonder.

("The New Spirit," *Three Poems*)

The use of prose elements in poetry, as in Williams and Pound, is so diffused a technique that it rarely provokes sensations of novelty, but Ashbery's intense employment is an adventure, as interesting as the day Jasper Johns remembers dreaming of painting the American flag. The prosaic elements in the early Auden influenced Ashbery; the touching qualities of ordinary speech and journalism and old diaries in *The Orators* were precursors. Collage elements for Ashbery's poem "Europe" were taken from a book for girls written at the time of the First World War. The book, entitled *Girl of the Biplane*, which he picked up by accident on the quais of Paris, is one reason for much of the placid plane imagery of "Europe." At the time, Ashbery was "collaging" a great deal as a symptom of an imagined "dead-end" period in his writing, and also due to the fact that living in France he felt cut off from American speech. He often received American magazines and manipulated their contents as a stimulus and pretext for further poetry. The grand collapses often noted in "Europe," its dashes and discontinuities called a "new poetic shorthand" by Koch, are one result of his *collagiste* direction. Though Ashbery's poetry has led most recently to a calm clearness, it began with the presentation of "objects" and "idioms" in explicitly dislocated form.

> sweetheart ...   the stamp
> ballooning you
> vision I thought you
> forget, encouraging your vital organs
> Telegraph. The rifle—a page folded over.
>
> More upset, wholly meaningless, the willing sheath

("Europe," *The Tennis Court Oath*)

His poetry had something of the "pathos of obscurity" as Lovejoy speaks of it, and the "pathos of incomprehensibility" was very much part of the mystique of such writing, though Ashbery always pointed toward principles of cohesion by discontinuity, if using the concealments of riddles and hints:

> She was dying but had time for him—
> brick. Men were carrying the very heavy things—
>   dark purple, like flowers.
> Bowl lighted up the score just right

("Europe")

Stein furnishes a specimen source for the opacities of this text. One must with Ashbery discriminate carefully between the nongrammatical, the nonsensical, the semantically inappropriate, and the tabooed. In the manner of a linguist obtaining the "feeling" of the limits of a grammar, Ashbery has developed the theme of "unacceptability," and related it with great wit to allied concepts of *absurdité, sottises, bétises,* and *l'absurde*.

There are a plethora of analogues in the associated arts. At the time Ashbery was writing as art editor for the International Edition of *The Herald Tribune*, de Kooning, Kline and Pollock with extreme dash and discontinuity were calling attention to the expunging of the copula and the coherent figure, and to the thematic of composition itself. Later the New Realists were to revive Duchamp's abrupt presentation of everyday objects as an introduction to what Ashbery called, in a comment on the New Realists, "the colorful indifferent universe." The self-conscious mid-progress shifts of narrations in Ashbery's *collagiste* poems are distinctly and masterfully of the age in which Jackson Pollock threw himself on the canvas, a proof and "permission," though Ashbery unexpectedly characterizes himself as more aural than visual, despite his participation in the art world.

The influence of psychoanalysis, permitting a more or less watery relationship with the unconscious and everyday mind, and corollary devices of "dipping into" an almost completely associational stream ("What else is there?") is another common heritage of technique

Ashbery shares with the abstract expressionists and surrealists. The Arthur Craven translation, "Elephant Languor," was interesting to Ashbery largely because he felt it resembled certain associational, disjunct narrations that he had already achieved. Ashbery has called attention to more than one neglected poet, and as a matter of fact has considered editing a kind of anthology of Neglected Poets, one that could include Wheelwright, David Schubert, Samuel Greenberg, and F. T. Prince, bizarre cousins or in-laws of Ashbery, all applying the same "syntax of dreams" for dramatistic purposes.

Ashbery's work, begun with kinds of *disjecta membra*, coalesces at certain periods in big coherent works: "Europe," "The Skaters," "The New Spirit," "The System." The development from collage of seemingly despairing fragments to unbroken paragraphs of di Chirico-like prose (Ashbery admits to di Chirico's prose, not painting, as an influence, of which more later) may be likened to the development of one of Ashbery's favorite composers—Busoni. "Busoni wrote a piano piece entitled 'The Turning Point,' and all his later music fittingly seems different from music earlier than that piece." The disjointed and indecisive has the look, at least, of a highly unified music. Ashbery's large compositions achieve this "look" of compositional unity while remaining what Coleridge has called a multeity. Composition in these works is not random but more a matter of parsimoniously distributing disparate images and tones and parodies than of unifyings and harmonizings. Ginsberg found the tone of Pope in "The Skaters," and the mock-heroic here does sometimes bear resemblance to the highly polished surface of "The Rape of the Lock." The highly polished surface in Ashbery, however, is less a social hint than a *memento mori* of the veneer of a world of manufactured objects and smooth, unbroken concrete. "The Skaters" may be thought of as a radiant porphyry of a variety of rhetoric, including imitations of Whitman, Baudelaire, science textbooks, William Hung's Tu Fu translations, Theodore Roethke, and John Ashbery. As he has described them, his intentions in respect to "The Skaters" were "to see how many opinions I had about everything." The most alarming feature of this style is the way it keeps upsetting our charming equilibrium and understanding of tone. After a quaint satire on the classic Oriental story of the failing student, Ashbery announces: "The tiresome old man is telling us his life-story." To some, his meditations upon or within meditations of self-laceration add more to the absurdity of the universe than interpret it, but these are finally friendly satires which point to the fact that unity, as we dream of it, is not realizable. One dreams of the perfect language within the fallen universe. Ashbery's deceptive drifts and accumulations of parody always erupt in the dramatic return which surprises and regulates, as in Proust. By his grand multeity in unity, his surprising simultaneity in unity, and a type of probabilistic unity, he achieves something of the misery and joy of a Jacques Callot baroque. He has always avoided the vanity that, as Señor Borges warned this writer once, derives from purely random techniques. But the specter of indeterminacy and uncertainty shadows his structural convolutions and involutions, if only in the numerous, self-lacerating dwarfs that appear and disappear throughout his poems.

Ashbery called my attention recently to a discussion of reticence by the poet Margaret Atwood: "I don't want to know how I write poetry. Poetry is dangerous. I believe most poets will go to any lengths to conceal their own reluctant scanty insight both from others and from themselves. Paying attention to how you do it is like stopping in the middle of any other totally involving and pleasurable activity ... to observe yourself suspended in the fatally suspended inner mirror." Ashbery has been most extreme in his reluctance to pad his poetry with what he calls the "stuff of explanation," just as he has been reluctant to be anything but a "practical" or "anecdotal" critic of the arts. He has, however, for one of his central *topoi*, the one called for by F. S. C. Northrop in his discussion of the future of poetry—the breakdown of causality in the nineteenth century sense. His discontinuities tend to throw us most clearly in the middle of the century of the Uncertainty Principle; one in which Whitehead called for the expunging of copula for a clearer style. The montages of Pound's cinematic Oriental translations are part of this lucid tradition of juxtaposition. Most of the best passages of Ashbery's poetry, moreover, like those of Stevens, deal with the practitioner's point of view and *praktik*, however veiled. His poetry, though not vulgarly explanatory, is in the manner of the "action" painters, a criticism of poetry itself as much as of life. A dice-playing God does indeed reign over the "sly Eros" of Ashbery's kingdom.

Ashbery's first book, *Some Trees*, is already filled with revitalizations of forms that had become connotatively encrusted. His sestina, "The Painter," an early example of such revitalization (1948), is influenced by Elizabeth Bishop. Her sestina in *North and South* employed certain common-end-words such as "coffee" and "balcony" that charmed Ashbery, and certainly the meticulously comical, soft-voiced rhetoric shows the rapport between them. Ashbery has elsewhere spoken of his love of Bishop's more recent "Over 2000 Illustrations and a Complete Concordance," a properly Pierre Meynardesque title which culminates in the—for Ashbery—inexhaustibly numinous line, "And looked and looked our infant sight away." The copula of "and" and its *mysterium* in repetition is part of the theme of Bishop's poem, and of Ashbery's poetry in general. The sestina form, therefore, with its arbitrary and sometimes comically stiff canon, is a fitting "receptacle" for the play of discontinuity and copula. Ashbery's sestinas, as opposed to the more coherent ones of Auden and Pound, make much of a purposeful barrage of the unusual mid-progress shifts and blurred drama. Another example of disjointed and spiky writing within rigid form is the eclogue published in *Turandot*:

> Cuddie: I need not raise my hand
> Colin: She burns the flying peoples
> Cuddie: To hear its old advice
> Colin: And spear my heart's two beasts
> Cuddie: Or cover with its mauves
> Colin: And I depart unhurt

("Eclogue")

"This poem was written after a bleak period of unproductiveness in 1951, when I was in publishing. I was somewhat awakened by a concert of John Cage's music." This music, more than anything then happening in painting, shook him and seemed to give once more the permission to find a form in the fertile formlessness into which he had wandered. There is a kind of simultaneous irony or depth to Ashbery's work, as if a critic paused to announce that he was invalidating all his critical statements including the present one he was making, and yet continued. His simultaneity is also that of chamber music, in which the "narration" of four voices can seem, as in Haydn, to recreate the coming possibilities of a domestic quarrel over the dishtowel. His domesticity and Firbankian penchant for gossip can be seen further enlarged in his collaborative venture, *A Nest of Ninnies*, which received the comically negative critique of Auden that it was one of the few contemporary novels that lacked sex. His pantoum, in *Some Trees*, inspired by the one in Ravel's "Trio," is another example of a witty use of an arbitrary and musical form. Again, it is music not the rhyming dictionary (though see his "Variations, Calypso and Fugue on a Theme of Ella Wheeler Wilcox" for some canny couplets) that inspires Ashbery's poetry. He is averse to "melodious poetry," though not to melody itself; he is most interested in sound as it joins and soon flies apart from the meaning of the words, a disjunction reminiscent of the practice of Webern of setting a poem with a meager amount of imitative music. Busoni's music appeals to Ashbery in the sense that the notes, in his judgment, seem to imply that they could be "any notes and they just happen to sound this way." They have a "built-in arbitrariness that is not aleatory." Opposed to the pedanticism of Reger and the synthetic cubism of Schoenberg, the music of Busoni seems to Ashbery to enjoy the double status of generating a new grammar and then commenting on it.

Although Ashbery's own intellectual music is associated journalistically with O'Hara and Koch, and there were and are certain useful reasons to link them, the discrimination of their differences is equally useful. They were at first pragmatically and conspiratorially joined against poets of a different aesthetic (e.g., Wilbur). While they also share a common *traditio* of French surrealism, a taste for Russian poets of revolution, and a somewhat similar procedure by montage, the characteristic Ashbery tone is not that of either, and we cannot be detained here by such considerations. Suffice it to say that Helen Vendler's characterization (in *The New York Times*) of the poets of the so-called New York School as "cheerful and Chaucerian" does not stand alongside the meditations of Ashbery, no matter how much he may be seen to lack the transcendental quality.

As for "the melancholy subject of Poetic Influence," Ashbery has indeed digested the influences of both Stevens and Whitman. He particularly loved the long poems of Stevens, on which he wrote a paper for F. O. Matthiessen at Harvard. His ubiquitous third-person narrator may very well have been derived from Stevens as a way of "entering" the poem, as in "Esthetique du Mal." The dreamlike imagery of "He," however, does indeed derive from a veritable dream; some have been envious of Ashbery's dreams, and one is reminded of Eliot's dictum on Freud and the *Vita Nuova* that those who expect much from their dreamlife will receive it. Much of the clumsy appropriateness of dreams is imitated in Ashbery's poems, though the flat lyrical catalogues of "Grand Abacus" derive from the long lines of Whitman, Ashbery being more spellbound by Whitman's technical virtuosity than by the spontaneous image of the bard mumbling in his beard. Ashbery's marvelous catalogues, like that of musical instruments in "The Skaters," also derive from Webern's "Cantata," where things "go bumping and rumbling for a time after you thought they were going to stop." One also associates certain elements of Ashbery's *catalogue raisonné* with prose, and Cage's noisiness:

> True, melodious tolling does go on in that awful pandemonium.
> Certain resonances are not utterly displeasing to the terrified eardrum.
> Some paroxysms are dinning of tambourine, others suggest piano room or organ loft
> For the most dissonant night charms us, even after death. This, after all, may be happiness: tuba notes awash on the great flood, ruptures of xylophone, violins, limpets, grace-notes, the musical instrument called serpent, viola da gambas, aeolian harps, clavicles, pinball machines, electric drills, que sais-je encore!

("The Skaters")

As Ashbery says, "Cage taught me the relevance of what's there, like the noise now of those planes overhead"; however, he would hardly imagine the sole strategy of his poetry to be the capture of a probabilistic everyday, no matter how prehensile the poet. His poetry sees the everyday in its relation to the supreme moment, the in-between moment, the pedestrian moments, "and one cannot really overlook any of them." Ashbery's divinely drab modulations and equitably and imperturbably distributed polarizations between these instants have led one critic to the delusion that this is "a poetry without anxiety," but it is actually more intense than decorative, and, while rococo in parts, it has much of the Laforguian quick shifts of pose. It is not merely a deliquescence into an *exercice de style* along the lines of Raymond Queneau. It is a less whimsical palette of possibilities.

Certain of the poems, "Clepsydra" for instance, combine along with a drabness a quasi-religious tone and some almost impenetrable details of landscape. Ashbery admits to having the Valery-esque experience not of a vague rhythm but a vague vision previous to a poem. "Clepsydra" was favorably foreseen as a "big slab, with no stanza breaks and like a marble slab down which a little water trickles." The tone-feeling of the poems is not equally stony, as a lot of exalting of the prosaic goes on. He utilizes a repetition of "after all" as a replica of a hack journalistic digression in:

> It had reduced that other world,
> The round one of the telescope, to a kind of very fine powder or dust
> So small that space could not remember it.
> Thereafter any signs of feeling were cut short by
> The comfort and security, a certain elegance even,
> Like the fittings of a ship, that are after all
> The most normal things in the world. Yes, perhaps, but the words
> "After all" are important for understanding the almost
> Exaggerated strictness....

He also refines a kind of legalistic diction, as in: "And it was in vain that tears blotted the contract now, because / It had been freely drawn up and consented to as insurance...." One thinks of the sweet transpositions of legal diction in Renaissance argumenta. Surely, here too is a poetry ready to be accused of yoking disparate tones and images with difficulty together, but the Johnsonian criticism tends to falter under the steady and sensible pressure of such thoughtful and feeling lines as Ashbery's, in which the strange connections and obscure jargons are, after all, quite beautiful.

Though classic parody has a target, these modulated parodies do not quite break their lance against ignorance or excess. They are targetless parodies which attempt to annihilate the idea of parody, since parody is, for Ashbery, almost an indecent idea. He is interested in flattening out all parodistic devices, using multiple and shifting targets of parody to blur the Bergsonian function of intimidating the inelastic target. Ashbery successfully reinstates the poetic qualities of all possible sources—journalism, degraded ditties, bad poetry, etc.—by implying that there is no such thing as the *poetic*. His poems are not ready-mades, as in the tradition of Duchamp, and he feels little kinship with Duchamp, "who was a supremely glamorous negation of everything." Ashbery negates "so that we can go on to what is left." The urinal of Duchamp is a witty negation of art, but Ashbery is trying to enucleate that negation among many (thus the fragments of readymade poetry within his poetry). He finds too many supreme culminations and duplicate negations of everything Duchamp did in today's art and literature. There are now certainly some duplicate negations of Ashbery. His newest work, *The System*, is couched in the clichés of devotional and pseudo-devotional writing. "One may be depressed by reading the fine print in the 11th edition of the Encyclopedia Britannica, with long prose passages in eight-point type, and feel as if one is drowning in a sea of unintelligible print—and yet that this is one's favorite ocean, just as drowning is said to be delicious when one stops struggling." Ashbery reproduces that delicious sensation. His poetry starts with a sensation, as does Valéry's, and ends with "a riot of perfumes."

New ways of writing were also opened for Ashbery by *Hebdomeros* of di Chirico, another instance of what he regards as neglected work of high quality. Ashbery was admittedly moved by the interminable digressions and flourishes of di Chirico's prose, which tends to burst out in terribly long sentences that go on for pages, and which are novels of one character. The scene may change several times in di Chirico's sentences, as in Ashbery's, and the course of this sentence is as a cinematic flow, under which the writer is pushing further and further ahead, though camouflaged by one of those "urgent masks," which may be, for example, Sir Thomas Browne.

John Ashbery's work is much concerned with, and has a true solicitude for, "the bitter impression of absence," and this poetry that speaks of the "fundamental absence" of our day should certainly be more sufficiently celebrated. With their fluorescent imagery, disjunction, collages, two-dimensionalisms, innovations in traditional forms and "simultaneous" use of an aggregate of styles, John Ashbery's poems today constitute a revitalization in American poetry. He is not a mere prestidigitator of devices, but a poet of the stature of Wallace Stevens.

Imago Mundi

Jasper Johns translated Buckminster Fuller's world map into a painting for Expo '67 and then metamorphosed that painting into a Jasper Johns; the result will be on show at the Modern Museum.

Note: Remarks in quotes are from Shapiro's conversations and interviews with Johns.

A people of rare capacity is said to have a good sense of direction but no maps; there is a tribe, moreover, with a multitude of maps, but all are of hypothetical kingdoms, and how to get there; and Borges reminds us of the most careful cartographers, whose works grew in precision to be the country itself. Bartolommeo Fazio, in his *Book of Famous Men* (1456) praised Jan van Eyck's *Map of the World* along with his portraiture. One thinks too of the love of certain poets, like Whitman, to include the entire world, if only by means of a *catalogue raisonné* within the poem. Jasper Johns however registered some reticence about beginning his map of the world; he could not submit to a cartographical fascination with the clarity that lured early Netherlandish painters, of whose microscopic and telescopic perspectives Panofsky speaks. He feels he might have rejected the initial commission but for the fact that it was to be located in Buckminster Fuller's U.S. pavilion at Expo '67, Montreal, and could be, appropriately, a Fuller map within a Fuller dome.

ARTnews, Volume 70, Number 6, edited by Thomas B. Hess (October 1971). Jasper Johns' *Map* can be viewed on the MOMA website: **https://www.moma.org/calendar/exhibitions/2654**.

But Johns' reticence also involved Fuller's inclination toward a brand of philosophical optimism the painter does not exactly share and Fuller's distribution of clear information. Johns moves in an altogether different direction and includes the possibility of disastrous relationships.

The tendency to create deliberate figures of irony and ambiguity does not interest Fuller. Thus, in the first version of the map, Johns had a fear of appropriating Fuller's subject for other purposes and followed the map closely; in his opinion, too carefully. He never obtained a space to see the whole map assembled until it was installed in Montreal and, among other difficulties related to its size, it was worked on in a bending situation, conforming to roof and floor of the loft, which was 12 feet wide and thus never permitted more than 12 feet of distance for viewing. When it was installed at Expo in its huge space, he said it looked "like a map, unfortunately." From a distance, a map; from close up, a painting. He did not appreciate this look, nor has he kept it, but has with adventurous and all-embracing revisions translated it into a Johns painting. The first version looked like a blowup of Fuller's schema: an image divided into clear information of areas and place names, with no sense of it being a painting, colors representing what they represent by means of a color key. It lacked Johns' usual quality of doubt and of casting into shadow the idea of identity or unity: "It didn't have any doubt at all. It was just a big map of the world." He wanted both a map and a painting.

It has not changed much in terms of materials; it has changed in every other way. He is no longer intimidated by the Fuller map. Has it lost its optimism? "It's not gloomy. It just no longer has any clear information." The map now has more of the mysterious excitement that certain poets feel when dealing with works in a foreign language they only half-understand or choose to misunderstand; or delight in dipping into half-comprehendingly—as if in a dream the *Divine Comedy* were given to one in lyric hieroglyphs. The flicker of not knowing, or the flicker of knowing in double perspective, is part of the ambiguity of Johns, with its own simplicity and generality. The map of the world was made to be read (one must pardon the intentionalist fallacy); all has its meaning; one sees the names of the places and finds the distance between points; all of that is given very clearly in Fuller's map, but if there is not quite a violation of any of that, or very little, those propositions of the map's logic are not salient or clear. The very structure of equilateral triangles in Fuller's modular system did not appeal to Johns, who is "not so fond of modular situations." What he does "like" is the fact of one form transformed into another: the sphere of the earth transformed into the modular panels. This is a *topos* of his work: a play of simultaneous perspectives. But though the map is a readymade object, it was in a sense "too pleasing, entirely pleasing as it is," and so he was led to go on and manipulate it in remarkable, refractory revisions.

The transformations in color are some of the most striking evidences of Johns' tact in deforming or at least tessellating the original intent of clear information in the original map. The colors of the Fuller map follow by gradations of the spectrum the climatic zones of the earth and modulate chromatically to cold blues. The last version of the map is at the furthest remove from this almost bland chromaticism. It is a map of strange color distributions. "I decided that that was where I could take liberties. I applied colors purely arbitrarily in a subjective fashion." Color and its distribution, though, as Valery says impossible to speak of, are among the most interesting pressures and principles of this unprogrammatic work. The map, as it stands now, was painted over the map as it was in Montreal, with its chromaticism of climatic zones. One of the ways Johns made his color decisions was to tactfully disguise the former system of color. The luminous encaustics of the old map still add in shining through, however, which makes the map look a bit like a luminous Vatican possession fit for a future in which the world church could claim its possessions by means of such an image. "They didn't approach me." One can think of the original colors of Johns' map as systematic, and systematic too in its fidelity to the Fuller scheme. But his revisions of this system were properly exhaustive and meditatively so. He did not merely make local revisions but spent much time getting rid of the initial system of color—*secreting* the original as much as concealing. This disguising method reminds one of the "spy" motifs in Johns' notebooks. As for the organization of the colors, Johns did indeed distribute arbitrarily, subjectively—true—but tightly too within the triangles themselves. Originally, the color area ran through various modular panels. One could then more easily treat the map as a unit, but this led to diffuseness. In reworking, Johns made the decision to maintain a discontinuity between modules. And thus, at the meeting of any two triangles, the painting is in entirely different colors. A bit of information, when it crosses the line, changes. This stresses the triangulation but also by juxtapositions creates a music of color reminding one of the "arbitrary if not aleatory music of Busoni." Such a large picture divided into small parts could have become boringly repetitive in its metrical units, but Johns has manipulated these larger sections of triangles as decisive units. The triangles are not left truly connected to the next, and this Rimbaudian *dérèglement* is dramatic, but nothing of even a certain tininess looks too busy. There is, of course, no unpainted ground; nothing has been left but what is consummately covered.

Johns does not think of this map as necessarily continuous with any preoccupation with maps as motifs. Perhaps it does sound too hypochondriacal to be preoccupied with maps, but the metaphysics of maps still obviously intrigues him in a Borgesian sense. Johns remembers Robert Rauschenberg bringing him a group of mimeographed maps of the United States on 8- by-10-inch pieces of paper—"I don't know what for; I don't know why they are made or why he brought them to me; I think he brought a group of them, not just one." Rauschenberg has the first Johns map of America painted in modulations of grey. One of the problems with the mimeographed maps was that the image was in the center and Johns has never liked centered images: "I don't mind things having a center, but I don't like things to be centered—I've always liked the thing to be *the whole thing*." One day he painted the mimeographed maps and "liked" the idea of the preformed boundary-lines and that the main divisions were already drawn: a given metrical system. "And the reasons they were drawn were equally appealing in that they were different than the reasons for the lines of a flag"—designed by the earth in large part and not merely artificial or geometric boundaries. Some straight lines on a map, as on the world map, may seem arbitrary, but none of the curving lines seemed arbitrary to Johns, but pointed to geological propositions. "They describe some natural situation." As far as he was concerned, the lines might have been nonreferential, lying on the painting, but they were indeed given to him from a different and circumscribed area of thought. This changed the experience of painting: the meanderings of river lines and shore shapes—all determined by something which is different than that which determines a geometric system. "I wanted to make a painting. I wanted to work with a given division of space, in some sense. When the shapes or lines have a meaning, it's very difficult to work with it as if it had no meaning, only a visual meaning. And that was my intention, to work with it outside the meaning of locating points." One shouldn't take one of Johns' paintings (in what Harold Rosenberg might call "a classical critical *faux-pas*") and try to get from here to the West Coast. On the other hand, Johns had one of his flags given to President Kennedy on Flag Day. "And I couldn't believe it": the equivalent perhaps of his map of the United States used as a road guide.

It is difficult to get to the unbearable point of a completely self-referential painterly system. There seems to be almost always that stubborn bit of the referential, stubborn as the irreducible facts of William James, stubborn as the Pythagorean necessity, the stubborn bit of which the Viennese say: *It points*. Johns is one of the great dramatists of the difference between a purely pragmatic system—a map of heaven and how to get there—and a system of extraordinary self-referential sensuousness, like a dance. He has tended, he feels, to suggest that there are "at least these two possibilities, if not some others." His paintings "have no purity; they are not any one thing." These are the poles upon which his paintings twist.

The maps vary as the textures vary—encaustic, encaustic and collage, etc.—but no new texture was adduced merely for the world map. His use of newspaper may not be explained merely as Duchampian prose or as a colloquial or quotidian salvaged for textural celebration. He uses collage in many ways, partly because it is a way of filling up space without making anything but a "literal kind of condition." An area of newsprint in one of Johns' flags strives for the same quality of literalness that the flag has and achieves it with a certain shimmer. His divisions of space thus become the same thing as the total space. These divisions are in a sense echoes or metrical reiterations of the concept of the literal. His newsprint echoes give an ideal arhythmical norm or *ictus* to his paintings which permit the sudden releases and betrayals of his more arbitrary color systems. As to the "California and Florida Problem" of which Frank Bowling has spoken—the difficulty of conjoining arbitrary shapes in a pictorial system—Johns has indeed been trying to avoid distinctions in his maps between land and ocean. The landmass is divided into small parts and the ocean is not. "The ocean is just given." Johns tries to bring these things together without giving that different information. He is hardly interested that one is water and the other land—"since neither is, they're all just paint." He wants to avoid the little appeal that one is water and the other land, the little appeal of the centered image, so the water must be avoided as a ground.

One begins with the Fuller map, with its justness of projection and clarity of reading, its actual ease of reading, its minimum of distortion, every straight line representing the same distance. Fuller's map is an extreme disjunction. There is, however, nothing anecdotal or acrimonious to Johns' colors, as has been maintained; there is hardly an obvious "feeling-tone" to the color, though it has a certain "tragic" effect when one counterpoises its ambiguity with the map underneath Johns' map. "What might come to mind is the thereness of the map. Not the pragmatic use after reading. The idea of usefulness is destroyed in the painting."

The map remains peculiarly sculptural, an architectural victory which has mercurial kinematics. It has no top or bottom. But he didn't paint this as a bird but as a man, not hovering over the canvas, but painting it mainly on the wall. The thickly impastoed relief maps of geology appealed to Johns as a child. (When he was in the first or second grade, he remembers, the fourth or fifth grade had a map made out of salt and flour.)

The newsprint as collage gives not a quality of relief, of building up, but an experience of "the other side." One's primary experience with newspaper, Johns says, is that one turns it and reads the next page. Johns' collage is part of the sensibility that has refused to accept the surface, although the surface may be emphasized by such things. He gives us the information of the other side. It is not merely the pleasure of Duchamp's door that opens and closes at the same time. It is not the simultaneous perspectives of the Orphism in Delaunay. The inside-outside experience of frightening aspect is not it entirely. Johns' sense is of grasping things totally, not just from one point of view. One experiences, as with the world map, the possibility of positions in both object and viewer, and these possibilities "color" the experience of seeing the painting and bring a new kind of information. This value—that the painting is on canvas and can be turned about—is more than an unusual detail in Johns' work. Fuller's image is in a sense centered—one continent of all the landmasses of the world, with little left that is not rationalized into contiguity—but it can be broken up or folded up. It has an indeterminate number of possibilities of being used and seen. Johns wanted the map to make, when folded up, a three-dimensional form. So the three-dimensional qualities one still "reads off" the plane even now are intentional. It turned out to be "too clumsy, too heavy, too fragile" to be folded in that way, but in principle it was of indeterminate position and various triangles were worked on in various directions in the first version. "So there was no gravity; the drips ran in all directions." But turning this whole world was difficult as said before, he had no place to stand, like Archimedes. But he is uninterested in doing a smaller more graceful world map; because he knows already it can be done. Originally, when the painting was to be shown in Montreal, it was put together with piano hinges, and the canvases could be folded into a sculptural shape that accommodated the geodesic or other interior. It must therefore be called at first a sculptural unit. But at "Expo" it was hung vertically without piano hinges. All panels were jammed up against one another. Johns preferred the double sculpture, round and flat, as it has been designed by Fuller. Hinging, however, was impractical: the map was "too clumsy ... all the things it shouldn't be." He thinks it could have been painted on a lighter material, more airy and easily manipulable, like plastic.

In Fuller's map, the names are there so you can read them. Legibility is their *virtu*. Johns' version emphasizes by a different system the torn-apart quality of the sphere, reinforcing the lines of latitude, for example, with an indifference to legibility. Johns takes no steps toward legibility, though certain placenames were repainted to give a stronger character. Names go over other names and make other names illegible, not deliberately, but as part of the system; as in life, Newark may go right on top of New York, and that makes its own spectral emphasis. The names in Johns' map run in circles. When a name reaches the end of the earth, as it were, it continues on the other side of the juncture: it is shredded. Fuller does not break names, but the electricity of Johns' discontinuous work reminds me of Marilyn Monroe when she died reaching for the telephone. Johns does not regard the artist as manipulating the edges of meaning for pleasure. He regards this as a healthy-minded point of view "that leaves out worlds of possibilities." Johns thinks of art as a symptom and relates it to disease, just as masks may develop in character as part of pathology. The activity of painting for him involves metaphor in some fashion, which is "always a sign of illness"; the Fall of Man in *Paradise Lost* precedes the advent of puns … Johns does not imagine a perfect, unfallen language, but a perfect non-language or a perfect absence of language.

Johns rejects solipsistic privacies which can merely be unraveled, as in the incomprehensibly beautiful riddles of Duchamp: privacies which can be decoded, or otherwise plucked. He sees the "delay" in Duchamp as partly this unraveling process, a high if unrepetitive solipsistic iconography. The worst possible response, as Johns says, is perhaps for the viewer to have the painter's own. The large map is the largest painting in Johns' oeuvre, but it is not culminatory: it was large partly because of the requirements of a large space. He has worked almost exclusively on the map for almost four years and has successfully counterattacked any feeling of smallness of detail in it. The map seems highly unified with certain basaltic intrusions of crude blocks of arbitrary groups of color. These intrusions and sudden iterations defeat some of the highly unified elements and give it a "fertile formlessness." He has evaded the rigid aspects of the modular schema and has created sudden areas of erasures. The painting is mostly one of additions, however, not erasures. When forms are too absorbing, he undercuts with a logical laceration. Conveying Greenland gives little leeway, due to its moth-eaten coast, and one could be cranky with the edges of North Carolina—certainly a print might be too simple, since the world has no straight lines—but Johns has defeated the wrong kinds of finicky metrical arrangements and so the map reads as a Whitmanian catalogue of something, in which one can move one's hand for a foot along the world folded up.

Johns, I believe, like Van Doren's Edwin Arlington Robinson—a poet the painter appreciates—sees "life in that profound perspective which permits of its being observed from two angles at once." His painting, like the evidence of Brownian motion, reminds us that the universe in its smallest details is in perpetual agitation and yields a restless unity.

Transcendental Meditations: Review of *The Crystal Lithium* by James Schuyler

James Schuyler is our relentless empiricist and, like F. S. C. Northrop's depiction of Georgia O'Keefe in *The Meeting of East and West* as "unmixed with theory," Schuyler works masterfully and with minimum violations of rumination and false continuity. While the advantage of Impressionism, in Northrop's schema, is an aesthetic of immediacy and freshness, its weakness is that a world of blurred factuality lacks a theoretical or moral component. Schuyler, however, seems to sit as patiently before the phrase as T. H. Huxley's child before the facts, and his poetry includes a moral component in its strain against the moralistic. Not that the poet is merely a species of Sherlock Holmes, but he always observes vibrantly before any interpretation, and renders everything as vividly as possible. His songs of the everyday ("Light Blue Above," for instance) rescue what might otherwise have seemed inconsequent uncertainties of air, agitations of a "restless universe."

The Crystal Lithium (Random House, 1972) is divided into sections dominated by either sense of place or seasons and by details as sensuous as Elizabeth Bishop's. Schuyler treats the textures of things with the superb tact he finds in the paintings of Fairfield Porter. "What these paintings celebrate," Schuyler writes in a review of Porter's work for *ARTnews*, "is never treated as an archetype: they are concentrated instances.... Their concern is with immediacy. They seem to say, 'Look now. It will never be more fascinating'" ("An Aspect of Fairfield Porter's

---

Poetry, Vol. 122, No. 4, edited by Daryl Hine (July 1973).

Painting," *ARTnews*, 1967). "Empathy and the New Year" initiates the volume and evades the lovely looseness of some of Schuyler's work with a structure of trimeters and betrayed trimeters in columnar strophes, in which the poet modulates finely from discontinuous narrative to discrete or parenthetical colloquialisms and concludes with something shattered yet whole, like the fruit-dish of Cezanne. Like his elegy for Frank O'Hara, "Buried at Springs," from his previous book *Freely Espousing*, these are celebratory strophes that point through particularity to a *numen tremendum*:

>   Night
> and snow and the threads of life
> for once seen as they are,
> in ropes like roots.

Like Ponge and Pasternak, James Schuyler points constantly to the outsides of things as to a force always beyond, and yet anxiously and inexorably enucleated. His similes are never aspirational or imperial, a comparison of the lesser to the great, but are devices to personalize and domesticate: "The sun is high enough to have its plain daily look of someone who takes in the wash. / It dries the laundry" ("The Edge in the Morning").

Schuyler's detachment reminds one of the naval meaning of "detachment" as a dispatching of a body of troops on special service. His poetry, which may strike one at first as full of unfastened affections, is actually a "war of detail," canonically opposed to the gross or wholesale; nothing is *en bloc*. Bronowski has recently spoken of the chromosomal errors in copying, the quantum uncertainties that ensure wandering life rather than dead if growing crystals, and Schuyler's poetry is full of this uncertain and restless copying from a life full of error and perishability. This is not the antiquarian or botanist collaging whimsical detritus in a bleak period; his poems have the intimist distribution of a Schwitters. He proceeds, as Langer says of the dancer, from particular to particular, never pausing to generalize, because he has understood that therein lies the difference between dance and gymnastics, between poetry and proposition. "The Trash Book," for example, dedicated to the collagist Joe Brainard, is also dedicated to those democratic and perishable items like dry grass or "that stump there that knows / now it will never grow / up to be some pencils, or / a yacht even." His minute particulars may be comic or camp, possessing a *potestas* that dwindles or deliquesces when wryly observed, but all is presented as comically fit for "the trash book." The aesthetics of throwaway objects or poems is in some hands a throwaway aesthetic, but there is much to be said for the orientalist in Schuyler, as he redeems the visual and rarely over-frosts the poem with retinal detail.

The masterpiece of the book is perhaps "The Cenotaph," novel in its widely-spaced drab prose lines, end-stopped like a Roethke line but much less metrical or aureate. Whitehead has spoken of the expunging of the *copula* as necessary for a style that is not betrayed by false sequiturs. Schuyler redeems the touching possibilities of an almost journalistic prose or equally flat art criticism as tones in a monologue carried on in what John Ashbery has called a "tongue-and-cheek" manner, filled with Wordsworthian wise passivity, and receptive of all contingency, a free streaming over a concealed grid system. The theme of contingency is carried along by unexpected dislocations in the "monologue." The poem is at once a placid journal denoting island life, composed with the attentiveness of Sara Wordsworth or John Clare, and a crammed print full of the wretchedness and humor of a Jacques Callot. The third part, "The Edge in the Morning," is the musical summation of all this dissociation amid all this rootedness. Uncanny precision presented in fractured catalogue form culminates in impressionisms of fisherman and bay and an elegiac closure:

> Suppose I found a bone in the grass and told you it is one of
>   Marc Bloch's?
> It would not be true.
> No it would not be true and the sea is not his grave.

Like Marianne Moore (an early supporter of Schuyler's poetry and his novel *A Nest of Ninnies*, coauthored by John Ashbery), he is a poet always stark enough. His uneasy rapports with the personal, his delicate epistles, his reportage, his *catalogue raisonné* of the perishable, constitutes paradoxically a transcendental poetry without the divine term.

In Conversation with John Tranter

John Tranter: What was your involvement with the "New York School"?

David Shapiro: It's a long story, and in a sense it revolves around a kind of myth or dogma: on the one hand the phrase "New York School" was an epithet that was used by some art gallery people, a phrase that drew a parallel between certain poets in the 1950s and certain painters.

It didn't necessarily mean that they came from New York, it didn't necessarily mean that they stayed in New York, it didn't necessarily mean that their art had anything to do with New York, nor that they all wrote like each other, or thought like each other in any way. So one of the problems with these academic labels, like the label Post-modernism, or Modernism for that matter, is that it does become a kind of false can-opener, in a way. But at any rate, sometimes it's a decent device, perhaps, sometimes for promotional purposes in the Apollinaire sense of a group of artists who are at least going to link together.

My involvement was this: I'd begun writing very early, when I was about nine, as a violinist, and certainly by twelve I was attracted to certain things in John Ashbery's poetry that I'd seen. Then again in 1960 when I was thirteen Donald Allen's anthology [*The New American Poetry*] came out. I loved parts of it. I met Kenneth Koch when I was fifteen. I was still very much under the influence of Wallace Stevens, and many other poets ... including the French Symbolists. I

Meanjin (Melbourne, Australia), Volume 4, edited by Judith Brett (1984). Reprinted in *Jacket* 23, edited by John Tranter (August 2003).

remember that when he showed me John Ashbery's poems I thought ... in a way it struck me as horrifying, and I remember the moment when I thought, "This is horrifying, he uses the word "I" as if it was just any other word," and then I thought "How wonderful!" So I had almost what's called the conversion experience ... that is, a kind of Damascus experience, in which I hated "Europe" at least for half a day—this long, Rauschenbergian poem—then, I remember liking Theodore Roethke more—then, by the next day, as someone has said about painting after Jasper Johns, it's as if everything else was in a kind of ashcan—not so much of history, and I still love Roethke—but certainly this newspaper collage of John Ashbery's overwhelmed me, and the idea that you could ... what people loved in the cut-ups of Burroughs, but I particularly loved, in John Ashbery.

I then started to correspond with him, and he published me in *Art and Literature* and wrote me very beautiful letters, and I became more and more attracted to his poetry. It was just at this time that he was writing in a more Neo-classical vein, and when I met him, he recited "The Skaters"—almost an Alexander-Pope-like poem. I remember trying to convince Allen Ginsberg that he was a good poet. Allen didn't believe it until I recited some of his poems by heart, and then Allen said "Hmmm." He's always credited me with slightly convincing him that this poetry wasn't completely insane.

At any rate, the poet Frank O'Hara and I became close; and I loved Frank's more personal poems. But I particularly loved the vast odes: the "Ode to Michael Goldberg ('s Birth and Other Births)," and the very extended poems that are remarkably like de Kooning.... A lot of these poets weren't published easily.... I decided to publish an anthology of New York poets, because at the time this came out—it came out a little later—poets like Frank O'Hara (who was already dead when it came out)—it was very hard to get a publisher for them.

So one of the reasons I published the *Anthology of New York Poets* with Ron Padgett—we disagreed violently over certain poets—I wanted Barbara Guest in, for example ... I was once very embarrassed by the anthology. It is said you commit an anthology, like a sin. And I thought it was much too sloppy. I had a dream of some kind of Japanese perfection. But I'm glad in a way that Ron loosened me, perhaps, towards an anthology that wasn't quite that way.

So there are these problems with what the phrase "the New York School" means. It can mean a chauvinism. I think many of us felt attracted to certain ideas, such as keeping language in the freshest possible state, after Mallarmé, and after Pound. To me it's a kind of second wave of experimentation in this country. The twenties, and perhaps the forties to the sixties ...

JT: The first sign of that kind of poetry that a lot of Australians saw was the collection of it in Donald Allen's anthology. How do you see the relationship between the New York group of writers and the other groups of writers in that anthology?

DS: Well, when I was working on the anthology, I remember going through a period when—at least for a brief moment—I would like almost any poet that I read, in a kind of schizophrenia. Sometimes it would only take a week to be influenced by, to admire, then to hate, revile and renounce certain poets. I remember loving Charles Olson's work, and now I like very little of his work except for the variations in which he used Rimbaud. I didn't like what was merely a corollary to Pound. And I think there were poets who were closer than the so-called Black Mountain poets. Frank O'Hara had a strong personal affinity for Allen Ginsberg—he introduced me to Allen, and to Diane di Prima (who published me), and LeRoi Jones was very close to Frank O'Hara. [Later, Jones would change his name to Amiri Baraka.]

But I think there were differences. One of the things that is always said about James Schuyler—a very reticent poet—and Frank, and Kenneth Koch, is that at the very least their concern for painting links them. But I think even more it's the—um—decision not to make merely personal confessions, the decision not to make merely academic re-divagations, as it were, and the desire to press forward with some openness to humor. Helen Vendler called them "cheerful Chaucerians" when she reviewed my anthology of New York poets. She obviously didn't like it very much. It took her a long time to care for it, and she once wrote me that my poetry seemed nonsensical to her.

"Nonsense" is a very important concept, I think, for these poets, in the sense that things drained to zero degree of old meaning still involves these poets. Like Andy Warhol ... I sometimes think they're closer to Pop Art in one way than to Expressionism, that they're sometimes said to be linked to ...

That links some of the poets, that zero degree of meaning, what I called "the meaning of meaninglessness" in a rather turgid book I wrote on John Ashbery.... I did want to do a life's work of the Fool in *Lear*— Victorian nonsense—and at Cambridge [where Shapiro earned his M.A.] they said, "We have too much nonsense, too much of that," and they didn't want to deal with that.

But it is one thing that perhaps links New York poets that's not usually mentioned.... It's somewhat similar to Russian Cubo-Futurism in which language speaks in the poem, as Heidegger says that language is the center of the poem. There's an awful lot of *content* in New York poets—in a way they're very figurative and imagistic. Despite what the so-called "language poets" say—a group here that thinks they've established this for the first time—language is almost always the subject of poetry, but perhaps—in John Ashbery and Frank O'Hara and Kenneth Koch—it situated itself at the center in a way that was very remarkable for American poetry; in the sense that the aspect that is self-reflexive in John Ashbery—what's labyrinthine and parenthetical, in a manic way—is new in American poetry, greater than what's pious in Eliot. It's something that perhaps these poets get out of Wallace Stevens, who wrote to Kenneth Koch saying, "You should celebrate more." But what he celebrated was language, mostly. And I think Kenneth is like our Claus Oldenberg, and John Ashbery is like Rauschenberg and Johns put together.

The saddest thing perhaps is that Frank O'Hara, who was a Rauschenberg, really should have had ten, twenty, thirty more years of life to establish himself. But I did want to say, for everyone, that usually Frank is thought of as careless, and I remember asking him how fast he wrote his "Ode," and he said "Months, and months!" It's very useful to know how hard he revised. And I don't think that all our international friends know (because the manuscripts haven't been published) how much Frank O'Hara revised. There's the myth of him just sending it all out, as it were, and typing it all out at a party. But a lot of the great poems were done very slowly, and I was very moved by that when I was young, that everything was done with great care.

I think perhaps that began with Donald Allen's editing of the *Collected Poems*, which had an introduction by Allen, and a note by John Ashbery, both of which mentioned that a lot of the poems were dashed off at work, or during his lunch hour ... "Lunch Poems" ... but perhaps that's not quite what "Lunch Poems" meant. No; and I think that actually he has a lunch poem where he says "First Bunny died, then John Latouche, then Jackson Pollock, but is the earth as full, as life was full, of them ..." And the care in which ... The myth of the poem is that it's written during the lunch hour. Ted Berrigan used to say, "My poems really are written in the immediate present; that's the difference." And of course, at different times a poet such as Frank could "dash off a poem." It then had the twenty years' pressure behind it. So time in a poem is always different. But a lot of times there is the sense of speed in a poem; something that de Kooning loved, but a sense of speed arrived at very contemplatively. So one has to discriminate really carefully, in an O'Hara poem, between the topic of speed and immediacy, and something like spilt immediacy. And I think the danger of the influence of the New York School has been the idea that if you just say "It's 3:15, hullo!" that you get a good poem out of cardboard. I admire cheap materials, and I think one thing the New York poets did was to try to lower the materials, like the diction of the tribe, in the sense that some new architects use chain link as a building material; so in a way Frank was able to do that. But there are a lot of rare things stuck to that chain link, too. And ... his chain link is a necessary chain link; somebody else's cardboard is not turned into gold.

"Speed recollected in tranquility." I'm trying to focus on the difference between Lowell and O'Hara. They seem to stand for me at two points in the development of American poetry. I think Lowell's diction determines an approach to things which is serious and heavy and committed. O'Hara's diction determines a corresponding freedom.

I found beautiful things in Lowell. I met him at the end of his life, when he said that he found Ashbery's poems beautiful though meaningless, or something like that. I think he was opening up. His attitude towards surrealism was … wildly narrow. He would talk about surrealism in one of his books as just … it seemed to him just that which inverted sense. And he always had a meagre idea of the visual, it is said. But I think that he was bound by meter, in a way, whereas Frank arose from a huge prose tradition as much as a tradition of poetry. You know, one has the advantages of one's ignorance. Wittgenstein didn't know Kant, and therefore could have that leverage in British philosophy by whistling with a new model of things. And I think that Frank in a way didn't have all the echoes that someone like Lowell did have in his head, didn't have to wrestle with some of the same problems, and then got great leverage—Copernican leverage, Archimedean leverage on the universe. But they don't have to clink against each other.

I do know that Lowell is sometimes thought of as a horrible poet. Peter Schjeldahl writes a poem in my anthology that says, "Let's tell the truth, America. Robert Lowell is the least distinguished poet alive." And there are poems by Lowell like "Water," a very quiet poem, influenced by Elizabeth Bishop, whom everyone loves—at least recently, and John Ashbery has promoted her work a great deal—and Lowell can sometimes strike a quiet mood. What I don't like about Lowell is when he was purple, melodramatic, encrusted. But when he relaxes, which is rare, or when he translates Montale, who I think is a wonderful poet and somehow perfect for Lowell, that works.

But it is amazing how good—for example—a poet like James Schuyler has turned out to be, who might have seemed just a tiny footnote compared to a huge Lowell. I don't like comparing poets in the negative way, but I'm pleased that in the twenty years in which I've supported someone like John Ashbery or James Schuyler, to the constant ridicule of the universe, as it were, that that has turned out simply not to be the case.

That John, writing "Self-Portrait in a Convex Mirror," has shown how he can really take the highest kind of Eliotic tone when he wants to, and really, I think in that poem, invents a kind of parody of the academic masterpiece, that really is a masterpiece, in a certain way. I don't know how you feel about that poem …

JT: I feel very ambiguous about it. Really, it worried me when I read that. I thought …

DS: Because of its skull-like vanitas academic tone?

JT: Well … I thought, this poem has been designed to win a major prize, and it won three!

DS: I doubt that that's true, except—It's not true, of course—But I think it—no, but let's say that John sometimes designs poems … he is willful, and it's not so much the major prize that he designs it for, as … but—there's no doubt that one feels in John when he does something, this immense Wordsworthian confidence based, hilariously enough, on a kind of complete lack of confidence, which one likes … as in the *Four Quartets*, what I most like is the admission of uncertainty and failure on Eliot's part. And at his best, John is also confessing to this complete sense of doubt.

He loves Parmigianino. He found a little book; he was lonely in New England; and just returned and returned and returned to this … and so I think that what he thinks about that poem is not so much willful in a triumphant sense, as lingering … he once said, "I like the lazy self-exploration of myself." He compared himself to [Jasper] Johns. It's just that he can sometimes assume a tone … Fairfield Porter said it's the tone of a man who can write the most perfect business letters. And John does sometimes dress up in that suit that reminds us of T. S. Eliot dressing up like a cadaver," someone said, "to win England."

What I've tried to do is to combine what I love in Eliot—because I still do love Eliot—pace Harold Bloom—I love the Chopinesque in *The Waste Land* which I still can say by heart, and love … a lot of people don't … and I love Stevens. And I've tried to make a poetry out of something maybe even more Russian, Jewish, something that comes out of Pasternak … one part of Pasternak. And we have had some large poets, and so one sometimes worries … is one just a footnote to a footnote, as it were? But one does one's best.

The worry is that between the forties and the sixties there was a large American art, as good as Frank Stella, as good as de Kooning, these large splashes of great achievement. And is it now, as it were, like let's say Brice Marden's monochrome next to Jasper Johns ... I'm not sure that anyone in my generation has made a structural achievement in the way that I'm sure that John Ashbery did. Or John Cage in music. Or Elliot Carter. I know that Ron Padgett is a fine comic poet, and he's an important comic poet in certain ways; and I think Joe Ceravalo, a poet who lives in New Jersey, is a very fine Pierre Reverdy-ish Cubist. But whether there's this other thing, you know ... I'm talking now about the second generation of New York poets, and there are some very talented people—Bernadette Mayer and Alice Notley among the women I think are extraordinary poets to follow—very talented. Too often the poets then of the second generation seem like corollaries to corollaries, as it were, to the adults. And we may just have to wait and see.

John Ashbery at one time looked like a corollary to Wallace Stevens, and a mere ... something French and pretty that Auden was worried about; and so we'll have to wait and see. But I'm not convinced yet that my generation has produced a work that will last. One would like to think one's own work will last.... I can try....

JT: I get a feeling when I look at American poetry from the outside that there was a great argument between, say, Lowell and his "school" on the one hand—and there were lots of them, and lots of them were very good—and the New York School on the other. With a lot of other things going on as well—Black Mountain, the Beats, and so on. But it seems the major fruitful arguments were between those two approaches ... and I'm wondering has there been a synthesis, has anything evolved out of that argument that we can see as the next step in American poetry?

DS: Well, I'll give you my sense of where things are, what the state of poetry is today. What depresses me is that on the one hand ... there has been a lot of naturalism. Some of this uses a bit of Frank O'Hara, or some of it uses a bit of one part of William Carlos Williams, in the most horrible way, that one always expected, which is simply to list the factualities that surround one. Which is the least negating, the least critical, the least intransigent. And as one of my friends said about the New York School, a lot of that collapses into fey preoccupations that are really like whimsy of the merest kind.

So it still seems to be a few individuals, who are charming and tough, and have genius enough to resist the collapse into naturalism; or the collapse, in the case of a few young people, into a kind of anti-naturalism that's too empty. To me, the so-called language poets, who are doing "oink," "klok," "chomp," are doing experiments like those that were done by a few concrete poets some ten or fifteen years ago. They're whimsical experiments, and they're not needed. They're recapitulations of minor duplications of minor negations of the 1920s; it's just not needed.

So we only have still, amazingly enough, a few dark individuals; and maybe this is good. And the so-called synthesis that you see … and I would like to think, as probably one of the few who would say they have some sympathies for Elizabeth Bishop and Robert Lowell and for Ashbery, that's—I do attempt to weld … and it's almost conscious—one doesn't do it per poem, as it were, but stylistically I'm interested in a poem that's ferocious enough to contain the strengths of everything that comes out of Elizabethan meter, everything that was in Hart Crane, and everything that could be, also, from Pound, Williams, Eliot—um—crushed, like a John Chamberlain car part, and also kept delicate and musical. Those desires are probably the desires of many poets, but it's another thing to say, "Can it be done?"

The thing that's depressing is that there are no intelligent magazines … the publishers' lists are old-fashioned, good poets are unpublished, all the complaints are still there as they were when Pound might have listed them to Olson. It's an age of Reaganism; it's a very sad dark age.

JT: The St Mark's in the Bowery group of poets seems to have a strong sense of community; it interests me that there was a particular focus for a whole mess of things over a long period of time. What did St Mark's mean to you?

DS: You know, I taught at Columbia for nine years, so in one sense I was "uptown"; I still don't drive a car, really, and I've read at St Mark's many,

many times, and I'm also on the Friends Committee, and I support it ... while groups can be very useful, there can be problems with the very idea of a group. Some groups can be ways of ripping things down to so-called lowest common denominators. Poets like Pasternak have always been worried by parties, political and otherwise, and perhaps aesthetic. So one of the greatest problems with any center for poetry is that poetry is exactly that which is decentered, constantly marginal. Collaboration is a different thing. Rimbaud, for example, collaborated with Verlaine, but one hardly imagines him at ease with group happiness.

But there's a lot to learn from groups, and I don't want to be too easily anti-group, either ... to be more positive, it's very hard for poets to have any sense that what they're doing ... as architects have, for instance ... sometimes "noble rivalry" among poets who know each other is very useful. Maybe the worst that happens in New York is when poets know so clearly that they're not cared for that there's not even the sense of a rivalry. And places like St Mark's can make at least a little bit happen. But my personal tendency is to be by myself, to look at the venetian blinds.

JT: To look out through the venetian blinds ...

DS: No, to be stopped by the venetian blinds, with hopefully snow falling behind them. And New York—I think it is important that the urban situation does give—in the last thirty years—a tremendous sense of speed, of a matrix, of Broadway Boogie-Woogie, of what elated Mondrian. There's no doubt that in New York one could meet Bill de Kooning and feel that it was worth living in this century, and that great things could be done.

But the despair is ... a century, as Frank O'Hara said, that's too entertaining, the New York that drains one into whimsy, and that produces a poetry that just looks like a minor game. I have a very intense friend who says that art is not a game, and as a Wittgensteinian, I think, well, it looks like one; but his feeling is that it is not exactly played for stakes, and it's not merely amusing, it's not a divertimento. Sometimes poets play in these centers as if ... it's a fun thing to do, and it is true that poetry is among other things fun and entertainment, but I like what—who was it, Eliot or Empson?—who said that the great poems get written because you'd go mad if you didn't. Certain of the great poems this century weren't written in any way to win the prizes or to be heard at the Church [St Mark's in the Bowery]. Certainly one needs an audience; but perhaps the best thing in this country is to know that there is exactly, in a certain sense, none; and then to deal with that problem.

"David Shapiro, 1992, Riverdale" by Laurie Lambrecht. Used by permission of Laurie Lambrecht.

As a child Shapiro was a violin and literary prodigy. He decided at 10 to be a poet but would later insist that his greatest influence was "being born a violinist." Mentored at Columbia College by Meyer Shapiro, he also became with time a noted art historian and was the author of seminal monographs on the painters Jasper Johns, Piet Mondrian and Jim Dine. Included in these pages are pieces on Jasper Johns (p. 21) and Cy Twombly (p. 235) and a conversation with the abstract expressionist painter Michael Goldberg (p. 213)

Falling Upwards

A certain violinist had a beautiful violin
But before he had time to play her long and listen
To her tones as such, he was compelled to renounce music
And sell her, and go on a far journey, and leave his violin
    in the hands of the violin case.

What was there to do? It is said You cannot live your life
    in quarter tones.
What was there to do? It is said you cannot live your life
    in silence.
What was there to do? It is said you cannot live your life
    playing scales.
What was there to do? It is said you cannot live your life
    listening to the Americans.

What was there to do. It is said you cannot live your
    life in your room and not go out.
What was there to do? It is said music disobeys
And reaches the prince's courtyard ever farther than smell
    and grits its notes like teeth and gives us food and drink.
And orders a fire to be lighted, famished silk to hang over it
    and repetitions to be sharpened.

What was there to do? It is said it is the violinists who do not sleep.
What was there to do? It is said we think and don't think; we are asleep.
What was there to do? It is said music sinks into the mire up
    to its neck, wants to crawl out, but cannot.
What was there to do? It is said the violin was a swan,
    seized the boy, falling upwards to some height above the earth.

    —David Shapiro, *To an Idea* (The Overlook Press, 1983).

Toward Stevens: The Will to Poetry

Master of those who may not know, who cannot know, yet must know and are never satisfied with the facilities of certainty, Stevens today is surrounded by choral rings of a too-certain criticism. For example, those who complain of his limitations of emotional variety reveal the anesthesia of a reading. Like the unaccompanied sonatas of Bach, Stevens' lyrics are constantly implying an accompaniment or the dramatic lack thereof. Therefore, he is the most dramatic of poets and solipsism is for him both a *topos* and a stylistic struggle. The critics who have recently been complaining of whimsy or facility in the poetry of Ashbery will likewise be tone-deaf to the feeling-tone of suffering in Stevens, but it is there.

If Stevens makes a poet such as Williams seem complaisant, Williams himself speaks of that inner security that so changed him and his relations to language itself and its fundamentally, for him, mimetic capacities. Stevens understood the pressures of the new abstraction. Language is not a pencil. He could not copy the world as if poetry were a "secondary world," nor could the words relent with their bitter burden of irreducible referentiality. But the autotelic function of poetry he returned to—and returned in the most demanding and undemeaning form. Not in the form of a "New Critic *qua* poet," but in the form of a poet who returns to language in its binding phonological arbitrariness, as the pianist returns to the keyboard and Quince to the clavier. The poetry does not so much depend upon the world as become a world; does not

---

The Poetry Mailing List, Vol. IV, No.1, edited by Stephen Paul Miller and Kenneth Deifik (September 1977). This was a xeroxed single-poet journal.

so much point to its meanings as show them. The opposite of poetry is stupidity, and Stevens' "familiar language of poets" becomes our own radiant resource. In this sense one might agree with Bloom that writing poetry has almost become a matter of reading Stevens, and thus add that the most fruitful of Stevens' critics are our best contemporary poets. He is the central Lucretian explanatory poet in his minimal explanatory mode. And, too, by maintaining the nostalgias of cadence and structure, he remains our grand curator and conservator and provides a species of encyclopedism of texture and tone. What Kenner refers to wittily as the "worldview of the dictionary" is indeed his view, if one understands by that, not neutrality, but definition and redefinition amid the blur.

One has as much difficulty penetrating to the bare Stevens as he had in penetrating to and through the fatness of the world. We may use our [William] James as a reasonable guide to this pluralist of possibilities. James has his "will to belief" and Stevens composed throughout his life a series of poetic essays on the Will to Poetry. This generativity was a bafflement, a pleasure and a commandment in the flux of degraded public commandments and desquamated vocabularies. As James thought of truth not as given but as "in the making," for Stevens, too, the motley truth was the process of poesis. "Ever not quite" is as much a motto for Stevens as for James, but it is important to note that pluralism here does not become in time a parade of mythical optimisms or mere healthy mindedness. There is, as with James, a horrifying ground of blankness one sees, hears, and conjures in poems, from "The Snow Man" to "As You Leave the Room." Not the desiccated "positive thinker" he is often portrayed, Stevens recommends poetry, however, and it is to his credit that his worst work was written under the pressure of attacks of his more easily socialized and socializing critics. A sociology of the semiotics of Stevens remains to be written, along with his undaunted life as a businessman, but one may leave the vita to one side now and go toward the immense work.

He is, of course, more than the "poet's poet," whatever that might mean. Always providing new ways of looking and no single-point perspective, he is the master of a skeptical physics in poetry, in which everything is connected to everything else but in the most effective ways, never in mere collage but in the fusion that counts. While there are times that the hierarchical judgement tempts, in the mode of an Yvor Winters canon, one is reminded that Stevens is quite possibly, if ever not quite, the essential poet of the century. Credible and never credulous, unbudgeable but with sudden comic elasticities, he is our most musical of mourners. Successes in our own day seem intimist in comparison with his capacious clauses. He remains our Picasso and our problem, even if we have our Johns and our poetic partial solutions, rejoinders, dissolutions of the problem, footnotes. But one might think here of the joys of influence, the erotics of influence, for once, if I may transform those current terms. Above all one may want a view of Stevens as common hero, though fussy and the authoritarian of the Letters, still the poet who most, after Keats, reminds us of the heroism of poetry and the golden uncertainty that moves us most away from the miscellaneity he detested. He is the mediator on language who best affords us the taste of a maximalism. The morality of his means was his meditation upon his means. He did not use the "rotted names," and his attack on naturalism has merciless momentum.

Corollary to the criticism that Stevens lacks emotional modulations is the charge of lack of development. This is a sometimes-mollified charge, due to the realization of the canon beginning with works written in middle age. Nevertheless, the work of Stevens might well be praised in the same manner as Yeats by Eliot: a poet capable of an adequate poetry for each stage, and here even each nuance of emotional "development," a phrase one might well want to "deconstruct" anyway. Leaving aside the more insipid early works, and not forgetting the jaunty and dissonant early letters, the poetry accepts increasingly the *mortalia* and maturities that an Erikson might map in more schematic fashion but that the poet reveals in an increasingly sensuous way. Stevens' meditations are not merely "about" a mottled and divided self, "and yet, and yet." Certainly, a chronological disposition is not the worst for one species of appreciation of the master. Chronos is not Clio, and Stevens' own unity remains unassailable.

The claim that Stevens is not an especially visual poet bespeaks a limited sense of the visual in poetry. It contends, in most instances, that the poet does not copy nature *en détail* like a regionalist. This is demonstrated by a now canonic but misleading juxtaposition of the end of "Sunday Morning" with, say, "To Autumn" of Keats. The detailing of Keats, moreover, as Ian Jack has diligently discovered, arrives as much by the way of Poussin prints as by a direct "sketching." In an age of collage and montage, it helps to realize that Stevens bears in all the poems a burden of visual genius. His multiplicity of attacks on the single object is part of that "poetics of cubism" discussed by Kambler. He should also be placed in the post-impressionist world of instantaneities and liquified simultaneities. Not to see the visual as analogue here, as in Ashbery of the "Europe" period, results in much useless deposition. Fairfield Porter spoke of the Joseph Cornell box as that intimist construction in which the highest and lowest reaches of the human spirit could be entrapped like the prey of de Nerval. Stevens is capable, too, of thinking of the poem as an intimate enclosure. His imagery is not necessarily "after" the exterior mundo, because it is that mundo. This hermeneutics presupposes a criticism not simply responsive to the single grand precursor but the interdisciplinary many-sidedness of precursors in the associated arts, which have their indubitable sway.

Valery has said that prose may be "eaten up" in its discursive aspect but that poetry offers less perishable satisfactions. One's analysis is often too easily after the discursive, and in Stevens' extreme meditations, say, "The Man with the Blue Guitar" or "The Man on the Dump," the poet's non-discursiveness permits an inclusivity enucleating the profoundest derangements—an older romanticism with the most pithy nostalgia—if one may include an oxymoron that disturbs our dearest notions of nostalgia. Nostalgia itself is redeemed by Stevens and reminds one of Leavis' many mistakes concerning immediacy as opposed to rumination. The perils of immediacy are seen immediately in Williams and his quack disciples of no discipline today. The ruminations of Stevens have become, paradoxically, immediacies, and he has redeemed sentimentality almost everywhere by including it along with cliché itself among the possible perspectives in a world of perspectives. The mind inspects the given and the poetry becomes a volume, and more than a volume, in the chemistry of introspection. Lest I be misunderstood, I am not rescuing Stevens from or towards what Forster has called the verse of "Significant Nonsense," but I am suggesting that the poetry here celebrated musically loss of *logos* as its central theme in a world in which harmonizing codes have faltered. It is true that a book could be written on the "myth of absence" in our time, but it will not do to think of a more representational Stevens.

The erotic element in Stevens too often goes unnoticed, and it is a complex element indeed. One might turn to the early and exquisite, "In the Carolinas."

> The lilacs wither in the Carolinas.
> Already the butterflies flutter about the cabins.
> Already the newborn children interpret love
> In the voices of mothers.
>
> Timeless mother,
> How is that your aspic nipples
> For once vent honey?
> *The pine-tree sweetens mv body*
> *The white iris beautifies me.*

Note the punctuationless moment of ecstasy in the framed response concerning responsiveness. As Kessler has too crudely counted, Stevens often uses the southern and northern poles as models of the emotions. Here the southern imagery is extraordinary and ironic in its digestion of Pound's early erotic poetry, which is superseded in a supple manner. "Aspic nipples" is just the cacophony needed before the widening "i" sound in the pine-tree and the white iris. The parallelism here sets up a mild vibration of the Hebraic parallelisms of *Song of Songs*. Thus, the poem becomes even more stringently secular by its parody of a formerly sacred text, as Susanna is transcribed from the already apocryphal transcription. The sexual in Stevens, so lacerated in "Le Monocle" is revealed as a comical weapon as in the Third Girl's: "I shall whisper / Heavenly labials in a world of gutturals. / It will undo him." No doubt this eroticism, and repression itself as topic, remain part of the poetry, up to and including the late complaint "... as if I left / With something I could touch, touch every way." It would be unwise, therefore, to forget that this erotic element plays its part in that Prufrockian moment of fear in "Domination in Black:" "I saw how the night came, / Came striding like the color of the heavy hemlocks / I felt afraid. / And I remembered the cry of the peacocks." Like the hemlocks themselves, eroticism is for Stevens both medicinal and poisonous, if irresistible poison. There is no more reason to applaud the erotic in poetry than to applaud it in mathematics, perhaps, but one singles out this erotic element in Stevens as an oversight of those who are deaf to tone and *topos* in a many-sided poet.

Each of Stevens' aphorisms is a fine amulet of cameo, with this one's inner rhyme reminding one of the blurring of genre distinctions between prose aphorism and poetry (and in Stevens an aphorism can be in one place a complete text and elsewhere a first line): "There is no wing like meaning." As a poet of the preposition, of the colorful tendency, of possibility: "Everything tends to become real; or everything moves in the direction of reality." The voluptuousness of looking, and the pure act of taking a look at being, that most difficult act, in which "substance becomes subtlety" is suggested keenly: "A poet looks at the world as a man looks at a woman." Against naturalism and its desiccations, he makes the more final of his "anti-final" judgments in severe tones that he reserved elsewhere for the sociological critics of literature: "Realism is a corruption of reality." The suddenness of his metaphors reminds us of Coleridge at the highest page of his fusions or of his meditation upon such fusions: "The tongue is an eye." Again, these are not the commonplaces that Auden sought in Erikson, Weil, and Arendt; they are complete texts and universes; and their virtue lies in the haiku-like sense of the encyclopedism they condense and the contrasts they contain. His burden is ever and again the case against rationalism and its classificatory schemata: "Aristotle is a skeleton.... The poet must not adapt his experience to that of the philosopher." If definitive has come to mean final, affirmative and decided, the modus vivendi of the 20th century encyclopedist should be to make certain circumferences, deflate the sense of finality and keep an ear out for the nuances of claims and denominations. Stevens classifies but to demonstrate the incompleteness of vehement classifications.

In "Sunday Morning" the birds "test the reality / Of misty fields, by their sweet questionings." Stevens is a poet who invents structures as tests of poetry, sweet tests in which poetic truth is constantly being developed and re-examined. "All poetry is experimental poetry." To revise Protagoras, then, he invents a Poetic in which "poetry is the measure of all things." This is our "fictive covering," and protects us, as Arendt says the Greeks longed to be protected, from chaos within and without. In this sense, too, Stevens recalls constantly that there is no way to take fiction out of cognition. Like Poincaré, but in aesthetics not the laboratory, he invents an aesthetic of the working dogma (one thinks of his tercets, his experimentations with rhyme, etc.). He throws away what does not work for him, as if it were not "true all along." Thus, one sees him burnishing away such failures as "Owl's Clover" and the "social poems."

Who is the speaker in these poems? One could reply with Eliot's dictum concerning the three voices of poetry, but the best reply is Heidegger's singular one: Language itself. Here a quote from the philosopher of the Black Forest will help: "We would reflect on language itself and on language only." Already we hear the essential note, the anti-illusionistic note. To continue with Heidegger: "Merely to say the identical thing twice—language is language—how is that supposed to get us anywhere? But we do not want to get anywhere. We would like only, for once, to get just where we are already." (Trans. Hoftstadter). Stevens is the comedy of tautology.

"The Poems of Our Climate" reveals again the advantage of the methodology of reflectiveness in Stevens, for example, over the poems of William Carlos Williams until the late period. "Pink and white carnations—one desires / So much more than that." In Stevens one has the carnations and the desire, the exteriority and the interiority in necessary measure so mixed nature might stand up and say something. Here is the advantage of relativities and ruminations over more rudimentary immediacies. The "never resting mind" returns again and again, not to some perfect language dreamed of by the younger rabbi but to the uses of a decidedly fallen tongue: "flawed words and stubborn sounds"—this last phrase used aptly for an Elliot Carter document. Carter who has spoken of the "theme of abruptness." Stevens makes his abrupt topic the fallen quality of language, as if to remind us that puns in *Paradise Lost* begin after the fall, or as Proust has it, the real paradises are the lost ones. "The imperfect is our paradise." His poems are the dissonant *Quartets* of our times. He is always able to yield the Eros, the vitality of this imperfection, as a suddenly ardent phrase: "Since the imperfect is so hot in us …" Language is not a camera, as in the worst of Williams, but an apparatus that Abrams has underlined, for emphasis, the lamp.

"Mozart, 1935" is a neglected masterpiece in which Stevens shows how much of the tone of a depressingly real surround he can summon. The past and present make their collisions but the poet as hero remains inclined to continue his practice of intellectual music. Just as Zhivago raised the congruence of medicine and poetry, where the hero poet cures in a variety of ways (and poetry is, as Heidegger reminds us, concern) and establishes his peculiar authority amid crisis, so Stevens summons the poet to the task. The poet is reminded that poetry is not merely divertissement, but neither is a divertimento mere (particularly if one considers late Mozart and a divertimento that is not exactly "background"):

> Poet be seated at the piano.
> Play the present, its hoo-hoo-hoo,
> Its shoo-shoo-shoo, its ric-a-nic,
> Its envious cachinnation.
>
> If they throw stones upon the roof
> While you practice arpeggios
> It is because they carry down the stairs
> A body in rags.
> Be seated at the piano.

But the deposition of an easy surrealism or antinomian attitude is sudden: "That airy dream of the future, / The unclouded concerto …" In Stevens there is never merely ecstasis as in some reduced Éluard: "Elle est debout sur mes paupières." There is a Shelley raging here and a real misery at heart and in the surround—now in magnificent measure mocking: "Be thou the voice …" The conclusion is one of Virgilian melancholy. "We may return to Mozart. / He was young, and we, we are old. / The snow is falling / And the streets are full of cries. / Be seated thou." What is being summoned is the sufficient belief, the "starry placating" that might, but does not, let one forget the indigestible evils.

"The Man on the Dump" is the most exacting of laments, indeed a doleful dump in a variety of pragmatic tests. Nothing more horrifying exists in the canon of language's gaiety than Stevens playing his own Fool. This fool gives us, as Jarrell remarked of Frost in that admirably blank "Provide, Provide," the minimal worldly wisdom but with the minimal conviction. The sense of tedium vitae is never more sordid and Roman than this and, paradoxically, more pure: "The freshness of night had been fresh a long time." Here the attenuation is an articulate pang: "The freshness of morning, the blowing of day one says / That it puffs as Cornelius Nepos reads, it puffs / More than, less than or it puffs like this or that." The picture of the poet as Chuang-Tzu or the Taoist holy fool in the percussion section (modern poetry as Barzun lashed it and we revere it): "One sits and beats an old tin can, lard pail. / One beats and beats for that which one believes. / That's what one wants to get near. Could it after all / Be merely oneself ...?" Of the last utterance Vendler footnotes her dogged differences with Doggett, a difference I find offering no satisfactions. "To me, Stevens seems contemptuous of the 'the' while to Doggett he seems to be praising it." To me, to dissolve this seeming problem, there is no Rilkean polarization of lament and praise. All is presentation here and difference, itself. The "the the" is *objet trouvé* and the given of language, answering the question "Where was it one first heard of the truth?" As in "Le Monocle" "fluttering things have so distinct a shade." Language is *the* place of difference, and that truth is isolated like the atoms and italics of another poet of *reticéntia* and thirst, Dickinson.

The admission of ignorance comes from Stevens in "Crude Foyer" as elsewhere, an admission we have seen almost institutionalized in our own day in the Principle of Uncertainty. The aesthetician has remarked that we eat bread, not electrons, and that uncertainty in the macromolecular world must remain the proverbial uncertainty of everyday life, psychological uncertainty (as in illness, romance, etc.) F. S. C. Northrop would dispute this and find exactly a basis for indeterminism in the Heisenbergian principle, but this does not need to be argued here. Stevens makes himself the master of the feeling-tone of uncertainty and the desire for more:

> Thought is false happiness: the idea
> That merely by thinking one can,
> Or may, penetrate, not may,
> But can, that one is sure to be able—
>
> That there lies at the end of thought
> A foyer of the spirit in a landscape
> Of the mind, in which we sit
> And wear humanity's bleak crown;
>
> In which we read the critique of paradise
> And say it is the work
> Of a comedian, this critique;
> In which we sit and breathe
>
> An innocence of an absolute,
> False happiness, since we know that we use
> Only the eye as faculty, that the mind
> Is the eye, and that this landscape of the mind
>
> Is a landscape only of the eye; and that
> We are ignorant men incapable
> Of the least, minor, vital metaphor, content
> At last, there, when it turns out to be here.

Eliot achieves this tone only in the confessions of failure in the *Quartets*; one leaves him when he turns to the iconic ballet of rose and fire. This is our landscape, without rose or fire. The secret strength is impotence and the theme, the most fertile one for Mallarmé, sterility. The poem bent always towards the poem.

"Notes Toward a Supreme Fiction" is not dedicated to Henry Church, as some have presumed, but to poetry itself. The poem as divided is a parody of Dantesque dogmatics and reminds one of our bitter lack of sequence. Godard has put it somewhat like this: We have beginnings, middles and ends, but just not in that order. Stevens' worst passages rely on narrative or fable. The best are the least obviously anthropocentric and the least allegorical. Here the poem has become a species of the university, the didactic poem for restored students who would become ignorant men again. It is his most deadly playful poem: "Phoebus is dead, ephebe." The erotic is not excused: "The philosopher desires. / And not to have is the beginning of desire." Elsewhere Stevens has called Leibniz a philosopher without flash. It is not his problematic: "The poem is a meteor."

The precisions of "Notes" are precisions made bolder by the portentous use of the tentative as topic and style. The musical sprezzatura is here and his pragmatic, kinetic faith. Abstraction, change and pleasure are the equalities of his civilized and civilizing pragmatism. One is reminded of Whitehead's sense of adventure, zest, and truth as qualities of civilization.

What is more complete than this poem, with its irresolute resolution: "Fat girl, terrestrial, my summer, my night." The poem has begun and ended heated toward poetry, the interior paramour. The poet is the Don Juan of the poem and now, masterful, he speaks to and through his own cadence: "You become the soft-footed phantom." He reserves his last lament for the mad monists conjured in the uncanny: "They will get it straight one day at the Sorbonne." Nothing is more endearing than this end in which Prospero announces his victories over the too-rational distortions:

> We shall return at twilight from the lecture
> Pleased that the irrational is rational.
> Until flicked by feeling, in a gildered street,
> I call you by name, my green, my fluent mundo.
> You will have stopped revolving except in crystal.

The rest, though with superb propriety, is epilogue. Rarely has the poem described itself more vigorously and named itself more vitally. For those who think that poetry about poetry is endpaper or tertiary at best, a symptom if not the whole disease, one refers them to this masterpiece of praise.

The last poems of Stevens make their appeal for a completion despite all incompleteness. "The exact rock where his inexactnesses / would discover, at last, the view toward which they had edged." The important note here is the verb and the prepositional phrase "toward which," its sense of crawling toward Dover to be born. It was James who spoke of the color of prepositions, a discovery a Radcliffe student [Gertrude Stein] made much of in her work. Stevens sees himself in a Valery-esque position, abandoning, more than finishing. The world must be abandoned with some sense of integrity and a peacefulness that does not exclude a pedagogical zest. He saves his most erotic meditation for the faithful mental Penelope, the interior paramour, poetry, his wife, his destiny and death. The amazing epigraph of "The World as Meditation" comes from the violinist Georges Enesco, both performer and creator, like Quince:

> *J'ai passé trop de temps à travailler mon violon, à voyager. Mais l'exercice essentiel du compositeur—la méditation—rien ne l'a jamais suspendu en moi ... Je vis un rêve permanent, qui ne s'arrête ni nuit ni jour.*

The classic anagnorisis, the recognition scene, is the tentative one of the sweetly testing Penelope. The pragmatic Penelope has learnt by unweaving, by deconstructing her bed, as we would say today in France. "But was it Ulysses?" And the answer, in this world of flux, in which one doesn't sail the same Aegean even once, is the only one poetry can make, the unanswerable dissolution of the question in a kind of contradiction: "It was Ulysses and it was not. Yet they had met ..."

> She would talk a little to herself as she combed her hair,
> Repeating his name with its patient syllables,
> Never forgetting him that kept coming constantly so near.

Stevens himself has voyaged constantly so near, meditating on his violinistic poetry. He has approached in an almost interminable adventure, making of his poetry the true logo-therapy of our time. Like Kafka's distant friend in Russia in the explosive "Judgment," he has his own divided self, the most distant and nearest of companions. Its consummations and final fortunes in the poetry of *The Rock* are consummations of an inconstant many-minded Ulysses edging toward a view of a constant cunning many-minded interior Penelope. Living in this permanent dream of practice and desire, the poems are paradoxically as final even as they announce "beginning" more than ever as their topic. "... Wanderer, this is the pre-history of February. The life of the poem in the mind has not yet begun."

Suzanne Langer has seen in man exactly that period of autistic babbling one never sees even in the recent thinking-chimps of the Emory Laboratories. They, darling and thoughtful though they be, identify fairly discursively what lies about them and then proceed, discursively once more, to beg for milk and apples. They are realists of a dismal science. It is difficult to find the animal that lies, except for oneself, as Wilde pointed out a while ago, though some animals have rudimentary non-linguistic strategies of deception. Nevertheless, the solipsism in man's early years seems to us to lie at the heart of a private poetry, which is not a dismal science, but a gayer knowledge. "Such tink and tank and tunk a-tunk-tunk, / May, merely may, madame," etc. The defense of ululation, of susurration is the least stagnant element in Stevens: "The gaiety of language is our seigneur." This does not make him a babbler, but it lends him the theme of a childlike *regressus ad parnassum*, a wise Wordsworthian passivity. Valery said the most wide-awake activity is the recording of dreams. The phonological element abiding in Stevens, seemingly regressive, is his most adult momentum. Joseph Cornell's boxes were once called "Toys for Adults." It is only adults who need humor, as Freud sadly reminds us. When he needs to, Stevens has achieved the most vigorous flat catastrophes: "At dawn / The paratroopers fall and as they fall / They mow the lawn." It is not contempt here, as elsewhere it may be; nor is it naturalism; here is the rigorous geometric exposition Weil found in the Greeks. Stevens, the babbler, is also capable of the poem of force. The paratroopers fall in rootless splendor.

F. W. Dupee once commented upon the fussiness of the man revealed in the Letters, the instructions to the daughter, etc. One also knows and is revolted by the levity and laxness of the remarks upon Mussolini to be found therein and the sexual distantiation of the late letters.

Nevertheless, the letters as a whole reveal no simple reactionary and no Poundian pomposity of invective and bias. For the most part, I would recommend them on the grounds of their fastidiousness, distance, and desolation, splendid documents and more than documents, remarkable simulacra of that desolation, distance and demurral one finds in the poems themselves. Thus, the necessary texts remain *The Necessary Angel, Opus Posthumous*, and both the poems and letters. I would place certain of the early and late letters with those of Keats for practical insight into the consequences of what is now called "creativity."

In the *Angel* there is almost too much to recommend. It reminds one, too, that Williams had too much the angel of reality and too little the angel of imagination. At any rate, the essays are constant illuminations for students; for example, the remarks concerning Cezanne. Here the attitude of Stevens is rigorously affirming work and art as that prodigious work which "searches appearances." The poems are always *towards* and thus to hail the longer pieces as crowning strains seems wrongheaded. Stevens' longest poems are never "seamless" successes. He is the master of parataxis and adduces new criteria for continuity and success. Just as Matisse and de Kooning raised the tentative mark and smudge to a new validity, Stevens makes valid a new discontinuity. The "masterpiece" is a notion for the apprentice of idealism and beaux-arts approach.

Speaking of the poet in an austere "Answer" for the *Yale Literary Magazine* in Spring 1946, Stevens says this: "... he (the young poet) is not a private figure. On the other hand, it does not mean he must allow himself to be absorbed as the politician is absorbed. He must remain individual. As individual he must remain free." He is not referring to the freedoms of business. At about the time Stevens is writing, American abstract expressionists were planning with every "unplanned" gesture a new freedom in touch and scale, the freedom celebrated in every canvas of Pollock and de Kooning, the freedom that Lukacs may depose as a disease of potentiality. Meyer Schapiro has found an adequate reason for the private and associational vocabulary of the abstract expressionists, in that the age was bewildered by degraded public rhetorics. Stevens and the expressionists became, despite themselves and all Rimbaldian revulsions, rhetoricians, but they planned and give us a rhetoric which has confidence in the body and its contingent streamings. Stevens' confidences are likewise American if not libertine. His liberties are taken towards authority, of course, and towards a revaluation of authority and "the hero," as in his poems on the Presidential statue. The thirst for cognition is explicit: "We never understood the world less than we do now, nor, as we understand, like it less. We never wanted to understand it more or needed to like it more." His poetry concerns the ecstasy of incomprehensions and constitutes, too, an appreciation of the sufficiency of a poetry in a tragic time.

Of Stevens' struggle with the problematic of private language, Bloom seems correct in his recent *Figures of Capable Imagination* when he quotes uneasily Wittgenstein: "What the solipsist means is right." Actually, a meditation of the limits of private and public realms of language, as begun by the British analysts but never carried over into the more difficult terrain of poetry, is exactly what would best illuminate the limits of Eliot, Stevens, and say a contemporary such as Ashbery. I am amazed that an appreciation of this particular gloire of Stevens does not lead the critic involved to a re-evaluation of that analysis in Eliot's *Quartets* as elsewhere. Stevens' labyrinth, like Eliot's prison, is often more pleasant than the maze recently projected by a contemporary enthusiast, a maze of ice that would appeal through the appalling possibility of death by exposure. The possibilities in Stevens' probabilistic poetry are more invigorating perhaps, but nevertheless concern continual and exhausting truth-in-the-making. (Moreover, it seems to me that both Eliot and Stevens contribute to the growth of any so-called "strong poet," today, such as Ashbery, and it is a poor study of Ashbery that would neglect one for the other.)

Stevens' best poems are often love songs to reality and the reality of the imagination. "Say it is the serenade / Of a man that plays a blue guitar." His blue guitar is not the sentimental one of the young Picasso's poverty-stricken guitarist, and one must laugh with Stevens at the idea of using one as easy explication. The fundamental *topos* (with or without Huizinga) is that "we choose to play / The imagined pine, the imagined jay." Here the poignant choice is to savor the imagination as real in every way. This is his letter to the world of an unrelenting audience asking him to play other tunes. Note that in Eliot the "unreal" is used to mean false, haunted, ghostly, degraded, uncanny, sordid, purgatorial, and partner to the end. The unreal in Stevens may take on the positive connotations of uncannily fresh, carrying and constructed, paradisal, the satisfactory complement of the real.

Just as Piaget has his graceful protocols with children, Stevens conducted a meticulous lifelong protocol with himself. He is a man constantly aware of his unawareness and this is, paradoxically, his central Socratic, humane, cognitive element. Just as the letter "C" can become the true hero and center of a central poem, so poetry itself becomes the common hero and center of the collected works. The permanent poem, the rock, the mountain, yields the view toward which all this consciousness and proper unconsciousness edges. Stevens is the best poet "alive" today. In his modesty we find our truer grandeur. One may or may not have an affection for the affectation even his wife lamented, but in his proclamations of the advantage of ignorance we find our independence and irresolutions.

On a Villanelle by Elizabeth Bishop

The New Yorker magazine published a masterpiece on April 26, 1976. Elizabeth Bishop's "One Art," a poem later reproduced in her *Geography III*, is a convincingly drastic approach to the archaic French form. It shows what drabness may do for an all-too-golden repetitive form. It is superior to the maudlin manias of Thomas, finer than the cerebrations of Empson and still severe, and takes its place along with those of Auden, James Schuyler, and a few other premonitory practitioners' specimen stanzas.

The title is "One Art," and it identifies for us the integrity and lack of integrity that remain the polarizing tensions of the poem. It is indeed a poem of explicit art, of many-minded cunningness. The poem reminds us, as Freud does in his chapters upon the theme of forgetting in *The Psychopathology of Everyday Life*, that the most buried life corresponds in its dynamic aspects to writing, to *expression*. The poem is necessarily self-referential and self-reflexive whilst it never gives up its bitter burden of referentiality. The art of losing seems a mere theme, but it is also the central and active theme of themelessness, affording such a space of absence to the poem. The title is reserved and masterful. In a poem which conceives of mastery in the most negatively thrilling terms, it stands as a Keatsian "lone star" of hermitage over the poem. The title is an unadorned handle and forgets nothing.

A villanelle may be said to be the classic form of repetition and persistence. Like Kierkegaard, Bishop broods about the repetitions possible upon this mortal earth. She is part of the "dreaming tribe" Keats

The Iowa Review, edited by David Hamilton (Winter 1979).

brooded about and nearly deposes in his "Fall of Hyperion" and she persists in brooding. The poem is both an homage to poetry, a defense of poetry, and a terrifying lament about the weaknesses of poetry in relation to *mortalia* that touch us in the Virgilian sense. Each repetition furnishes a new twist of suffering. Rather than producing a stream of repetitions to remind us of voice or consciousness, as in Stein's explicit meanderings, she composes and decomposes with repetition and persistence to give us a very palpable thickness (in Jakobson's senses) of attention.

The poem is filled with palpable dissonances of off-rhymes that link Bishop with the tradition of orality, desire, and dissonance, in Dickinson and Moore: fluster/master; gesture/master. These dissonances each lead to the incongruous congruent rhyme of master and disaster. It IS disaster that is the large fate of the master. As Heidegger has it of Nietzsche, so Bishop of herself, the *topoi* are the circle and suffering. The poem is a circle from which we cannot escape any more than Borges can escape from Odin's disk in his phantasmal story. The poem and its archaistic form are themselves a fine and almost comical fate. One modulates from dissonance to dissonance, as in Charles Rosen's sense of the "classical style," too often perceived as a constant turning towards harmonies. The harmonies are small interpolations in a prose world of suffering.

Bishop never speaks too much. Montale has said, "The false poet speaks." Her poetry is not the falsely deceived one of utterance. But her diction is properly humiliated and low in a Wordsworthian sense; she never rises too high or aspires too magically, though the whole is sublimated magic. She begins with art and ends with art, "The art of losing…. (Write it!)" and so the whole poem is an essay as much as it is, in Ong's slightly too mystical and logocentric sense, a cry.

Bishop is involved with difficulty. The art is one of making an absence palpable, and she draws attention to her poem constantly in the way the Russian formalists never tired of presenting. She is, moreover, a presentationalist; and thus, she is even more filled with pathos at the theme of presenting, in Ashbery's phrase, a fundamental absence. Within the poem, she offers advice, but as Frost does in

"Provide, Provide," as a battered self, making small invectives out of the world's demands. When she asks us to "Lose something every day," we understand this as a collapsed soliloquy and, along with Jarrell on Frost, we are most moved by her very lack of confidence in the injunction. The whole poem does throughout make a confidence out of a failure of Mnemosyne. Since poetry is memory, the art of losing is a form of anti-poetry which she transmutes most naturally into the poem. To forget is in a Freudian sense even more a symptom and displacement and metaphor than a memory. Forgetting traces our own shapes. It is Bishop's triumph to write it out in such disappearing ink.

Bishop is concerned with mastery, self-mastery too as a metaphor for mastery within form, not over and above form. She plays upon the versions of the word "loss" too with the erotic playfulness of Andrewes in those sermons that so charmed Eliot. The whole poem is one of drastic advice to the *ephebe*, as Stevens reminds us that writer and reader are in an essential Socratic relationship of rapport and disrupted rapport. The poem reproduces something of the hysteria that precedes the desire for mastery, just as Empson has noted that the negatives in Keats' "Ode to Melancholy" remind us how much the poet was tempted to *go there*. "Practice losing farther, losing faster," writes Bishop, and by the spatial and temporal modifiers she reminds us that we are going into the hallucinatory modality of the *ephebe*'s first negative way.

Indeed, the poem as sacrifice is part of Bishop's puritanical *traditio*, and the verbs are verbs of sacrifice. We must lose, we must offer, but along with Kierkegaardian man we must never ask for unhappiness but wish for more. Every time the poem names some *thing*, it is not a public thing, but a private care or treasure, or if public, like two cities, the public seen privately and treasured as a dwelling. Like Heidegger, she is the homeless one seeking a home and understanding that to dwell is to be, to be is to build. The little villanelle is a "mirror on which to dwell," a building to inhabit, an emptiness built upon emptiness. We are reminded always of her constructivist bias, her architectural gifts, as it were, as she shatters the form and fuses it simultaneously.

A reading of the poem shows it as a *grammatology* in Derrida's sense, a scene of writing given to us as an analysis of writing itself, with all the whims of an almost absolute negativity. What one must remember is to write. What one must remember is that one will forget everything else, that one will lose everything but the faculty to write. Writing is not negative in relation to sound or to voice. Writing precedes everything in the most unexpected way; without the art, there is nothing. In the writing there is a beginning.

Thus, we are watching an almost scientific unfolding of the magic writing pad. Bishop is a writer dedicated to the fitting proportions of consciousness and unconsciousness. She has separated herself, like Auden, from the French tradition of automatism and surrealism. Yet both no doubt have undergone an interpenetration with that system of thought and thoughtlessness. One thinks of Auden's debt to Saint-John Perse and Bishop's own relations to Valery and even Laforgue through Auden and Eliot. She is constantly warning us, and warning us against *bêtise* and *sottises*, but her poetry therefore and nevertheless bespeaks an extraordinary interest in the buried life and the drunken boat of possibility. "So many things seem filled with the intent / to be lost" is a phrase that seems to have wandered out of the haunted wood of Baudelaire's "Correspondences." We correspond and respond indeed in a haunted universe to objects and subjects that seem to have no other object but to haunt us. Bishop is all too often in the *pays des merveilles*.

Throughout the poem, one imagines a certain congruence between text and psyche, until what we are astonished by is that this has indeed become a text of transgression and madness. The poem has not at its coda but at its very non-Aristotelian heart the art of losing oneself, the art of losing a self, the art of almost losing a text, the art of losing the shifty shifter "you." Bishop is involved with the dangerous theme of solipsism, and she shows us the horror of private language in her parenthetical asides that are a tribute to her reticence: "(the joking voice, a gesture / I love.)" She tries to keep these parentheses as Proustian delays, as suspenses, as adornments, but what they seem to come to mean are multiplicities, transversals, as argued recently concerning Proust and in relation to Deleuze's meditations upon the multiplicities of desires in the writings of that master. At any rate, her parentheses function paradoxically as breakdowns of the syntax and as rhetorical abundance and advantage.

What is appalling in the poem is that one comes to see indeed the facility of mortality, the easiness of oblivion, of mastery. The art of remembering is hard; the art of forgetting is the natural one of any *ephebe*. Of course, the irony throughout is one which a Kierkegaardian critique might depose. But one is not able to use here any ethical critique as a check against Bishop, just as Bloom argues elsewhere that the ethical will not check Keats unless it comes from a poet who equally honors the earth.

This is a poem that is not tied down to things nor morbidly dependent upon the earth, though it is filled with a tension created by the feeling-tone of dependency and passivity and self-doubt, recently called by no less a journalistic purveyor of cliches than *The New York Times* the attribute of an addict. Like Emily Dickinson, Bishop is indeed part of the tradition addicted to possibility, "a fairer house than prose." The poem, however, must be argued as abstract, a poem of sullen surfaces, a poem of shattered facets. It is a villanelle, not because as Graves would have it as regards the sonnet, Bishop wandered into the sonnet and woke up when it was half-finished. It is a villanelle, that most plotted and formal of *probabilistic* gardens, because suffering could demand no other strategy than the abstract choreography of the villanelle. It is not a dance of tensions along Cleanth Brooksian lines, it is not a well-made urn, but a kind of well-wrought emptiness. It begins with the abstract statement "The art of losing isn't hard to master" and it concludes with the force of syllogism: "It's evident / the art of losing's not too hard to master." The little difference of the colloquial "not too hard" is all the difference in the world. It's not too hard, one reads, and why this significant difference?

The poem is about falling away, disaster, and as we fall towards the conclusion, we realize that poetry itself affords us a mastery. While we cannot handle anything within the poem but imaginary door keys and uncomfortable or anguishing hours, within the poem we may keep these things by naming them.

Throughout this poem there is neither unmastered irony nor mastered irony. There is the presentation of the process of trying to master irony. Mastering irony is the present tense of this poem. The poem is a series of brilliantly tragic asides to the *ephebe* who is still oneself, and to the text of the eternal *ephebe*. The poem is not the poem of an aesthete, but it is the bitter novel of the self-poisoned one. The poet like Hyperion has lost not just a realm but a self, and a self that was a realm and a *you* that guaranteed the poignant sweetness of this realm. All this is gone before the poem starts.

The disaster of the poem is a self-reflexive one, like the self-reflexive breakdown of syntax at the end: "the art of losing's not too hard to master / though it may look like (*Write it!*) like disaster." The immense repetition at the end bespeaks all trouble, all dreads, all stutterings that Freud said speak of mental contradiction. Here is the level of ambiguity Empson shied away from when he spoke of mental contradiction in the poetics of Gertrude Stein. The disaster is seen and grasped in the speaking music of the poem. Beyond the appearance of mastery is a Goethean statute of limitations. The poem is perceived as an erotic transgression that commits the poet to the poem. In the imaginary, in the construct, is a poignant redemption that redeems all losing while forgetting nothing."(*Write it!*)" It is a poetry of parenthesis and pathos, of exclamation and the exaltations of falling.

Elizabeth Bishop is strong enough, and not necessarily in Harold Bloom's sense, to accept the canonic and the arbitrary and the given. She accepts the given of the form in the way that Jasper Johns accepts the dark given of the design of the American flag. There is nothing more arbitrary and almost stupidly arbitrary than the villanelle. Whitehead says that tragedy and science grew hand in hand. We may be killed by rules that loom out of the dark; they make us and mar us, not the other way around. In such a way, the more we discover the invisible rules of form the more we doubt and yet insure our only form of human mastery in self-encouraged, self-acknowledged Socratic failure. To write poetry is to die, as much as to philosophize is to learn how to die. This little poem is a little death, as erotic, as vital as any death, as filled with suffering and as vast as a glimpse of a new continent. It is a glimpse of the oldest continent. It is no longer a travel poem in any easy exotic way; it is not a translation from any Portuguese but the psyche. "There is no frigate like a book." Just as Mallarmé brooded on the other, the burnt breast of the old Amazon, Bishop broods upon the other, the text, the furthest and the fastest text. The funniest rhymes (last or / master) remind us of the friction of experience within the Imaginary. The changes within the poem are vital admissions ("I miss them, but it wasn't a disaster") but never melodramas of the confessional. It is the anti-theatrical, a wordless theatre played between the stanzas. The poem has its ethos against any easy deception "I shan't have lied." Within its opacities, its labyrinths, the poem overcomes all obstacles to achieve a final pathos. Mastery must always be mastery of disaster. There is no need for mastery except on the horizon of dread and death. All of the things lost within the villanelle are indeed metaphors for this death, this final divorcer, in Keats' great phrase. While writing itself seems like a separation, it is dedicated to the most final of separations. The poem achieves a mastery within a pathos in the classical framework of Aeschylus: *pathei mathos*. Here wisdom is not wrought from suffering alone but from forgetting, too. Oblivion is a temptation and Elizabeth Bishop puts her cunning against oblivion. She says, wittily, Are you afraid to lose? afraid to forget? afraid to die? Then, with Frankl and his marvelous theories of paradoxical intention, she murmurs, Then lose, then lose door keys, lose hours, lose everything, and then you will become a master. Hard advice, but "how witty's ruine."

Review of *Days and Nights* by Kenneth Koch

The cover of my copy of Kenneth Koch's *Thank You and Other Poems* has fallen off from use, but the achievement of the poet has not been publicly and sufficiently underlined. While his influence among some poets has been enormous and fruitful, it isn't accurate to limit him to this influence, and it is interesting to note that he has consistently and to date suffered because he is our reigning comic poet of intelligence. Since his poetry is one of affirmation among parodied forms, it has not appealed to rationalists. His new poetry, however, of, say, the last few years, has become increasingly open to the theme of suffering, memory, and limitation, and his mastery exhibits itself even more fiercely with these new topics of disunity. Like the late Fairfield Porter, who abhorred abstract antinomies, Koch's poetry is always at once abstract and realistic, always concerned with process but never careless, always embodied with the light of the particular.

Days and Nights (Random House, 1982), Koch's latest volume, is a disturbing and enthralling book. It begins with a masterful collection of short variations, "In Bed," rivaling Koch's own early "Collected Poems," as a way of making something solid as an Alex Katz cut-out of Gertrude Stein. In the midst of parodies, philosophical beds, art beds, suicidal and futurist beds, and beds referring to the beginning of the poem itself, Koch floats this tender couplet:

> The bed lies in the room
> The way she lies in the bed.

The Poetry Project Newsletter #99, edited by Greg Masters (October 1983).

And, in case you thought all this was obfuscation through metaphor, he includes "Psychoanalytic Criticism in Bed": "What are you trying to avoid talking about / When you talk about bed?" It's a little diabolic series of cadenzas: a dictionary of beds to wake you up. The next poem, "The World," is a very brave poem about unhappiness. It seems as if Koch is applying the same audacity to suffering and its sequels that he wanted to apply to affirmation: "Saying I ought to see / Suffering is simply that / A thing for every day. Can one person cure me? / Am I sick? I am / Unhappy and I think / I shouldn't be. / ... Poetry, my enemy! / Why can't you do everything? / Make me young again. / Give me that hand in my hand." The difference between Koch and other confessors to suffering is that he bribes us, as Freud says, with a public form to his private intimacies, a consciousness that mediates all cliche: "Sic transit ego / And sic fugit this poem."

One of my favorite poems in the volume is the explosive and explosively titled: "Girl and Baby Florist Sidewalk Pram Nineteen Seventy Something": "Sweeping past the florist's came the baby and the girl / I am the girl! I am the baby!" It's as if he started with a little genre scene and then shattered it with every cubo-futurist device known to humankind: "Florist stands whistling / Neither inside nor outside thinking about the mountains of Peru." Poetry has probably never had a person as learned as Koch as willing to scramble and sacrifice. I can think as a comparison only of de Kooning sculpting a dog or elegantly crushing a clam-digger. He celebrates the child, but as an adult.

If Koch's largest moods used to be presented in the present and future tense, his new mode, as in "With Janice," is the past in elegy: "The leaves were already on the trees, the fruit blossoms / White and not ruined and pink and not ruined and we / Were riding in a boat over the water in which there was a sea / Hiding the meanings of all our salty words." "I loved the texture of your talk ..." "Plate glass was nowhere around." "You were / A blue coat ..." Like Frank O'Hara's "A Step Away From Them," it is a celebration of the fullness of life, however, rather than an academic frightening us with allegorical skulls: "I wore Leonard's jacket and my clothes, then shoes / Meet yours, advancing, so walk about the best / Final of beach, to not notice numbers /

Except when they are speaking, as we stopped less / When all this was around." Koch once said love induced him to a new clarity, and here it induces him to a new complexity. "Twenty Poems" has the Catullus-like ambivalence again: "Then he loves her no longer, / For one second." *Days and Nights* is a startling, extended "meditation" on poetry and its possibilities amid all this worldliness and multiple emotion: "The idea of Mallarmé / That / Well that it was so / Vital / Poetry, whatever it was / Is inspiring / Is I find even more inspiring / Than his more famous idea / Of absence …"

Koch's prose piece, "The Green Step" seems to me to be one of the most limpid and yet replete stories any poet has written since Koch's own perfect "The Postcard Collection." It's as complicated as "Letters from Tula" and is both a love story, music and architecture criticism, and a description of itself. The philosopher Ted Cohen says metaphors are used to create intimacy, sometimes destructive. What Koch gives us is a tense artistry that is at once extraordinarily intimate and yet also public, even epical in scale. This polarization is the secret, I think, of his great art. We learn from his green steps the way the surrealists learned from de Chirico's blank arcades.

Proverbs

In my family, the Bible was inextricably bound up with music, with the singing of my grandfather, the cantor Berele Chagy, whose sweet tenor voice in performance and recording gave me my first sense of Kafka's comfortless spiritual world. It is no surprise to me to find in Hebrew a lack of words for poetry but an abundance for music, nor was I surprised that, when my grandfather died while singing, the grandchildren were told that this was the best death: to sing until the end. It is always with some wonder that the commentaries I read on the poetics of the Tanach delete this sense, though I am aware of the difficulty of importing it to our discussion. But it is a personal impossibility for me to think of the "Scriptures" as writing without tones, without utterance, and without the improvisational pathos brought by the great singers. While reading even the most austere of the prudent counsels of our book, I hear always the elegiac embellishments of the golden chazzanim (or cantors): Chagy, Sirota, Rosenblatt. If Kafka speaks in his diaries of the "unjust Judges" and of how the pages do not flutter for him, yet for me they move most with the sense of a singing performance, not ethical discursivity, but the real chamber music of the synagogue.

There is a dazzling note in Kafka that reminds us of his sudden pietistic twinges, not unlike our own: "The Polish Jews going to Kol Nidre. The little boy with prayer shawls under both arms, running along at his father's side. Suicidal not to go to temple." This is the correct

---

Congregation: Contemporary Writers Read the Jewish Bible, edited by David Rosenberg (Harcourt, Brace, Jovanovich; San Diego/NY, 1987). The Revised Standard Version is used in this essay.

beginning for the studenté's sense of Proverbs in our time: the distance from, and nearness to, the children the writer feels, the destructiveness in our ironic interval from ritual, our need for a temple, and the comical theme of its exoticism in those fluttering prayer shawls. Just as there is passionate hesitation in the interpretation of Kafka—Scholem finding in Kafka all allegory and, recently, Deleuze admonishing us to look for nothing but social surface—so the Proverbs remain as a constant problem. On the one hand, for many they seem to be a scribal textbook plagiarized from Egypt, or a textbook to be plagiarized by even later Egyptian clerks; however, for others they are the most explicit binding together of allegories, explicit and concealed, and of Wisdom—and not merely prudential understanding, but the Wisdom that initiates worlds, the Wisdom that presides over the irreducible evils of Job. Coming to the Proverbs, most contemporary writers are disturbed by their conservative norms, and such a penetrating reader as Northrop Frye suddenly calls a strophe on discipline one of the most harmful of sentences. No allegorist will be likewise stopped by the theme of discipline, a constant in all mystical literatures. Is this an anthology like Benjamin Franklin's bourgeois success stories, or is this a garland of enigmas?

More than one author has suggested that the book has sunk in reputation in our century because of its confident tone and its lack of doubt. Yet this is particularly annoying as a view of Proverbs, since students of the so-called Wisdom movement have been led to see aspects of it as essentially an anti-pietistic movement, if not of doubters, then of international sages instead, who stood apart from the priest and prophet. There can hardly be a formulated skepticism without the kind of resolute attempt at principle exfoliated at such a scale in *Mishlé* (Hebrew for "Proverbs"). Just as Kafka confines his most fideist dreams to some marginal reflections despite what seem to be the labyrinthine doubts of his novels and tales, so the proverbs here speak of a tension with skepticism. Embedded in many resolute adages is a remarkable realism: "Scoffers set a city aflame.... A fool gives full vent to his anger.... If a wise man has an argument with a fool, the fool only rages and laughs, and there is no quiet" (29:8; 11; 9). "He who robs his father and mother and says, That is no transgression ..." (28:24). The first wave of this last horrifying phrase is enough to convince the ephebe that moral perversity exists. Principle alone and quotation by itself are not sufficient: "Like a lame man's legs, which hang useless, is a proverb in the mouth of fools" (26:7). One does not expect a fideist collection to announce that it must be used wisely and with a sense of humor, but *Mishlé* repeats itself on this point: "Like a thorn that goes up into the hand of a drunkard / is a proverb in the mouth of fools" (26:9).

Here is a book without covenant, history, or revelation, but a book that teaches us how to read: "to understand a proverb and a figure, the words of the wise and their riddles." The world is to be decoded by the most strenuous deciphering, and the beginning is reverential anxiety. Immediately there is a picture of a violence that destroys all codes: "Like Sheol let us swallow them alive and whole, like those who go down to the Pit ..." (1:12). The structure of this book concerns receptivity: "Making your ear attentive to wisdom"(2:2). All utterance must conform to this ideal, deriving from divine speech: "Put away from you crooked speech, and put devious talk far from you" (4:24). In a sense, the search for a perfect language begins and concludes with the admonition to "pay attention." The world is broken into fragments like these many proverbs, but the hidden spark-gatherer is Wisdom, since it alone seeks such unities as are possible. The wilderness of worldly proverbs baffles the imprudent reader, who loses his way among such badly infinite perspectives. But Proverbs relies on a resolute envelope, as at the conclusion: "Every word of God proves true, he is a shield to those who take refuge in him. Do not add to his words ..." (30:5). Reading is an activity that makes a difference, and this difference cannot be minimized or foreshortened: "Like a madman who throws firebrands, arrows and death, / is the man who deceives his neighbor, and says, I am only joking" (26:18). The ethical life is not a dream, it is barbed like the arrow of time and rushes forward with a mortal tempo.

A simple hypothesis concerning *Mishlé* is the possibility that it was performed in schools, with one line sung out by a teacher and the couplet oratorically finished by a student. Certainly, this approach could account for some of the "literary" embellishments of the proverbs, where folk sayings are famous for their savage unity; by contrast, our collection is replete with more "writerly" forms. What is significant for Proverbs is not simply that the book was meant in part to be performed, but that the performance is in strict accord with the theme of the book, which is familial unity with the divine. The *ephebe* is constantly addressed, and mother and father are unified in the most drastic sense. "There are those who curse their fathers and do not bless their mothers. There are those who are pure in their own eyes …" (30:11-12). The Lord is to be feared like a father, and not, as one psychoanalyst has admonished, because without such fear He will castrate like a father. The Lord is to be shown reverence because He has created the multiple perspectives of a miraculous world, the world in which the "Good Wife" can be conceived and the world in which the industrious ant reproves all sluggards. Meaninglessness is not a problem here, nor in Job, but, rather, the proliferation of meanings is a problem. Merleau-Ponty was right: we are condemned to meaning; and Proverbs at its darkest condemns us to language, meaning, and the "comfortless" spiritual world that Kafka reflected.

There is an extensive anthropological and linguistic literature that has developed on Proverbs, and we have learned much from it that might be of use in our reading of the canonic texts. Joyce Penfield, in her extensive studies of the Igbo peoples, who are much given to quotation and proverbs, has discovered in the field, and with the help of the Prague formalist Mukařovský, that the proverb is essentially a device of depersonalization, of distance and control, of a contextual indirectness. She has discovered in the proverb a route toward "group conscience," a means to control violence and shame with the most condensed means of prestige in formulation. The metaphorical proverbs force the listener into acute "processing," and yet are as specific, despite all ambiguities, as recipes. As a matter of fact, David Robertson, who argues for a non-Aristotelian reading of Proverbs, also suggests this sense of situational specificity. A proverb in our text seems to float above and beyond situations. But really, as Robertson suggests when trying to dissolve the knot of a famous contradiction—whether to answer a fool according to his folly or not, and our book suggests doing both—the scandal of the proverbial method is its worldliness, its ineluctable link to surface despite metaphor and ambiguity. The anthropological suggestion is to read this encyclopedia of formulations with all due attention to its fractures, indications of a wilderness of eruptive contexts. Proverbs demand places.

When we think of proverbs as demanding persons and places, we realize the scandalous difficulty of reading this seemingly ahistorical book without history. And yet the archives of archaeology are not that potent here. Despite beautiful parallels found in James Pritchard's extraordinarily useful anthologies of Egyptian and other Near Eastern texts, there is no certainty in Wisdom scholarship as to whether we are dealing with an essentially Egyptian text "collaged" onto a Solomonic frame, or whether Israeli Wisdom was diffused into later Egyptian scribal forms. At the least, however, the parallels, including the too-congruent use of the number thirty in organizing one section of our text, remind us that universalism here finds both form and content interfused. The proverb is a cosmopolitan form, though one anthropologist has discovered that urbanity tends to threaten the form. Still, we may find in Proverbs a truly Solomonic urbanity, and the howl of Wisdom takes place "at the entrance to the city gates" (1:21). We are impressed that more than one student has remarked on the relation of the condensed proverb to the establishment of the alphabet. The proverb is as much early science as ageless prudence. It stands with Solomonic architecture as a tectonic vehicle: the building up of character in an ambiguous school.

The poet Wallace Stevens is said to have collected volumes of proverbs in much the way Walter Benjamin is said to have searched for collections of psychotic world-systems. Our book does have a problem at its core: the massing of the microcosmos. Yet to us, reading this fractured so-called list of lists; we are surprised at the unified power of this disunity. The book announces itself with a mighty framing device:

> That men may know wisdom and instruction,
> understand words of insight
> receive instruction in wise dealing,

> righteousness, justice and equity;
> that prudence may be given to the simple
> the wise man also may hear and increase in learning....

[Proverbs 1:2-5)

And the ode to the "Good Wife" stands as the other ferocious framing of this book. To begin at the beginning, instruction in the reading of all codes, and to end with the "fruit of her hands," suggests that the late editor of this text knew how to make a recipe book seem intently focused. The last acrostic, since the "Good Wife" is organized by the alphabet and its mystical resonance, seems to make a whole poem into a proverb, if we recall that *Mishlé* comes out of a matrix of words for "analogy," "metaphor," and "figure." In a book in which the *ephebe* is to learn how to decode life's wilderness, it is fitting that the last figure is the powerful wife who "opens her mouth with wisdom / and the teaching of kindness is on her tongue" (31:26). The maximum affirmation is made through the minimum alphabetic technique.

The book has been decried for its repressive constancy, its fidelity to fidelity. No doubt the wise man reads the Book of Proverbs and turns to Job, where we have a rather skeptical indictment of false comfort. It would seem too easy to describe Job as the inversion of Proverbs, and the false comforters as those who have learned our book too early and too well. Here it is significant to recall that our Proverbs contains a tremendous worldly darkness: the world of panic to those who have refused wisdom, but also the simple strictness of the relative world itself, where a woman is charming but leads to an accessible abyss. Those who have seen in Proverbs a fear of desire, a fear of woman, a misogyny at the core, must be corrected. The book does have some of the great representations of the slipperiness of desire and its discontents, but in that it shows the moral realism that releases us to a new knowledge of woman and her stature. There is a fundamental finding of the Other here, the wife evaded by both Kafka and Kierkegaard, and both adulteress and householder are seen and fully revealed as forms of divine power glimpsed within the ordinary companionate dream. Proverbs contains a loud psalm to woman—divine, thus terrible—and what is refused is the "rehearsed response," as if we knew how to read her. The adulteress is portrayed as a demon as glidingly powerful as any girl of Avignon. On the other hand, the "Good Wife," charitable, working and loving, is a finale, radiant as a fundamental eulogy—I still recall the effect of the rabbinic recitation at my grandmother's funeral. Woman is the key to our seemingly opaque allegory.

S. R. Hirsch gives a fundamentally sound, if pietistic, reading of the meanings of *Chochmah* (Wisdom) in our Wisdom text: "The terms ... are found also as applied to God. In fact, they can be applied in their truest, deepest and fullest sense only to God. The share that people get from this spiritual essence of wisdom, understanding, and knowledge—emanating from it and made possible by it—is merely an infinitely faint echo of the Divine...." The Book of Proverbs may be said to be divided into those passages that give worldly advice as to the conduct of business, politics, matrimony, friendship, affairs of state and heart, and those maxims that most stringently concern the spiritual rapports. But the book attempts to create an inescapable self-reflexiveness: "The beginning of wisdom is this: Get wisdom, and whatever you get, get insight" (4:7). There is a link between the high and the low, between world and spirit: "Prize her highly, and she will exalt you; she will honor you if you embrace her" (4:8). "It is the glory of God to conceal things, but the glory of kings is to search things out" (25:2). This is a cunning counterfoil to Einstein's remark on God's subtle lack of malice. *Deus absconditus* might indeed be the first and final incitement to all science and all poetry. We find in mundane suggestions simply the arithmetic for the conduct of a life tied to the divinity, hidden like gravity and as constant. Just as Walter Benjamin dreamed of a book entirely of quotations that would reveal a whole city, so Proverbs in multiplicity reveals the divine city, a place in which the good woman's "works praise her in the gates" (31:31).

The Proverbs are a constant reminder of the inclusivity of Judaism, an inclusivity Freud discovers in linking Moses to the universalist vision of Akhenaton. The Proverbs begin with prudence and end with happiness: they are a poem to the earth in the ethical dimension as much as the Song of Songs is the earthly ode in the aesthetic and erotic dimensions. There is little of the tribalist in our text, and yet for all those who have seen this collection as internationalist, it is also important to think of it as yielding a national collection, a group anthology that fosters unity through memory. Here analogy is more significant than chronicle, and the book foregrounds a constant present tense. It is the present tense of these shocking analogies that functions as such a contrast to the epic past of the great histories: "Like a gold ring in a swine's snout / is a beautiful woman without discretion" (11:22). The analogy is correct and is always correct, like gravity or the alphabet. And the future tense is not one of prophecy but, rather, is one announcing the exact causalities: "He who trusts in his riches will wither." The prophet may find himself quoting a proverb, as Ezekiel does (16:44), but the condensation of the proverb functions much more like a rule than like a warning or revelation. It is the man-made scientism of the rules that gives them so much modern force in the aphorisms of Ludwig Wittgenstein and Karl Kraus.

The French negative theologian par excellence, Jacques Derrida, has remarked in a dialogue that the theological motif is always homogeneity. If this were indeed so one might profitably think of Proverbs in its eclectic "collage" state as part of the Jewish critique of idealism. One's face is rubbed in *the near*, as Leo Baeck has put it—the nearness of the divine, the nearness of the world, the nearness of the uncanny fusion of world and divinity. There is no wisdom without the fear of God, but also no wisdom without the fear at home; the fear of home, since we are those who may be exported in haste to a dim underworld, as materialist an underground as has been conceived, a world called Sheol, derived etymologically from the small, cramped grave. *Mishlé* is a heterogeneous text and obdurately so, because it bears upon its "speaking" side the sand fissures of all the contexts that make its demands so exigent. Proverbs is a cadenza of prudential severity, and it may indeed be misconceived as the authoritarian necklace, chain, or crown to which it refers. Actually, it may come to seem closest to a book of dreams or jokes, with the kind of prudence we feel in Freud when he suggests that children should not be sent to the Arctic with summer clothing and maps of the Italian lakes. Proverbs, said to be the most sublimating book in the Bible, is, rather, an eruptive text of a restless shrewdness that does more than balance the idealism of priests and prophets with the cunning of the "elders." Commandments are finite; the Proverbs are infinite and remind us that attention must be so. The Book of Proverbs is not simply the site for craftsmanly counsel on cunning, though some have analogized it with the efflorescence of the arts under the imperial Solomon. Like the so-called Wisdom psalms, this book contains a tone of strenuous searching that links it with the PreSocratics. It is true that there is an overwhelming worldliness in some of the chief topics, such as avoiding violence and adultery and drunkenness, but we also note, as in chapters 8 and 9, another theme, so grandly stated as to force the mundane, as it were, into allegory: the theme of a personified Wisdom. "Wisdom has built her house, she has set up her seven pillars" (9:1). One does not need the traditions of Zohar and other hermeneutical vehicles to enjoy the multiple perspectives of this allegorical architecture: "She has slaughtered her beasts, she has mixed her wine / she has also set her table" (9:2). This is a wisdom that can only be described at the risk of the most drastic revisionism, as in a new genesis: "The Lord created me at the beginning of his work / the first of his acts of old" (8:22). This "wisdom" seems as if it would appeal to the latest neo-Platonisms of the Wisdom of Solomon, most probably written under Hellenic influence. A series of idealizing odes forces the inner collections to be read through their irradiation. Although one might agree with Mark Van Doren that the Song of Songs is "merely" human and erotic, *Mishlé* here offers a tremendous rebuke to any reductive reading.

Let us accept that many of the inner collections in our canonic text emerge from an international matrix of prudential counsels. Let us even accept that these inner collections function as modest and moderate rote learning for a new civil servant: "To impose a fine on a righteous man is not good; to flog a noble man is wrong" (17:26). Those who have seen this book, like Robertson in a recent essay on its "syndetic" quality, as being without beginning or end, miss, the fundamental insistence on Wisdom as Beginning. I do not think it improper to share my sense that those who have called this work a collage mistake or misconceive the nature of collage or even *bricolage*, as Northrop Frye has called the whole Bible an ingenious *bricolage*. The collage has its own unity and is particulate despite ruptures in texture and changes of density and direction. A collage is not, moreover, beginningless or endless. The Book of Proverbs has many recipes, it is true, and Robertson is right in suggesting that we must learn how to apply our little directives. But the book also has some enormous principles and pressures, and these cannot be mistaken even if the form is turbulent, and the punctuation of the form is restless, anomalous, asymmetrical. The book that is said to end nowhere concludes with woman as language and happiness. The book that is said only to accumulate begins with a proliferation of absolute oppositions between wisdom and folly. It is a modernist misreading to conceive this book as "accretion without development." Wisdom signifies development.

It is fitting for the melancholy poet of disunity, the Jewish Catholic Hugo von Hofmannsthal, to have written a prose poem on Chapter 30 of Proverbs and the mysterious figure of Agur. Here we have a sudden skeptical darkness that seems to yield an endless undertow to our book: "I have not learned wisdom, nor have I knowledge of the Holy One. / Who has ascended to heaven and come down? Who has gathered the wind in his fists?" (30:3-4) This is the fabulous cadenza of answerless questions that we have heard in Job's whirlwind encounter: Here it initiates the great numerological poems on the wonders of the world. Like the great choral ode in Antigone, it foregrounds the wonder of man himself, and yet it does this with the constant Near Eastern decorative zeal of linking the whole animal kingdom. How much the lyric poet Antonio Machado was to learn from the modest singing tones of this mystical numerology: "Three things are too wonderful for me; four I do not understand: the way of an eagle in the sky; the way of a serpent on a rock; the way of a ship on the high seas; and the way of a man with a maiden" (30:18-19). Machado in his "proverbial poems" speaks of things that are not useful at sea: one, rudders; two, anchors; and three, the fear of shipwreck. This prudential and uncanny lyric could not exist without the wonders of Agur. And Agur's erotic underlining of the way of man and woman speaks against those who find Proverbs' prudence antierotic. Prudence leaves space for wonder.

Just as a proverb may seem a humble or mean or quotidian form but turns out to be a focusing of attention that is in itself a delight, there is a congruity in the imagery of Agur with the focus on the seemingly insignificant. The ants are a humble people—one might say, a comically tribal bunch—but they are also rationalists for us to stare at. The badgers look fallible and frail, but they invade mountains. The locusts may look anarchic without a king, but they are Prussian in their orderliness. And, in the last insidious image of paradox and strangeness, Agur yields the immortal image of eruptive power: "The lizard you can take in your hands, yet it is in kings' palaces." These are not proverbs but extended numerological miniatures that remind us that Proverbs is *not* simply a collection of proverbs, but an anthology of diverse forms. And it is diversity that Agur celebrates, a diversity of power that encounters the worst without blinking: "Under three things the earth trembles, under four it cannot bear up: a slave when he becomes a king, and a fool when he is filled with food; an unloved woman when she gets a husband, and a maid when she succeeds her mistress" (30:21–23). There is a Shakespearean tone of the aristocrat's privilege here, but what is most available to us is the sense that some tolerance is paralyzing. One cannot tolerate one's own negation (as my own mother used to remark about the limits of pluralism).

This is the one text that can make contradiction explicit, as in the famous, scandalously opposing advice on answering fools (26:5–6), because the world is presented as a wilderness for wise men to garden. The cultivated reader is not provoked by a contradiction but understands that the symbols will be applied tactfully to the situation as it arises in the murk of multiplicity. The Wise Man, like Joseph, decodes dreams like brothers and becomes a ruler by such decoding. And brothers are indeed a theme: "Better is a neighbor who is near / than a brother who is far away" (27:10). Charles Peirce went so far in his semiotics as to say that man himself is a sign, and that would be acceptable to Agur among his wonders. A wonder, a sign, a figure, an analogy are methods and means for an encyclopedic text on the subtle but not maliciously designed world: "Faithful are the wounds of a friend; profuse are the kisses of an enemy" (27:6). Prudence is not the stairway to a Machiavellian *Realpolitik*; it is a means of avoiding the falser Machiavellis who surround the wise man like hidden snares. It is relationship, in reading, friendship, and speech, that is the canonic Buberian hero of our nonstory: "Iron sharpens iron, and one man sharpens another" (27:17). The proverbs in mosaic sharpen one another, as later the fragments of a *Minima Moralia* are sharpened with Theodor Adorno's juxtapositions.

Our book is not concerned with success so much as it is concerned with health itself. Emerson was influenced by this book to become a great aphorist on the theme of health, and yet few have noted, despite Emerson's essay on prudence, that we cannot have our strongest native transcendentalism without a grappling with the problem of prudence. The inconsistency and the eruptiveness beloved of Emerson, as of Whitman, were not an infantile discontinuity but one founded on an attention to the divine as a focusing device. *Mishlé* counsels us in a myriad of ways to avoid infantile paradises and to grow up toward the difficulty of "real life" seen in almost penological perspectives. There is no easy way to avoid the theme of punishment, because this book tries to become "equipment for living," and it would be a saccharine collection indeed if it refused the perspective of punishment. "A wicked man earns deceptive wages" (11:18). At the least, the book concerns itself with our illusions, and for those who think *Mishlé* is not worldly enough to note the success of the unrighteous, we might add the Freudian note that money does not guarantee happiness, since it does not reward an infantile desire. "He who troubles his household will inherit wind" (11:29) seems to suggest that the book is a constant critique of infantilism. If there are no constants, there is the drive toward constancy. The book may, at least, be seen as an anthology of utopian and, paradoxically, materialist idealizations. These ideals, as William James has said, create the real. The real world depends upon a comparison.

Throughout our century there has been a positivist desire to search for a perfect language. One has only to think of the tension in the master of *figura*, Ludwig Wittgenstein, who sought for a language whose propositions could be laid next to reality like a ruler. This pursuit in

Wittgenstein finally cracks into his later, mature mode, which revels in the anthropocentric infinitude of so-called language games. We might say that *Mishlé* is already ruled by the tension between the pursuit for a perfect language—the divinity, seen allegorically as Wisdom, the Sage, the Good Wife—and the resolute acceptance of the shattered world of forms—glimpsed in the multitude of prudential adages. Proverbs insists, as a text, that metaphor cannot be escaped, though there remains the immortal desire for an escape from metaphor. Metaphor, with its compacted insistence on difference as much as identity, is the single method for attaching word to object, man to thing, and person to divinity. We might say that the Tanach, with all its aniconic zeal and the anti-idolatrous urge, could not help being negative toward the metaphor as eidolon. Yet Solomonic glory resorted to a decorative architecture, and this late book (sixth century B.C.E.?) is a Bible of metaphors. God speaks in metaphors: "I also will laugh at your calamity; I will mock when panic strikes you, when panic strikes you like a storm, and your calamity comes like a whirlwind" (1:26). Out of the whirlwind come questions and metaphors. Those that would purge us of analogies would purge us of architectural models to which we must cling. Just as the word "metaphor" is metaphorical, the very word for "proverbs" is a compacted figure of figures. Borges speaks of a book of analogies which splits into infinite pages, and so the form of this book is purposely of its monotonous magnitude. The scale itself is an allegory of the extent of wisdom: Solomonic numerology.

 The Wisdom movement is usually viewed by scholars as polarized, so that the skeptical authors of Job and Ecclesiastes seem to admonish the repressed conservator of Proverbs. But again and again there are flashes of a dazzling darkness in our book that rival the darkness of those "strange books." One does not merely want to create a rudimentary contrast of pessimism versus optimistic faith, but since this is a theme so harped upon in the commentaries, I would like to remind the reader to remember these gloomy adages: "When the wicked rule, the people groan" (29:2). Of course, this is only the last part of the dystich "When the righteous are in authority, the people rejoice." But the undaunted realism of the groaning people remains and stains the whole dystich. Elsewhere, the entire adage is Hobbesian and brutish and short: "If a ruler listens to falsehood, all his officials will be wicked" (29:12). A lack of receptivity is death itself, the final disunity, seen in the most corporeal of images: "He who is often reproved, yet stiffens his neck / will suddenly be broken beyond healing" (29:1). All the comical inelasticities that Henri Bergson speaks of at the heart of wit are summoned in the images of excess and psychopathology: "A miserly man hastens after wealth and does not know that want will come upon him" (28:22). Rashi speaks in a commentary about sexual intercourse that is discreetly summoned in this infuriatingly sly image of the impure: "This is the way of an adulteress: she eats, and wipes her mouth, and says, 'I have done no wrong'" (30:20). This portrait, with its unbending mimetic punch, is an example of a realism beyond hope or despair. These things are so because the earth and the emotions are laid out with the geometrical zeal which will appeal later to the lens maker in Amsterdam (Spinoza): "Wrath is cruel, anger is overwhelming: but who can stand before jealousy?" (27:4). Rather than repression, sublimation, or conservatism, we find in Proverbs a contempt for illusions: "A continual dripping on a rainy day / and a contentious woman are alike; to restrain her is to restrain the wind ..." (27:15).

Boris Pasternak's freshest collection is called *My Sister Life*; I know of no one who has drawn attention to the great Biblical figure parallel to this: "Say to wisdom, You are my sister, and call insight your intimate friend" (7:4). This is how the peculiar narrative on the impure woman is initiated, and it leaves us with a less embittered sense than without it. Robert Alter has spoken of the extended power of this little secular poem, and we are amazed at its spatial precisions, its rhythmic finesse (both in Hebrew and in the King James translation, moreover, a translation to be wondered at, unrivaled, in itself untranslatable—though for my discursive purposes, I cite here from the Revised Standard Version), its tremendous forward motion and tragic close. "For at the window of my house / I have looked out through my lattice / and I have seen among the simple, I have perceived among the youths, a young man without sense ..." (7:6). The repetitions are horrifying, and they deepen the turbid atmosphere like glazes: "in the twilight, in the evening, at the time of night and darkness" (7:8–9). The woman is dominant: "She seizes him and kisses him, and with impudent face she says to him: I had to offer sacrifices, and today I have paid my vows; so now I have come out to meet you, to seek you eagerly, and I have found you." Like Pharaoh's wife in the Joseph story—perhaps written in Wisdom circles, as current scholarship has it—this woman unites a false aestheticism with ethical betrayal: "I have decked my couch with coverings, colored spreads of Egyptian linen.... Let us delight ourselves with love. For my husband is not at home" (7:19). And the victim follows, like an ox, a stag, and a rushing bird. So much for those who cannot decode the Other and the others.

Proverbs may seem to be the greatest case of what Hermann Broch once referred to as "I"-suppression. It should be noted, however, that the collection is constantly pierced by the dialogic tone of father to son, and thus is not the tedious string of decontextualized adages it may seem to be to those who plunge into its midst. Theodore Reik has spoken of Jewish wit and its idiosyncratic self-lacerating tones, and he suggests that a "powerless" people may develop the signs of pathology that Freud speaks of in his essay on "The Exceptions," those who behave as if early suffering gave them antinomian privileges. But our book is the least antinomian and has about it the most empurpled sense of doom and mortality: "A little sleep, a little slumber, a little folding of the hands to rest, and poverty will come upon you like a vagabond, and want like an armed man" (6:6). Perhaps it is the concreteness in the condensed majesty of these lines concerning the absence of all control that goes to making the "personism" of Proverbs. Because we come to see teaching itself as something bound physically upon our hearts and necks, we do not find the book sepulchrally impersonal in any lateRomantic sense. This physicality is present everywhere: "Can a man carry fire in his bosom, and his clothes not be burned?" (6:27) "The words of a whisperer are like delicious morsels; they go down into the inner parts of the body" (18:8). We understand by the indirect admonition against slander that the book is to become part of our body. Reading is vascular or nothing.

Robert Alter is correct in pointing out how much of the pithiness of the Hebraic proverb is lost in the smooth unraveling of the

English mistranslations. Alter understands that the authors of this book regarded linguistic facility as the gateway to Wisdom: "If we are not good readers, we will not get the point of the sayings of the wise" (Alter, page 168). And he is most adept at calling attention to the morality of the "smallest verbal movements" in the precepts and riddles of our text. His analogy with Alexander Pope, moreover, is correct, if one recalls the true ferocity of that great satirist. This book is not one of elegance alone, but of the sanity that derides false luxuries and none-too-subtle adulteries. Elsewhere, Alter derides some of the formulations for having the hackneyed predictability that could be expected in schools of rote devices. But note that a poetry of prediction and predictability is not so far from a poetry of fate and causality. The smoothness of the road to adultery slips into unsurprising doom. In many ways, the music of law—indeed, of predictability—is a resonant one here. If a modernist is mostly attracted to adages with stippled surprises or sudden reversals, it is also true that wisdom demands a stern regularity: "A just balance and scales are the Lord's; all the weights in the bag are his work" (16:11). Proverbs demand patience.

There are many things for a poet to learn from Proverbs, even that perverse pleasure in condensation and *non sequitur* that appears in the "perverbs" of our contemporary Harry Matthews, who with delight takes Canonic maxims and deranges them. What is extraordinary in *Mishlé* is, however, the scale of its *extended* narratives, as in the extended homage to the Good Wife, where the woman becomes anagrammatically the whole language. "She rises while it is yet night," and becomes a constant like a sun. "She is like the ships of the merchant," and effectively annihilates space and time, like wisdom. But it is always wisdom that is being praised in the elongations of *Mishlé*, as in the final tribute: "Charm is deceitful, and beauty is vain, but a woman who fears the Lord is to be praised" (31:30).

Drunkenness, too, receives its opposing extended and physical fugue: "Who has woe? Who has sorrow? ... Those who tarry long over wine, those who go to try mixed wine. Do not look at wine when it is red, when it sparkles in the cup / and goes down smoothly. At the last it bites like a serpent and stings like an adder (23:29–32). There is an eidetic physicality to the rush of this vertigo: "Your eyes will see strange things, and your mind utter perverse things. You will be like one who lies down in the midst of the sea, like one who lies on the top of the mast" (23:33). Such self-violence is the opposite of reading.

The drunkard antihero cries from within this vertigo as one who is indeed simple, simplified, and, etymologically speaking, wide open: "They struck me, you will say, but I was not hurt; they beat me, but I did not feel it. When shall I awake? I will seek another drink" (33:35). There is a grave circular comedy being enacted here and by the "intimate yell" that another poet has discovered in great Russian admonitions. Here the intimism is intense and relentless; the ephebe is caught up in the repetitive folly of a minor ecstasy. Note how difficult it would be for the Hasidim to reverse the enormous canonic weight of these admonitions against immoderate states.

One does not want to call this book merely Apollonian in its calls to order and sobriety, but surely there is a parallel to Greek wisdom in its rebuke to excess and its parallel call to self-knowledge. It might be part of the glory of the tragedians and the authors of Mishlé that self-knowledge is seen exactly within boundaries, relations, and balances, as opposed to any infantile Rimbaldien *dérèglement de tous les sens*. All the senses are to be part of the ruled world, a world created in number, weight, and measure. Thus, the drumbeat of the measured proverb is like a genesis of its own, dismaying to drunkards, a web woven in honor of exigent Wisdom.

What remains for us today of Proverbs is perhaps surprising in its abundance. We do not think of its fideism as part of a slothful false comfort known to Job's friends, since nowhere is there counsel that the promises of rewards are calculated as insults to the suffering. As a matter of fact, we might cite a host of proverbs that speak of kindness, empathy, tact: "A poor man who oppresses the poor / is a beating rain that leaves no food" (28:3). Job's friends give the right cliché at the wrong moment, but the whole lesson of Proverbs concerns the tact of utterance and rapport. Ecclesiastes, too, that "strange book," is not more strange in its distressed materialism than the abundant materialism of our book:

"As a door turns on its hinges, so does a sluggard on his bed" (26:14). And as for Blake's proverbs of drastic de-sublimation, there remains the exuberant: "Better is open rebuke / than hidden love" (27:5).

Freud speaks in his *Moses and Monotheism* of the soaring abstractions of Egyptian thought and the savage particularities of the volcano god of later tribal tradition. In Proverbs, we have both the soaring particularities of a late, cosmopolitan universalism, and the fundamental monism of the Wisdom allegory. We may be moved by the sweep of this book, as by the great analyst's most labyrinthine case histories, where a rage for order and a tolerance for concreteness support one another. The analytic wisdom tradition includes the imperturbable doctor of our shattered Soul.

No contemporary reader has much problem with the so-called moral realism of Proverbs, as when the melancholy Agur summons up images of greed and infantile fantastics:

> The leech has two daughters;
> Give, give, they cry.
> Three things are never satisfied;
> four never say "Enough.":
> Sheol, the barren womb,
> the earth ever thirsty for water,
> and the fire which never says
> "Enough."[30:15]

What is more difficult for some is the sense of pietistic hope in the seemingly simple theodicy: "He who walks in integrity will be delivered but he who is perverse in his ways will fall into a pit" (28:18). To this, the simple reader asks, Isn't this simply refuted by experience; is all this, as it were, pre-Job? Is not this that Ecclesiastes and Job were written to refute?

But I do not think it is so. A reading of the Psalms will show how often the great national songs include in them constant promise of reward for righteousness: "Blessed is everyone who fears the Lord, who walks in his ways! You shall eat the fruit of the labor of your hands; you shall be happy, and it shall be well with you" (Psalm 128:1). The link of Psalms and Proverbs in these seemingly naive counsels is the tone of pathos and desire. Both Psalms and Proverbs are stating the counsels of the wise as the dream of righteousness. It is obvious from the darker maxims of Proverbs, as from the dark exilic hymns, that the wise men knew quite well of the triumphs of the wicked; many formulae sketch this perverse triumph. The theme of righteous reward is not in contradiction to the suffering of a Job. Job himself is crowned with a final reward, if only *ex machina*. Is this unsatisfactory? (My mother used to say, with some "moral realism," that Job never got back his original children. This I take to be the height of the prudential tone in contemporary Jewish wit.) Reading Psalms and Proverbs together, one learns how often a proverb is a song.

We conclude that David Robertson is wrong in suggesting that *Mishlé* is a syndetic book, mainly involved in creating, like libraries and museums, a non-developing accumulation of recipes in random order. It does develop, it is synthetic, it does indeed reconcile opposites. I think no reader of poetry can miss the sustained and alarmingly tense opposition of Wisdom and Folly, of the Adulteress and the Good Wife. This volume is an extended homage to Wisdom in its perpetual militancy against sluggard inattention. The longest and most seemingly random of the collections has at its heart the sense of prudential insight as reaping reward and being its own self-reflexive joy. The climax in the acrostic poem clearly underscores the idea that the logocentric universe is indeed well-ordered, like the family in its true dialogues. Whatever is minimal in the prudence of *Mishlé* is accompanied by the Tremendum: "Better is a little with the fear of the Lord / than great treasure and trouble with it" (15:16). I think it is straining to modulate from the early interpretations of this book as being a conservative scribal textbook to the new vision of it as a whimsical collage of popular art. The folk sayings are indeed derived from popular sayings but are transformed into a unity of supernal power. It is not a unity easily glimpsed, but it is a delirious mistranslation to seize in it only disunity. For its exemplariness Coleridge might well have yielded us his neologism, "Multeity." The radical multitudinousness of Proverbs always points to a vision, and a vision of vision: "The eyes of the Lord are in every place." It is because these eyes are everywhere that the book may seem to some to be bursting with everything. It is a strange recipe book that supplies the food.

Review of *The Complete Poems* by Edwin Denby

Edited and with an introduction by Ron Padgett and with essays by Frank O'Hara and Lincoln Kirstein. Photographs by Rudy Burckhardt.

Edwin Denby's *Complete Poems* (Random House, 1986) brings before the public, in an edition superbly edited and introduced by the poet Ron Padgett, a poet who has avoided the canons and anthologies and deserves a permanent place. Padgett gives us some of the pertinent and suggestive facts: Denby was born in 1904 in China, with the disturbing burden of being the son of the Consul in Tientsin; by 1908 was removed to Vienna, where he was educated in German and was enthralled by the puppet-shows; and later had a discontinuous career at Harvard. Analyzed by a colleague of Freud, Dr. Paul Federn, Denby seems to have finished a classic crisis by finding himself as a poet and dancer, and Padgett gives us the significant fact that he was a specialist in eccentric or comic dancing. From 1935 on, he was a denizen of New York, worked with Orson Welles, Paul Bowles, and Virgil Thompson, among others, and became a pioneer dance reviewer. Two books of his poetry, *In Public, In Private* (1948) and *Mediterranean Cities* (1956) appeared before Padgett and other second-generation New York poets brought out a *Collected Poems*, now supplanted by the current volume. A stoic and steady mind, he resented the final indignities of prolonged illness and took his life to save his friends and himself from further absurd distress in the summer of 1983.

Poetry, Vol. 150, No. 1, edited by Joseph Parisi (April 1987).

Denby's work first became known to me through the strange little magazine *Locus Solus*, where I saw the curiously jointed sonnets of his *Mediterranean Cities*. It was years later that I became aware that these sonnets, conspiring with the photographs of that accurate, masterful urbanist Rudy Burckhardt, had emerged as what Fairfield Porter called one of the most beautiful of contemporary collaborations. Denby's dance criticism, and some essays on life in the thirties among artists, are a model of an empirical yet passionate criticism. His poetry, praised by O'Hara and some of the younger poets, also seemed to constitute a kind of dry rebuke to expressionist cadenzas. Denby made a quietistic poetry of the subways that Lincoln Kirstein compares favorably to Crane. What sometimes is more appealing than most urban affirmations is Denby's understated minor key, in which cats, libidinous and melancholy bachelors, buildings, and historical traditions all mingle within some learned forms to create a jagged antitheatrical pose and poise.

If one looks at the sonnets, the form he evidently most admired and mastered severely, though he was capable of extended work in a variety of song-like modes, one realizes that he had the poetic equivalent of de Kooning's Dutch academic training. As a matter of fact, it is perhaps only slightly hilarious that such "academic" underpinnings helped make Denby a father-figure among Lower East Side Poets, who almost all foreswore the sterner reaches of scholasticism. Denby was the perfect anti-father figure because he used all his learning so gracefully. He avoided the pedantries of many others dedicated to elegance of form. His sonnets could become as crumpled as paper bags and as rigid as some synthetic fibers. He used the sonnet both as a parodistic resource and created a homage to the sonnet within each belated object of his craft, much as his beloved Balanchine took a lasting pride in pulling apart the conventions of classic ballet. Both Balanchine and Denby were masters of activating classic space with fresh gestures.

I had some contact with this dry and witty intelligence and can testify that his presence, sudden on the subway and magisterial if modest at the dance auditorium, was always an occasion for intense conversation. During a Utopian moment in my own conversion to a Tolstoyan pacifism, he made some lacerating comments concerning man's evil nature. I find his poetry filled with a very sophisticated sense of psychology and a refusal to become the dupe of competing systems. Dance didn't make him a hedonist but kept him an observer of all bodies and places. Criticism informs his poetry, as does psychoanalysis: he is one of the few poets to have written a sonnet about genitals, and it is subtle. Abstract expressionism influenced him, as did the "Pop" art of his many painter-friends, but his own poetry is a curious blend of the representational and the joyfully anti-mimetic.

On the one hand, many of the poems are bitter-sweet meditations on the power of New York, but the city never overwhelms the quiet bachelor with his obsessive love for cats. Affection in Denby is specific and overwhelmingly direct, for the cold streets of New York and for grey cats, for his friend's young son and for his friends, for Walt Whitman and for his legitimate disciple, Frank O'Hara. Depression gives him some of his gloomiest and most fractured moments of public torpor, but in the Sixties his sonnets are choppy and sophisticated meditations on old age and random joys in city life. Elegant always and disdainful of art without finesse, he ends by underlining the seductive sense of language itself: "Complicities of New York speech / Embrace me as I fall asleep" (untitled sonnet, p. 165). He is never as acoherent as Ashbery, but many of the late sonnets have a bizarre short-hand style that resembles Chinese poetry in literal translation. He usually makes vigilance itself his theme, as could be expected from a man whose professional responsibilities were those of the eye: "Munificence I eye fearfully / Forest disorder dear to Rudy" (untitled sonnet, p. 163). Unlike Auden, he doesn't permit his urbane knowingness to diminish to dogma or pedantry. His "grotesque dancer" side seems to have kept him permanently alive to the devilish stupidity of things and the wonder of bright bodies in space. His poetry is a kind of eccentric dancing, and one could make an interesting study of how often he situates people and buildings as a theatrically activated series of presences. It's as if Hart Crane had followed the mincing tones of his "Chaplinesque" rather than a more pantheistic mood. In Denby, precision and energetic flair replace Romantic atmospherics. He is the Balanchine of poetry, to state it baldly.

To continue these impressionistic analogues, I would say that Denby's poems, particularly the sonnet-sequences, are cinematic, and the poet learned by making film-scripts and doing a little brilliant acting in films. Beyond certain formal characteristics, however, Denby's greatest strength lies in his ethos of the personal and the particular, as in a postcard poem brilliantly filled with the names of every possible friend. This homage to proper names is an anti-confessional homage to the promiscuity of language itself. I think one of the ways to praise Denby adequately is to remember that the sonnet form is fabulously difficult to "deconstruct," in the fashionable phrase, and that Denby is one of the very few American practitioners not to succumb to its Medusa-like terrors. He dismantles the usual sense of syllogistic charm in the Shakespearean mode and creates a personal and even diaristic use of the form that keeps it song-like but makes it also more cruelly continuous, prosier, and closer to urban reportage.

The tour Denby gives us of his New York and his Vermont, this non-narrative movie of tender tentatives, is one where collaboration is affirmed as the truest mode of poetry. The meaning of the city for Denby becomes clear as a fruitfully chaotic place where margins criticize the very idea of the center. Denby's poems are memorable— Elaine de Kooning startled many by her poignant recitation of them by heart at his memorial—paradoxically because of their multiplicity. Denby's poems resist the falser, easier coherences; they provide the solace of truly shattered and shattering perspectives.

Review of *The Happy Man* by Donald Hall

Donald Hall's eighth book of poems is a very powerful volume, and it makes a rare combination of phantasmal and shattering narratives with natural description of a high precision. His descriptions of cows, chickens, and some convincingly Chaucerian fowl are massed with the colorful modulation that make them more than impressionist. There is a reflexive joy in Hall's language that does not hinder an equal and impassioned joy in mimesis itself. Another poet I admire is conjured in these poems, James Schuyler, and the landscape here has a patient particularism and a grace analogous to Schuyler's but with an idiosyncratic melancholy that is quite identifiably Hall's: "It is good / to wake early in high / summer with work to do, / and look out the window / at a ghost bird lifting away / to drowse all morning / in his grassy hut" ("Whip-poor-will"). Since Hall is capable of a dense prose and can use this prosiness well within his poetry, one has to admire the winnowing here, the modest "clear brief notes" of a poem terse in its custom-made crispness, the summery laconism of the lyric lament that reads as paradoxical praise. It is not for nothing that this highly polarized volume, oscillating between calm representation and agitated introspection, quotes the mystic Eckhart on the power of Repose. Haunted by a father's dying face, the poet turns to "building a house" as a central sacred act in a world more profaned than the word. Building a landscape, building up a dream sequence, and constructing a sufficient dwelling are the soul-making tasks here.

Again and again, Hall shows his resonant power in constructing voices, as it were, voices placed in such a way as to give us a kind of rural

Poetry, Vol. 150, No. 1, edited by Joseph Parisi (April 1987).

antidote to the conventional urban *Waste Land*. It is a noteworthy and adequately multiple pastorale, and it is of course elegiac. The son recalls the exasperated father and his longings to do only what one desires. The enormously moving fragment, "Shrubs Burned Away," from a long poem in progress, keeps up a steady and ambiguous marriage of voices, childhood reminiscences, and a final mating on a joyful central bed. The image that an archetypal psychologist might hunt for most diligently is laid bare immediately: a secret house constructed by a brother and sister out of some precise *märchen*. But we are not permitted mere enchantment for long, as the poet gives us a father weeping in rage over the cradle, and the raveled children grow amidst adulteries and wars into the possible consolations of a craftsman's middle age. This long poem has the power of a novella, full of a strong *black-and-white* in the Japanese sense. One does not forget that, in the Chinese tradition, Tu Fu's central poem is that of his house blown to pieces by the autumn wind, where the poet dreams in an emergency of the poor scholars of the whole world and a house that could contain them like a mountain. Hall contributes to our most dignified sense, with his recollections of failure and interruptions of rapport, of a public dream of shared and secret space.

The poet has come upon a plain style that is still sensual, filled with parallelism and play, capable of solemnity and a flexible humor. The image of an inexhaustible joy contrasts with the Virgilian twilight that always touches his mind:

> From the Studebaker's backseat, on our Sunday drives,
> I watched her earrings sway. Then I walked uphill
> beside an old man carrying buckets
> under birches on an August day. Striding at noontime,
> I looked at wheat and at river cities. In the crib
> my daughter sighed opening her eyes. I kissed the cheek
> of my father dying. By the pond an acorn fell.
> You listening here, you reading these words as I write them,
> I offer this cup to you: Though we drink
> from this cup every day, we will never drink it dry.
>
> ("The Day I Was Older")

This marvelous elegy to the world without marvels is the final proportionate gift of the "happy man" of the ironic and truthful title. The guilty innocent son has outlived the imperfect, loved, entangling father. The poet reads the obituaries and is a professional reader, *at the sign of the signs*. The world has become as reposeful as the patrician landscapes of a Fairfield Porter, whose chief message, he remarked to this critic once, was: "Conclude every sermon with the words, Pay attention." The poet pays attention to each part of the kingdom: "A mink scuds through ferns; an acorn tumbles." It is a kind of ode to "To Autumn," a homage to unexplained and inexplicable particulars. But this poet cannot end without noting that the family is part of landscape and makes for the bread and wine of miraculous largesse. What Hall achieves here and elsewhere is a kind of psalm to the passage, as Freud put it, from hysterical misery to ordinary unhappiness. But ordinary unhappiness is our most appropriate form of happiness. This is a poetics of imperfection, one that regards all Utopian notions of purity as what Meyer Schapiro called a hypothesis. The imperfect reader, not Joyce's ideal reader with ideal insomnia, is offered the resource of the poet's desire for clear representation.

Buckminster Fuller once suggested a gigantic bubble over the metropolis of modernity to accomplish, among other things, the end of deleterious weather. Donald Hall, like Fairfield Porter, laughs at such a sad unwillingness to accept contingency, and his most sensual poems concern the wild irregular regularities of inner and outer weather. (The reader of his rich, almost Elizabethan "Twelve Seasons," might also want to look up Hall's prose homage to winter in the haunting catalogue for a show of paintings called *Winter*, published last year by the Hood Museum of Art.) Hall's love for particularity in nature would have cheered the empiricist in Fairfield Porter, who recounted to me his delight in watching the Fuller domes get tossed by the Maine breeze. Fuller was involved in the distribution of clear information, while art revels in "disastrous relationships." Hall is particularly thrilling on the happy disasters of relations, and the relative happiness of a starry fall.

After the New York School: Interview by Joseph Lease

Joseph Lease: Do you feel typecast by critics?

David Shapiro: Critics tend to typecast one. I've had the experience of writing a book in black paint, as it were, my almost suicidal *House (Blown Apart)*, and having critics begin by typecasting me as a New York School Poet of whimsy and cheerfulness. So it is, yes, dangerous. I think the New York School Poets may have less in common together than one thinks. Though there were some shared affinities—for Pasternak, for Stevens, for Surrealism—each poet now seems fairly distinct: James Schuyler, Frank O'Hara, Kenneth Koch of the older generation. And some younger poets may seem to have blurred, in critics' eyes, into mere epigones. This is simply part of the pathos of literary traditions, and I guess we're caught in it. My own sense is that some have tried to make the flux or the impressionism of the New York School into something "solid as the art of the museums." I often feel our task is a Cézannism of trying to fix the mere impressionistic empiricism of great poets such as James Schuyler and Frank O'Hara into something angrier, more sexual, whatever that might mean, less lenient with history. The impressionism of the New York School, much derided, actually has a great freshness. One loves the freshness of James Schuyler's poems and it's very hard to better that sense of exultation in them or in Fairfield Porter. It may be almost absurd to say one can do

---

Pataphysics Magazine, edited by Yanni Florence and Leo Edelstein, the Blue Issue (1990).

anything better than Ashbery in his rococo sense: that exquisiteness in "The Skaters" that I really love, the pathos of the labyrinth there. One simply tries to do what one can do, glumly. (Laughter.)

JL: How have you tried to make that impressionism angrier, more sexual, less lenient with history? What do those categories mean for you?

DS: Well from the beginning I was a violinist who was very interested in late Mozart. That is always already Romantic. The Mozart of the late Divertimento and late Beethoven, those are one's standards. Something that I love in Elliot Carter is his drive for polyrhythmic music, and he also defines the tempo of music in a way that I feel very close to. He talks about the necessity for rhythms that accelerate and decelerate, the variety of tempi that he wants to have acting together. And in my poetry one of the things that often annoyed older poets is that I was very interested in changing tempi. I think that one part of the steadiness of John Ashbery's poetry—to speak synesthetically—is its extraordinary perfect monochrome. And since one couldn't do any better than that in its own way, as John Ashbery said of Duchamp, one tried for a polychrome poetry. And it wasn't simply in response: I think at any rate it was a necessity for me to have a poetry of many rhythms, one that would not be as entranced with forms of monotony. Not that I didn't flirt with them, but one simply saw that masters of monotony like Warhol in a generation before me had investigated that, it seemed to me, had pursued that recklessly. What I was interested in was the darkness of the divertimento in which sequences would abut and create a kind of montage.

I was always interested in doing a philosophical epic, and I continued in "House (Blown Apart)," "To an Idea," and in other poems, such as "About this Course," and "Man Holding an Acoustic Panel" to create a sort of elegy to an America I despised. I had an anti-imperialistic theme, politically, that was very difficult to match with monochrome and I was less taken with camp than with Jewish earnestness and with prophetic qualities in Isaiah that were my first sense of poetry. There's a part of me—comically enough, and not everyone might see this—that even links to my old Newark friend Allen Ginsberg. There is an aspect of my poetry which irked the parodistic in poets such as Ron Padgett and Ted Berrigan, the part of me that's perhaps too involved with seriousness. But I was very taken with Rilke's idea that one should not be merely ironic, and I always told my students to dig past mere irony.

Not that I was involved with confession, but I was very interested (since my wife is an architect and we've lived together for so many years) in structure, in the kind of moral seriousness that you get in the great visionary architecture of John Hejduk, his penological cities, his analogous cities. Aldo Rossi's dream cities might seem to be an analogue, but John's are even more austere. That's why I put John on the cover of *House (Blown Apart)*. I've been interested in achieving the kind of depressing, massive sense of melancholy that one gets again and again in Jasper Johns (in many ways my aesthetic standard) and the mania for prophetic structures in John Hejduk's great imaginary cities. And I often dream of a poem that will be as labyrinthine as one of John's analogous cities.

That's all very far from the single lament. Jeremy Gilbert-Rolfe said to me that our theme together, as colleagues, painters and poets, is multiplicity. He sees it as Deleuzean. I don't know if that's true, but it seems to be one way in which my poetry is more "demobilized" and "nomadic" than one might think.

JL: You use elements of collage which are alive for you. They become charged with personal force. One feels in your poems not the systematic non-sequitur but something lived and felt.

DS: Gilbert-Rolfe once said to me, "So where's the collage in your poetry?" I said, "Well, I've transformed grammar and physics textbooks and played with their degraded diction." He said, "No, that's not collage." I said, "Well, I've taken Heidegger and changed all his words for 'being' into snow." He said, "No, no, that's not collage." I said, "There's 'A Song,' where I take parts of 'When A Man Loves a Woman' and turn them into a disco cascade with elements of *The Encyclopedia Britannica*." He said, "Oh yes, that's probably the only place where you use collage." He was teasing me because I kept trying to state the argument in terms of collage, and maybe that's not necessary. It's even more difficult to find what collage might mean in music, though I think it's a very important aspect of certain problems in Stravinsky and Schoenberg.

JL: What most readers associate with collage in poetry is a kind of a syntactic staccato mode, and you never abandon melody, though you do, as you say change tempi—nor do you abandon syntax, nor do you really abandon narrative, though dream-like narratives slide into one another in your poems.

DS: Collages to me suggest that a person is involved in appropriating from a variety of sources of textures, one might say. For example, my poetry sometimes does appropriate high and low dictions and attempts to have them explode. I am very interested in seeing what one word does to another word. It is obvious when Braque uses a newspaper against a piece of paint that he's interested in dissonance. But I don't think it's necessary to have breakdowns in syntax because I think that collage and this form of juxtaposition and montage can occur with forms of dislocation that we can make less trivial than mere discontinuity. A lot of the collages that I do often don't announce themselves as such, as in Marianne Moore, who really is a kind of collage poet (I think "Marriage" is one of the great collages that we have), but she was interested in the fact that collage could be a principal of continuity.

In other words, somewhat as Andrew Ross suggested that intellectuals could learn from mass culture, one can appropriate—and not for complacent purposes. One of the things I don't like about the montage of the eclectic "postmodernists" in architecture—one thinks of certain popularist architects, of whom my friend Arthur Cohen said they were trying to monumentalize their own vulgarity—is that one doesn't want only to say, "Las Vegas is enough," as the found poems of Oliver North do, or aspects of some of my contemporaries. One doesn't want to just parade mass culture, though I like the idea, as has been said by Ross recently, that one gets a certain kind of surplus value out of these seemingly degraded commodities. But I have been very interested in the explosion of a Menippean horde of a multiplicity of rhetorics.

I was very attracted early on to *The Waste Land* as the encyclopedia of consciousness. It seemed to me the most melancholy poem, the most haunting. I've always been amazed at those who have been able to give it up. Most New York School poets sort of laughed at me for my love of *The Waste Land* and even of *Four Quartets*. I hear Eliot in Ashbery. Eliot and Stevens combine in me. I'm always appalled at the critics who seem to have to make the choice between Eliot and Stevens. I love both of them and I find the feeling tone of suffering in Stevens and a great cadenza of Cubism in *The Waste Land*. I feel very sad that one would have to give up *The Waste Land*. It is a sort of principle of my poetry to continue to think about what a contemporary *Waste Land* might be. It may be that one of the things that I'm not attracted to in a certain form of the recent narrative poetry has been a return to a storytelling that *The Waste Land* seems to have "blown apart." I do think that if you're going to give up figuration, you're going to have to give an abstract work that is as good as Velázquez. I think if you're going to give up one form of storytelling, you're going to have to do it in another way.

JL: What is that "other way"? The two parts of the title *House (Blown Apart)* for example: one has "house"—domesticity, the inner life, the family romance; that one has "blown apart" in that sense of *The Waste Land* having blown narrative apart. How do you balance them?

DS: Well, remember that "House (Blown Apart)" is an allusion or a quote or an appropriation of a poem by Tu Fu where he tells a story about his house, a thatched roof hut. Tu Fu loses the roof of his house and watches—an old man being mocked by kids from the south village—and at some point, commenting on this emergency like a Channel 7 reporter, he turns, and after a lot of precision about the domestic crisis—his wife and son inside restlessly kicking their feet and the rain streaming down (he said that the war had produced a lot of insomnia)—he suddenly changes scale a great deal and, in what the Chinese regard as a great act of piety and an enormous poetic coup de théâtre, he says, "I am dreaming of a house with a thousand windows and a thousand doors. I would like to see this house before my eyes. There I would house all the poor scholars of the world. If I could only see this house before my eyes, I would die frozen, still satisfied." I like particularly the William Hung translation. What I've tried to do is use what's already bifurcated in Tu Fu. On the one hand it's very personal—"my house has been blown apart," and his reportage on the details—which is something I love to do. In psychoanalysis I love to keep dream diaries. I love that exaggerated sense of the personal—the extraordinary sense that something is really your world—that you can get in dreams and the sense of terror in dream diaries. And a lot of my poems do come out of dreams.

But there's another part: I've always presumed that the personal is public. My mother was very left-wing, a dissident in South Africa in her youth, so I was brought up with a strong socialist background, to say the least. I can't really imagine poetry without the political term. I do feel that a lot of works that look private have an extraordinary political term. The narrative, which implies the family that has a beginning, middle and end (children or mothers dying), and the public situation (which is framed most darkly by the Holocaust and the meaning of political oppression in our century up to and including things that are still taking place in the Middle East—the transition from victim to victor and back again in nation-states): those are the dark nomadic edges of my poetry. I meant *House (Blown Apart)* to have a very public, imperial sense of the American house blown apart, just as "A Man Holding an Acoustic Panel" was my funeral poem in 1968 to a whole generation that seemed to be blowing itself up in bombs. That's why Jan Palach—and the funeral of Jan Palach—is very central in that third book of mine. Jan Palach was a young man who burned himself to protest against the Russian invasion of Czechoslovakia and even to this day his grave, or lack of a grave as it were, is a very political situation. But a personal funeral becomes a public funeral: what his mother said was picked up by a microphone—"My son, my beloved son, I never thought this possible. I'll follow you on foot."

I was in the generation of '68 that thought they could do something. Lionel Abel has suggested that one of the lessons of the '30s was that people overestimated that they could do everything or underestimated that they could do nothing. Irving Petlin, the painter, said, "I think we held back the full force of the fist of the American empire." And that's something to be said for our generation. I think that the rage that's in my poetry (and you can feel it in the photographic cliché of my smoking the President of Columbia's cigar [the photo of Shapiro that appeared in *Life* magazine during the Columbia Uprising] was the enormous rage over the immoral war with the Vietnamese, of which I still continue to think in almost Manichean terms. The pathos of that war was still very large in me. And the yielding of the universities to that war, and the yielding of the entire society to that war. It's very hard for me when I see the wall in Washington not to think that we were trying to make those names less of a scroll. I regard it as a valuable part of my poetry—that rage against the American empire. I'm still fairly sure that the empire needs to be criticized. Poetry can have this anti-imperial theme as a part of it. I don't make it my topic. It's not my burden to be explicitly, dogmatically political. It's just that one does use it everywhere.

Walter Benjamin: A Lost Poem

after a dream

In a lost essay on poetry, Walter Benjamin had written, *I was born into a rich, perhaps too-rich and too comfortable existence in Berlin. Each time my family saw soot in the air we wanted to move to another vacation spot. Poetry today withholds too much. What does it withhold. At any rate, eclecticism, Prokofiev ...* The most Brechtian poem of Benjamin has almost been forgotten. It was published under the title *David*, with a section of a doorknob as a slightly Duchampian typographic oddity. I found the proofs, rare as the Redon for *A Throw of the Dice*, in a bookstore. The poem was fairly simple:

> David or King David
> How
> did you
> *done*
> your door

Unfortunately, many of Benjamin's remarks on poetry were now simple scratches on the cover of the book, effaced like the infamous magic writing pad and indecipherable as hidden love (as opposed to open rebuke). Some of his lost short stories appear in this volume. Scholem said, There was nothing like being alone with Walter Benjamin. *It made one want to read.* The source of that remark is also lost.

—David Shapiro, *After a Lost Original* (The Overlook Press, 1994).

Six Books of Poetry: A Maximalist Manifesto

Sun by Michael Palmer (North Point Press, 1988)
Fair Realism by Barbara Guest (Sun & Moon Press, 1989)
The Crystal Text by Clark Coolidge (The Figures, 1986)
Bitter Angel by Amy Gerstler (North Point Press, 1990)
On Blue Note by William Corbett (Zoland Press, 1989)
Sonnets by Bernadette Mayer (Tender Buttons, 1989)
New York on Fire by Hilton Obenzinger (The Real Comet Press, 1989)

There is no wing like meaning.

A poem need not have a meaning and like most things in nature often does not have one.
   —Wallace Stevens

Beginning a review of a group of books of poetry has its conventions, and while it is impossible to escape them all, it would be interesting to disrupt a few. The Polonius-like initiation of a review yields a time to state some views on the rise or decline of poetry in America or in general. The established poet may make a few gestures of contempt toward the mediocrity that lies about him. The younger poet, rarely given a chance to do much in the way of judgment, might make a few impassioned practitioner's comments and then praise a few colleagues whose style lies near his or her own. Eliot confessed late in life that he saw little in his own criticism but this species of practitioner's prejudice,

---

American Poetry Review, Vol. 20, No. 1, edited by David Bonanno (January/February 1991).

but still, how much was learned from a bias or "creative error." As a pluralist, one dreams of the critic who might, as Alois Riegl dreamed of it in art history, escape the specific gravity of his epoch's taste, but the dream of the escape from bias is itself a bias. The standard of receptivity may help us: William James was suggestive when he wrote that love gives us more knowledge than a blinding "objectivity." Few of us have been changed by a journalistic review, and yet we live drowned by it, as by *The New York Times*, which tends to be most convincing in those subjects where one is not an expert.

The "situation" or "condition" of the art usually emerges as the topic for discussion. Today, a gambit might be to think of the poetic spectrum as a political one: the "Language" poetries as a left wing and the "New Formalists" as a right wing become the clichés of a deposition. Except that there is no practitioner alive today who is not in some sense a "Language" poet, dedicated to the intricacies of self-focusing sensuousness of language, and there is hardly an experimentalist I meet who has not been obsessed, almost parodistically, with the palette of given forms. If we cede the extreme right and left to such groups, what remains for the one who is not a zealot, Puritan, or partyman? This is the place where Frank O'Hara admitted he was falling asleep with quandariness and that there was some anxiety in being dismissed as too calm or not crazy enough. Is there a place for *sophrosyne* or wholeness in a poetry that will not seem like some psychotherapeutic drive for balance? Is there a radical moderation, as the painter Lucio Pozzi has suggested, that will be a maximalist stance untrammeled by the drive toward reduction or dogma in aesthetics? Again, wouldn't this maximalism be a dogmatics? (See Charles Bernstein's letter in the *American Poetry Review*, September/October 1990.)

I have used too much preface already, but I might suggest my own biases, in the spirit of Jean-Paul Sartre who said he would put his cards on the table, if everyone else did—this, when asked why there was not more explicit sexuality in his works. Of course, one's cards keep changing, but I would like to suggest that my sense of poetry is the dynamic spin of all the aesthetic axes once enumerated by the restless pluralist Roman Jakobson. Jakobson, who is too often thought of as a microscopist of grammar, made a radiant mature formulation of poetry in which addresser, addressee, content, context, code and contact are all summoned forth as ineluctable parts of poetry. For me, a maximalist theory of poetry is one that includes the subtlest sense of the imbrication of these axes. We cannot escape the person in the poem, nor should we vulgarly try for the escape from the (*hors texte*) outside of the text, an abyss that leads to ahistorical "philosophies of indifference." Our "perfect" critic understands the imperfection of his own means, since criticism too involves addresser, addressee and the opacity of history and reference. There is the inexhaustibility of poetry in the wild rushing of these forces upon themselves. Poetry is not so much a self-focusing machine as the densest explosion of all the possibilities of a communicative system of multiplicity.

While this may seem abstract or vague—and crudely foreshortened like this, it is—the pluralist reformulation of Jakobson's famous schema has some interesting implications for the critic or reviewer. The adequate review would be one that is receptive to all the poles of an aesthetic. Biographical criticism of the subtlest variety—one thinks of Meyer Schapiro's psychoanalytic and skeptical investigations into Cezanne, or Jakobson on the suicidal syntax of Mayakovsky or Pushkin—would not be tabooed, for the sake of a sepulchral chastity or intrinsicality. The addressee would not be forgotten, and thus the contribution of a "reception criticism" such as Walter Benjamin's is one of our most precious possessions. The "grammar of poetry and the poetry of grammar" is not necessarily situated at the center, as in Jakobson's formalist scheme, but it would be seen in a dynamic ratio with author and audience, sometimes anonymous, often plural, but never entirely absent. And the referential axis of the contextual is only disdained by those who dream of a "zero degree" escape from the world itself. The political critic might learn from the meta-lingual; the grammarian might collaborate with the psychoanalyst. What is implied is that poetry is so rich and replete in its maximalist state that one critic is communally involved with another in what has been called "critical seeing," and what we will call "critical reading." An attempt would be made not to truncate, in advance, any of the richness of poetry. (Alan Dugan makes this suggestion pithily in *APR*, May/June 1990.)

This complaint against reduction has its comical aspects, moreover, since one knows how often wonderful practitioners have gained their ground by the "creative dogmas" of a variety of reduction. I have been inspecting the work of Mondrian recently, and it is poignant to see how often he painted flowers and yet tabooed the work, as if representation would stain the linearity of his drive toward geometric purity. But the flowers and the abstractions remain, and the critic tries to take into account the libido in both and in the dogmas of chastity.

Having made these remarks, one turns to the books at hand with the possibility of severely disappointing the reader. The books may be a kind of arbitrary selection, and one cannot necessarily praise those books that may recently have meant the most to one, in terms of poetry or poetics. (For example, this is not the place to say that I have learned more about poetry from Scholem's correspondence with Benjamin about Kafka than from most books of the recent past.) One cannot suddenly indicate the whole of one's private canon, except with bathetic results, and our own sense of the perfectly imperfect critic, the melancholy critic, is one who is constantly revising his canon. Eliot was sage in suggesting that he looked in reviews for those names mentioned that were not under review and that there he found the secret authorities or issues of the day. It is not insidious to suggest—as I once did to a veteran *avant-gardiste* who asked me who was the best living poet—that Stevens is still the best living poet, at least for oneself. That is a suggestion of limits, or standards. But in my own practice Stevens joins Eliot with a sense of shared feeling-tones of suffering, and the great Russian poets and surrealists combine in an erotics of "influence" that is perhaps a linguistic pantheism. One does not review "Pasternak," in looking at the poets of one's time, but *My Sister Life* is perhaps a secret form of comparison, a standard of pleasure, in [W. Jackson] Bate's sense; not an anxiety so much as a rule of admiration and excellence: criticism as *paideia*. (I am not discussing today Ron Padgett's unpretentious comedies, for instance, but they give me a Herrick-like joy and rebuke me for my bombast or sullen literariness.)

Criticism does not usually apologize so much, and yet theory becomes, over time, an apologia for our lives. It is perhaps not inappropriate to apologize that one's critique has not become a poem, as in Charles Bernstein's *Artifice of Absorption*, a kind of essay on rimelessness.

* * *

Michael Palmer's poetry seems to underline a sense of the maximalist adventure in poetry: "and on those words we have written house, we have written leave this house, we / have written be this house, the spiral of a house, channels through this house...." He is married to an architect—(as am I) and is married to architecture, that fragile art. His poetry is at the furthest remove from ejaculation or confession, and yet it is not impossible for him to use a momentum from a Freudian case history to achieve the feeling-tone of suffering: "A voice will say Father I am burning / Father I've removed a stone from a wall, erased a picture from that wall...." This is a dissonant poetry that comes "after," after the Holocaust, after Celan, after the taboos on lyric poetry itself. It is a lyric poetry at war with itself: "Because we are not alive not alone / but ordinary extracts from the tablets...." ("Fifth Prose")

His poetry is part of a relay of multiplicity, as when the first poem in the book is entitled, "Fifth Prose." His books keep inscribing themselves without a simple sense of Aristotelian order, and thus his Baudelaire Series begins with an involutional historical riddle: "*A hundred years ago I made a book / and in that book I left a spot / and on that spot I placed a seme....*" The vatic desire competes with a sense of desperate empiricism, or the desire for the feeling of factuality: "Mei-mei, here is the table / Who knows the word it...." He is inspired by the Judaic infinities of Jabès and Celan: "Dear Lexicon, I died in you / as a dragonfly might / or a dragon in a bottle might // Dear Lexia, There is no mind...." There is a late symbolist passion here, and the topic of childhood is modulated in a musicalist aesthetic: "Once I was a nice boy / but now I sleep for hours at a time / Snow, You must be my pillow...." But any sentiment is ruptured when the poet suddenly addresses the "Hateful City." The method of Cezanne's or Jasper Johns' doubt is conjured up: "Ideas aren't worth anything / This is a hazardous bed / called perilous night, some blues / some indigoes, some reds / other colors I forget...."

It is essentially the difficulties of the latest symbolist architecture that intrigues Palmer and is the burden of his work: "You, island in this page / image in this page // What if things really did / correspond, silk to breath // evening to eyelid / thread to thread…." This complete ideogrammatic poem is a kind of lament concerning the breakdown of any simple synaesthetic canon of correspondence. Palmer is aware of what Jakobson referred to as the "bachelorhood of the word," and the sadness of this critical series of poems lies in the harping on the dissonant impossibility of an affirmative lyric: "… by the name of Ceran / or Anlschel // 'blooming fields of weeds' / what letters displaced…." There is an uncanny play of doubles: "The secret remains in the book / It is a palace/ It is a double house // It is a book you lost / It is a place from which you watch / the burning of your house…."

Uncanny, too, is his sense of poetry as mistranslation, like a version of Rilke that is a wild re-tracing of "Orpheus. Eurydike. Hermes": "Some stories unthread what there was / Don't look through an eye / thinking to be seen / Take nothing as yours…." The lyric sequence is interrupted by a sudden carnival of prose: "Flashes from you. While the heads of their victims. Why is a word, for example, meaning violence. Or was it how. There are other words with the same meaning. Cloud-words staining the…." The desire or nostalgia for the transcendental is rendered with a Deleuzian joy in immanence: "How lovely the unspeakable must be. You have only to say it and it tells a story." Nor is this poetry a mere smooth skin, since the poet has an expressionist tradition to translate: "I am an architect in Vienna / dead and a writer / in a blood red bed…." It is not for nothing that the eschatological is appealed to in "Poem of the End," and two amazing minimalist sequences called "C," in which there is a marriage of the lyricism of Creeley, a constructivist modesty, and the chiliastic of Celan: "Unutterable // pages // of counterlight // in the fluid window…."

There is the need, in this fractured narrative of almost atonal lyrics, to build up a long sequence, a kind of unity seized in Romantic Multeity, or even more, to let Multeity be sufficient, and Palmer concludes his book with an anti-sublime sequence, "Sun." It begins with Bataille-like acephalous horror: "A headless man walks, lives / for four hours

// devours himself," and develops as a kind of philosophical-political questioning of the horror of our epoch. The sequence reminds me at times of the penological schemata of the great architect John Hejduk, who dreams of theatrical masques in which architectural ceremonies and poetry meet and more than mingle. In Palmer, poetry seems to be tracing a kind of architectural map where ceremonies of mourning might take place: "Day Three is X, Name of X, Name of N /// It is a spring day in a state of siege // I offer you a flat land // Sun flares, then divides...." Language contracts and cannot speak except with anomalies: "The throat read us this." Chomsky's anomalous is poetry.

Gershom Scholem spoke of the authoritarian manner in Benjamin's prose, a style of revelation. This is the method in Palmer, and what is lenient in its revelatory tone is the admission of an erotic lyricism in which the body is affirmed: "Then I knead my breasts so that milk spurts out / across his face and neck, silver // coin under the tongue...." But the poem is mostly one of terror: "but fortunately I am perfectly dead / and can see into the past with a lens...." The relentless coda uses the full range of prophetic, anti-imperial denunciation: "Write this. We have burned all their villages.... // Write this. We have burned all the villages and the people in them...." It is significant that our latest symbolist should find the necessary words for a social vision in "pages which accept no ink." The private shattered house is open as a window: "Pages torn from their spines and added to the pyre, so that they will resemble thought." Those who think a critical poetry of linguistic doubt hedonistic and mere should consider this very serious cadenza.

* * *

Fair Realism, astonishingly beautiful title with multiple meanings, is a book by an author who has distinguished herself in the lyric and in critical prose—including an important, unsentimental biography of H.D. abounding with civilized verve—and who has been neglected as an important precursor of the "Language" poets. Indeed, when one looks at work Barbara Guest accomplished in the late 1950s and early 1960s, one finds pieces that often seem to have been written yesterday, if not tomorrow, and would be regarded as "advanced" in their paratactical disruptions even today. (It was a youthful indiscretion that

Ron Padgett and I were not able to include her in our motley *Anthology of New York Poets*: a misjudgment we have apologized for over the years and an indication of the lopsided dogmatism of youth.) She recently read for Poet's House in New York a translation of Horace, and this translation reminded one of how elegant her syntactical decisiveness can be, and how her moderate and sweet tone is, in a certain sense, a classicism. The usual Horace translations emphatically lose the "poetry" of this balanced and elegiac pastorale, and her urbane mixtures were able to get the Latin concisions more than any other I have heard. I would hope she would give us a volume of these translations one day. Until then, one might keep Horace in mind, when reading Guest, as an inter-text of some explanatory power.

The Horatian inter-text reminds us that pastoral is always an urban mode, by paradoxical indirections: "Wild gardens overlooked by night lights. Parking / lot trucks overlooked by night lights. Buildings / with their escapes overlooked by lights...." Guest has a narrative motion in her poetry that combines with her acute sense of landscape and landscape painting:

> I take from my wall the landscape with its water
> of blue color, its gentle expression of rose,
> pink, the sunset reaches outward in strokes as the west wind
> rises, the sun sinks and color flees into the delicate
> skies it inherited,
> I place there a scene from "The Tale of the Genji.
>
> An episode where Genji recognizes his son.
> Each turns his face away from so much emotion,
> so that the picture is one of profiles floating
> elsewhere from their permanence,
> a line of green displaces these relatives,
> black also intervenes at correct distances,
> the shapes of the hair are black.

("Wild Gardens Overlooked by Night Lights")

The whole poem is both a lyrical apologia for the precisions of the great early novel—we have at least two magisterial translations by

Waley and the extended one by Seidensticker—and an apologia for the lyric and its peculiar *realism*:

> Thus the grip of realism has found
> a picture chosen to cover the space
> occupied by another picture
> establishing a flexibility so we are not immobile
> like a car that spends its night
> outside a window. but mobile like a spirit.

("Wild Gardens Overlooked by Night Lights")

The lyric as a descendant of sacred commentary enters by the margins of an Oriental scene of recognition, but increases our sense of opacity and by means of a very accurate architectonic theme of the screen:

> Screens were selected to prevent this intrusion
> of exacting light and add a chiaroscuro,
> so that Genji may turn his face from his son,
> from recognition which here is painful
> and he allows himself to be positioned on a screen,
> this prince as noble as ever,
> songs from the haunted distance
> presenting themselves in silks.

("Wild Gardens Overlooked by Night Lights")

This is the indeterminate, obscure space of the Guest lyric: the poem functioning as a screen of scattered and scattering surface rather than as a focused mechanism of simple still life. "The light of fiction and light of surface / sink into vision whose illumination / exacts its shades...." It is a melancholy realism which knows its own uncanniness: "the decision of changing / an abstract picture of light into a ghost-like story...."

Roman Jakobson has spoken of the variety of competing "realisms," and it may seem that with many contradictory meanings, it might be time for the term, like Romanticism, to come under a taboo, but it is useful to add this relatively irreal "fair realism" to our encyclopedia of nuances. There is in Guest a humorous self-consciousness concerning her stylistic tensions and the analogues in the history of modernism: "An over-large pot of geraniums on the ledge / the curtains part / a view from Kandinsky's window" ("The View from Kandinsky's Window"). We remember that Kandinsky has been said to modulate from "pictures of anything"—Monet's haystacks—to "pictures of nothing," the first abstractions. (Henri Zerner and Charles Rosen have written incisively on this subject in *Romanticism and Realism: The Mythology of Nineteenth Century Art* (Viking Press, 1984)). But Guest conceives her project as a way of synthesizing the "anything"—humble, democratic bits and pieces, shards of language, detritus of New York—and "nothing"—atoms of language, grammar self-focusing, a poetics almost of zero degree. She knows this subject-matter so well that she is able to reduce in scale to a little parable as neat as Stevens'"Jar" [Stevens' poem "Anecdote of the Jar"].

There is also, suddenly, an expressionism in her work that makes this self-conscious humor into something much more intimate and carnal: "Welcome brutal possessor / of the memory cards, / on the wall under wainscoting / a nail holds the thread" ("The Thread"). Eroticism spelled out in the negative is even more ferocious: "We have not taken heroines / to snow, thrust hair under waterfalls, / we sent them to museums / they own splendid eyelashes, / giantesses who wear no clothes." This Baudelairean and splenetic eroticism is suggestive both of Laura Riding and of H.D. and has a peculiarly musical modesty: "This concern for time exists in memory cold / it is innocent of earth that suggested you."

This is a book with a mature variety. For example, "Ilex" is a shattered Greek narrative that often yields pools of *stained language*, a linguistic analogue to Helen Frankenthaler:

> white palms.... molded lattice—
> Sirius—are his watchers
>
> we wait in bronze liquid air
> with the pull of soft knots

The poet emphasizes, however, her story in its broken condition as much as the condition of her linguistic medium. In another poem that gives us her title, she suggests a mode of disequilibrium: "an emphasis falls on reality." Of course, with this mood of "envy" for egregious realism, we realize how much the poet understands the "bachelorhood of the word" or the dream-logic of floating signifiers. We end like painters who can only trace and re-trace in passionate hesitations of thought:

> The necessary idealizing of your reality
> is part of the search, the journey
> where two figures embrace
>
> This house was drawn for them
> it looks like a real house
> perhaps they will move in today
>
> into ephemeral dusk and
> move out of that into night
> selective night with trees,
>
> The darkened copies of all trees.
>
> ("An Emphasis Falls on Reality")

A poet with such a disturbing sense of space and perturbed sense of a "late" style remains polarized, as it were, between forms of representation and abstraction. She uses her Stevens-like tercets to give pressure and principle to this topic of restlessness.

* * *

Two of the poets under discussion had a special relationship with the painter, Phillip Guston, and in the works of Clark Coolidge and William Corbett one finds, despite their immense differences in style and themes, a particular receptivity for the modes of the visual. Both collaborated on the most amazing poem-drawings, to use a clumsy phrase, with the painter, and Coolidge's drawings are the site of a significant catalogue (The Berkshire Museum, Pittsfield, Massachusetts) that should be scrutinized by anyone interested in the history of collaboration. Corbett's collaborations have appeared in a remarkable issue of *Notus* magazine (Fall 1989). In Guston's late drawings, we find the most primary shapes—pyramid, shoe, hand, clock—creating a cartoon commentary on the poems, or creating a Van Gogh-like humble illumination of the poems. The writing of Coolidge and Corbett was permitted by the painter to become a full partner of the line. The painter establishes a space for language that is one of the most compelling I have seen outside of the Oriental "marriage of the perfections." Guston's swerve toward the representational, an audacity so powerful that it came under a variety of denunciations and taboos, makes any phrase by Coolidge exhibit its vascularity. Coolidge's phrase: "To release it needs a grip so strong / one is possessed to come free," stands in brute capitals under a rudimentary clock with two arrow-hands and a dark-armed creature seen in one-eyed profile. The word "grip" is heightened by the upturned arm and hand, and the timepiece in its gravity seems to stand for all the impossibilities of release. There is little simple illustration, but there is an immense empathy with the representational mode lodged within Coolidge's most extreme riddles. For a Corbett poem on Richard Nixon, the painter of the most poignant color-abstractions of the fifties is capable of wild satire, chillingly specific about Nixon's phlebitis-afflicted leg and monstrous as a humorous Saturn. In both poets, Guston's drawing opens the text rather than closes it and yields us an image of the "sister arts" as relentlessly fine as anything since Denby-Burckhardt [Edwin Denby and Rudy Burckhardt].

Coolidge is mostly known as an "experimental" poet, as if there were any poetry that were not, as Wallace Stevens joked about its vitality. The phrase "experimental" or some such epithet seems to remove Coolidge from his human burden. Actually, he is a musical poet in love with jazz, and his poetry is often an explicit homage to jazz and to certain improvisational writers he loves. His love of geology emerges in many of the poems, and also his geometric drive toward the crystalline formally. His patience and his love of the stoical humors in Beckett are qualities that endear him to many, and his long poems are usually diaries of observation, as in his book *At Egypt*, even if the humor of this "linguistic" writer being a documentarist produces many of the twists and turns of the volume.

His early work was a kind of extreme sequitur to the mad shards of the cubo-futurism of the New York School in Ashbery's "Tennis Court

Oath" period and Koch's "When the Sun Tries to Go On." He caught the ideal that Koch used to preach in classroom and poem: the fresh word delivered, in Gertrude Stein-like persistence, as woody and humble as a ruler. This paratactical quality still irritates many of the critics of that poetry, but actually it is extraordinary how fractured narratives were able to build up in new tectonic shapes from these exercises in fission. "Europe," by Ashbery, is still a neglected *Waste Land*, full of a joy and perplexity that permitted the later classical Ashbery to have such a perturbed line. Coolidge was able to make a frozen music out of the difference between "trilobite" and "trilobites" in the microcosmos that became his peculiar linguistic creation:

>ounce code orange
>a
>   the
>   ohm
>trilobite trilobites

This infuriatingly dense little poem, shorter than a Webern but filled with variety, is a provocative pleasure: a Joseph Cornell box of insects, fruits, and science.

The early "reduced" work of Coolidge has led to his being type-cast as the dogged abstractionist in poetry, whereas actually his little lyrics always had the very firm construction of a Serra, say, a kind of density that was sculptural. He arranged poems without dithyramb because he liked observing their properties, as a minimalist observes corten rusting or neon brightening. These reductions were, moreover, equivalent to a kind of sensuous materialism in language that spoke erotically to many. (And politically some might place it in the context of the anti-authoritarianism of the 1960s, but this gambit has its weaknesses as well as charms.)

The mature Coolidge seems to speak to us in an almost Cézanne-like mode in the long poem, "The Crystal Text." A friendly and greying face looks out from us from the cover, but the contemplative poem is not in any easy sense, genial. It seems to be a yoga-like accumulation of meditations about the "active possibilities" of seeing, writing, and thought. Rilke's *Orpheus* furnishes the book's quotation, and one senses that Coolidge's rage to see is as erotic and frustrated as an Orpheus. He has taken the side of things, like Ponge or Jasper Johns, but is filled with doubt about what makes a thing: "The thought to weigh things / and then rush back to them." The desire for a Menippean satire is very strong, as if Pynchon were a lyric poet: "I hate history because it has never entered the / world as a life. It has no direction / but back into the fold. No touchingness / very following to its black boxes. I would / want to walk out and say, The History of / the World. I would need a stream through / my head like the quartz crystal in the sunshaft / on the desk of a following wood." The subject is seen as *consolatio* and yet possibly false: "Meanwhile, and over miles, we console ourselves with cut stones.... The misgivings of solace." The poem reads as the notebook toward a sketch, the pluralist sketch of a crystal that could become a self-portrait, that smiling face on the cover. But a shattered portrait alone suffices.

This book could have become sentimental in an age in which the healing powers of crystals have become a degraded industry. Coolidge becomes a translator of the crystal and releases it from any easy kitsch.

> He sees the fire in the crystal
> as a network of cracks in the air.
> And the wood of its rest should flinch.
> Or enbrown itself in rising heat.
>
> The next thought of an ice cut gem.
> A hand emblem that will not stay to hand
> but drop off into endlessly pursuant space of all the angles.

He is constantly being saved from dullness or sentiment by the lively, fresh American language that reminds one of Thoreau. There is a homely vernacular here that is a sharp analogue of the humiliated items in Guston's late palette of images. The surprising fissions of the early poems come back as if to explode in little percussive dissonances:

> What do you see when you look out with your language?
> A pile of hooted buckets.
> A loose laugh spoon.
> Miles of adroited pain paper.

Lungs full of glass beads.
A list of nodyles knowing of nameless.

The question might have been an annoying crypto-philosophical rhetoric, but Coolidge already knows it is and is not. His answers might have been whimsical surrealist capers, but they become, by turns, concrete, real, surprising, and finally expansions into a dignified homage to immanence. For those who think Ashbery's cubo-futurism was a wretched Dadaist joke, and for those who think that of the whole enterprise of late linguistic experimentation and exhaustion, this book should come as a maximalist rebuke: "The sentence is of durenamel, but the people handle it and do not read it." Coolidge has gone a long way toward expunging all the false coherences, all the lesser whimsies:

> And what is one's own death, locked as firmly as
> a bubble in a crystal? A darker line I had
> not seen before ... A question is a hand reaching. The crystal.

I can't do justice to the immense and paradoxically lonely pluralism of this serious work.

* * *

Amy Gerstler recently collaborated with the artist Alexis Smith on a hilarious and sad encyclopedia of "Past Lives," in which a diverse collection of chairs was manipulated to gain a group portrait of contemporary and historical characters. Gerstler has a beautiful note, which should be read by all historians, about the function of the object:

> Objects soaking up and then giving off the complicated fragrances of the personalities and lives of people they come into contact with is not a new idea ... As a child, I thought a certain pair of dilapidated straw sandals in a glass display was one of the most wonderful things I had seen, because an ancient Egyptian, someone who worshipped Isis ... actually wore them on his or her surprisingly small feet ... that humans confer some of their essence on the inanimate objects they use, and that these allegedly lifeless items may later radiate human qualities they absorbed.

This notion of Gerstler's is not just the commodity fetish used for a new pathetic fallacy. It is the same humane insight that led Van Gogh to picture his father as an open Bible and himself as a shrunken Zola novel, or to find Gauguin in a live candle and himself in a withered tobacco pipe and pouch. Poets, also, learn to make of objects a self-portrait or the portrait of a whole culture: "the pure products of America / go crazy." ["To Elsie" by William Carlos Williams.]

Gerstler's poems are not reductively oriented to the everyday. She makes a surrealist cadenza out of "Sirens," and turns this morsel of the salon into something frenzied and real:

> "Pale as an August sky, pale as flour milled / a thousand times, pale as the icebergs I have never seen, / and twice as numb—my skin is such a contrast to the rough rocks I lie on, that from far away it looks like I'm a baby / riding a dinosaur." August, flour, and dinosaurs are part of a diction that lies roughly against the litany of pale and fictional icebergs. The poem deserves and needs both high and low diction, fair surrealism and dark realism mating for an impurism.

There is a tone of domesticity in the poems, but it competes with the surrealist sense of escape and vast spaces. Guston's ferocity of figuration is present in Gerstler, also, a kind of din of images:

> I've an uncommon calling.
> I was born without immunity to this din in the air:
> the sad humming of the long lost.
> Imagine not being able
> to help hearing every word
> that's been moaned in this kitchen
> for the last thousand years,
> and random sounds too, from snorting
> in the stable that stood here
> before your house was built,
> to the croaker's whisperings
> at the bottom of the pond
> which filled this hollow before that,
> when this country was all swamp. The song
> of every being that passed through here
> still echoes and is amplified in me.
> The sour spirits of the drowned

who imbibed brackish water
remain huddled here, dripping,
in your kitchen ...

("Clairvoyance")

The ambition is to become a kind of popular Cassandra and howl in the "damp precincts," but of course the howl is now a complex series of whispers. Morton Feldman, the great American composer of pianissimo, once told a student: "Just because it's called a loudspeaker doesn't mean it has to be loud!" and he made an immense monochromatic music that was his own analogy with Guston's sublime. In Gerstler, we see how effective a quiet, ruminative and contemplative poem can be, though Leavis trained many of us to think of poetry as the opposite of such rumination. On the other hand, Gerstler has a series of complex, humorous prose poems which can be as immediate and imagistic as a germ: "A few germs float up the baby's nose while the mother reads, making the infant sneeze." Hers is a poetry that Jeremy Gilbert-Rolfe has evoked as part of an "Erotics of Doubt":

> How should I know what moves you—
> who shivers in your distance,
> a prostrate mirage on the cheap
> green bedspread in the only
> air-conditioned motel in town—
> the one with the hole punched
> through the bathroom door?
> You're afraid of your own thoughts.
> You keep staring at the sky,
> where one magnificent fleecy doubt,
> several miles in diameter hovers
> just above that spot on the horizon
> also known as the vanishing point ...
> where the sun begins to burn off all you ever held dear.

("Doubt")

It's not only the erotics of doubt but the anger at disconnection that keeps this satisfactory poem of dissatisfaction going like a

Guston clock. The hole in the door stands for all the possible ways of a scopophilia—the love of looking that keeps us mesmerized by a poetry of images, and yet the poet knows that all such images are insufficient. The formalist in Gerstler lets her make a poetry of naked devices, where the vanishing point self-reflexively becomes the disappearance of the poem's subject itself. There is a wandering and aggressive use of figuration here, as if the poet were poised always with the eraser fluid that might demolish the architecture of the poem. She knows "the malice of objects" and fills her prose-poems with their aggressive and humorous speech: "No one can blame them for their hue or cry, their metallic jealousy. The ache of silver. Plastic's pang. The anger of glass. We cast and sand them into bowls and plates we guzzle from. Turn graceful organic shapes into another form of our incessant babble" (from "The Malice of Objects").

But Gerstler's poetry becomes most complex when it speaks of the difficulty of love, naming, and all such investiture: "What does such mute profundity disclose? Speak to me, one of you. The objects' fettered language, in the throes of erosion, sifts beyond my hearing. Under duress, or torture, they only break, never name names." One does not *exactly* know what these objects can name, and the poet is left with a species of elegy to the signature. The poet has a variety of poems and prose poems concerned with the erotics of language, but none is more gripping than a last smoldering elegy. It is as if the dark subject of masochism, as Karen Horney once spoke of it, had received its apotheosis in a lyric of self-laceration. The homesickness in the following poem seems to be for a time when objects spoke more clearly, when a connection between men and women might be clearer, and when home itself in linguistic terms was less uncanny. The poem is one of Romantic crisis, and all the ominous monotonies of Gerstler seem to conclude in its troubling, Proustian wound. It is as if, as we grow older, we know little except Kafka and Proust: the moral disorder without and the starry chaos within; a social world become a labyrinth and a private world an atonal abyss:

> Few realize this glittering hour exists. But you do.
> The sky molten, the clouds so aroused

> they remind you of your mission:
> to huff and puff and blow down
> the old forms, then erect new altars
> from mud, breadcrumbs, and pollen.
> Your course, shooting star,
> becomes clear for a minute.
> The day begins to warm up. What's distant
> from us is perfected, I guess. A wind
> from the abyss ruffles your hair.
> The air thickens into your body
> as you move through it.
> You never believed a word I said.
> Nor were my hands of much use.
> My love for you so akin
> to homesickness, that tonight,
> instead of clouds, the sky looks full
> of crumpled bandages and blindfolds.
>
> ("Overcome")

* * *

There is a fine melancholy to William Corbett's poetry, and the poet has been capable of extended works, such as his "Columbus Square Journal," where the documentary of the day alternates with anguished memories of an abandoning father. The whole, however, is always as democratic, demotic, and truth-telling as the Phillip Guston with whom Corbett collaborated on such a little elegy as:

> Walker Evans dead
> The rooms empty out
> Many thousands gone
> No survivors unseasonable spring

(Cover illustration, *Notus*.)

The reference to Walker Evans is interesting, because we find in Evans the man who could transfigure the rejected object and make the debris of American landscape and the glamorous nothingness of an American billboard into something as seemingly permanent and significant as Zen tea-ware. The Guston that accompanies this has, significantly, an inverted shoe that shows us its sole. It reminds us of the still-life of Van Gogh in which Meyer Schapiro finds the artist creating a species of self-portrait through still life. Corbett's forte, like Guston, is making the factualities of everyday life into a humanism.

Some of this transfiguration of empiricism comes from the best of O'Hara, say, "A Step Away from Them," and the walks of William Corbett represent partly an homage to our best flaneur of New York, but without the infantilism of so many attempts at the unmediated freshness of that master:

> Passed Gilbert Stuart's grave
> where one night
> we saw rats at play.

("Walks")

> Boston cleaves to the river
> hooking out of sight.
> ....
> The bridge trembles, It's the whooshing
> cars underneath, their passing
> never ceases.

("Crossing the Footbridge over Sorrow Bridge")

> I was out before this rain
> turned to find silvery slits
> in the dark river water.
> Waiting beneath the tangle
> of a plunging willow
> I return to absent friends
> call their names, indict each one
> for his or her infidelity
> and complete a cold divorce
> on my side. Over and done.

> What pleasure is this?
> Home, hair dry, tea made
> I sit to write soon aware
> of rhythmically splashing water.
> My neighbor's broken gutter!
> Bastard! The drops march on
> after the rain has gone.
> No revenge but to brood.

("Beside the Charles River")

This poem has the meditative realism of a Rexroth translation from the Tang period. Each observation adds up, and there is a general love of sensuous fact that places it in the tradition of Peto or Harnett: *trompe l'oeil* in poetry might mean that we are made to believe a real gutter is being broken and the poem is a diary. But accents fall here on a fairly unreal realism. The poem is made with the grand artifice of alliteration (silvery slits) and little half-rhymes gutter/water/aware; one/done; on/gone) and a lightly pressured rhythmical balance of three and four feet. Absent friends, infidelity and divorce are at the center of the poem and that flux reinforced by the impressionism of river, gutter, and rain. This poem is not about the hedonism of surface but is an American homage to the classic Chinese poems where friendship, as Waley put it, has the place of Western eros. Except that here, friendship is eros and combines in a dark tangle. The poems are in the tradition of Demuth and Williams in their freshest sense of the drab:

> The trees *are* drab
> Their leaves trashy
> like cheap bright clothes
> washed once. The truth hurts.
> Halloween tomorrow so why
> wear your mask today?
> Ghost of the face to come?
> It's a free country
> children say try and make me!

("What Did You Expect?")

Interestingly, this fastidious poetry of urban and suburban fact becomes, over time, a machine of defiance. The children add to the bare landscape their cry of liberty and intransigence. Again and again, there is a secular prayer, as in Berrigan and Padgett, for a hedonistic laziness that might have been applauded by Mark Twain:

> When white haired
> unsteady on my feet
> near deaf, half blind
> soon to breathe my last
> may I still enjoy
> the guilty pleasure
> come from a movie
> into bright summer sun.
>
> ("Prayer")

But the same poet can write with complete insidious rage about antisemitism, wounds, and circumcisions: "A lick / of the whetstone / to bless the knife / to thin the blade / that cuts painless / and seated in your armchair / you wonder at / the worm of blood" ("Within Memory"). In other words, the drab style is so filled with conviction that it can be used where the usual aureate lyric would fail. His elegy to a minister is a poignant psychological study of a child's love for the adult and the adult's perfect imperfection:

> You will not rise so high
> in another's eye as you dreamt
> of rising in his who stood
> so straight in chapel preaching
> his sermons, arms at his side.
> By this morning's light
> John Duane Verdery
> seldom wore the Reverend's collar
> was something of a ham
> a good decent man
> who enjoyed himself.
> Service and care were his texts.

("JDV 1917–1985")

Corbett can "get away with" the colloquialism of "ham" and he can also suddenly use "service and care" because the montage is a completely convincing sense of conflicted humanitas. He doesn't need to make the vibrato more heated for such a closure; the "talkiness" here is more singing than if he sweetened the line. This is the lesson of factuality, or the feeling of a humiliated factuality, from Williams to O'Hara and Creeley. (Jasper Johns once told me of a dream in which he was working in water, but Marcel Duchamp told him he was working in a less expensive material: air! The parable is to use degraded materials rather than turning gold into cardboard.)

Two of the pleasures of Corbett's book are his gift for a swirling or fractured storytelling and his practice of poetry as art criticism. The poem "The Shoe" is a wild memoir of a draft-dodger's departure, where Corbett does or does not act courageously, in a grotesque and politically apt gesture of waving a shoe aloft. This "shoe" becomes a sacrificial "thing" and even the poet announces his ambivalence about its status. The whole poem is a masterly unity and should be read by those who think narrative comes only in decorous shapes. It's here, and in the remarkable analogues to Guston's art, that Corbett finds a factual art filled with the reparations of feeling and art:

> Now it is Phillip dead
> and in the roots
> I grip and tug
> caught is a nail
> hang forged like
> those he painted
> common and austere.

("Postscript")

* * *

The sonnet is one of the immortal conventions before which even the mature Williams slightly crumpled. The fate of this form is remarkable, because practitioners are always arriving to freshen it up, amusingly parody it, have their revenges against its muscular voids, and delight in a tradition that, none too paradoxically, becomes more adventurous with its continuance. Ashbery punctured it in prose, returned to it in sixteen-line irregular-regular units in *Shadow Train*. Koch used Roussel to gain the flattest, driest diction as of Larousse in his narrative cycle, "The Railway Stationery." Edwin Denby tried and achieved a dry dissonant and prosy sonnet in his urban and international series. The sonnet is part of our libertine tradition, that is to say, and I mention this because the sonnet is too often claimed as a kind of conservative refuge. Actually, sonnet, sestina, and villanelle have functioned, for this practitioner and others, as tectonic possibilities to be manipulated, subverted, and gloried in rather than as shrines to be venerated or rule-systems to be obeyed. Rimbaud, one recalls, uses the form to create his most obscene sketches after the genital organs, a sonnet whose conclusions and questions still fire us: "Oh to be naked like that, seeking joy / And sleep, turned to the glorious part of you / Both of us sobbing, both of us free?" In 1962 or so, when I translated that using many French trots, I thought of the sonnet as part of a kind of practice, as in scales, but also knew that the arpeggio properly played turned into its own concerto. Like anyone else, I started with the refulgence of Shakespeare's infinite cycle and concluded with Mallarmé's etiolated enharmonics. As a pluralist, I resent any particular group claiming it; and the "modern" project against it is contradicted by the uses of it within Rilke, Yeats and the Symbolists. Jasper Johns has spoken of his admiration for Ted Berrigan's logical cycle of "Sonnets" and made a painterly homage to one. Johns' chief admiration is for the sullen sonnets of Edgar Arlington Robinson. Such, such are the joys of this form!

Bernadette Mayer's cycle immediately announces its theme of transgression in its purposefully slangy diction of eros and carelessness: "Love is a babe as you know when you / Put your startling hand on my cunt or arm or head / Or better both your hands to hold in them my own / I'm awed and we laugh with questions, artless...." The humor of this so-called artlessness is in how succinctly and wisely the poet knows how to phrase a self-consciousness: "All torn and sore like a female masochist that the rhyme / Of the jewel you pay attention to becomes your baby born." That may not succinct enough for some stylists, but elsewhere she calls the male genital organ "your succinctest cock" and we will grant her the pleasures of that specificity. Often her poems delight in a photographic sense of New York that does seem to come out of the dense love of Denby, Rudy Burckhardt, and Berrigan: "As if by the scattering of light rays in a photograph / Of the softened reflection of a truck in a bakery window," and it would be interesting for a student to trace the history of the city within the sonnet as context and contextual analogue for love. The eternally renovated and renovating city is the burden of much of these poems and becomes a kind of defense for the sullen and joyful rips at the fabric of the form—for example one sonnet which is seven unrhymed couplets with a constant deposition of Dante, and this sonnet followed all too logically by one which deletes the annoying logical couplet at the end.

The happiness in Mayer's poetry is a happiness of the city and its proletariat, with the marginal poet throwing in her lot, though without sentimentality: "It was hard to have no money today / I won't even speak about the possible flowers and kinds of lingerie." The tendency, however, is for Mayer to associate poetry with a Utopianism, and she has called her work "headlong sonnets":

> Francois Marie Charles Fourier said in 1880
> This planet should be sent to a lunatic asylum
> But it's not poetry's fault
> For being so concerned
> With love beauty sex and ideas, money
> All the preoccupations of the philosophers, thieves
> & prostitutes, I myself make no image
> When I say anything including saying
> Let's get on with our non-paying work as always

Her poetry delights in the idea of the gift not as part of power but as part of the charitable sexuality of the headlong modern poet: "Sex, where's the couplet? / The concluding modern thought's a warm winter scarf." There is a constantly teasing archaism throughout the sonnets, and an audacity that permits her this kind of marriage of politics and love, urban photography and the whimsies of an anarchist sonnet:

> The landlord was thrown out of the rent-stabilization group
> Because he did so many wrong and bad things
> We don't know what this means yet
> & whether our rent will go down or up
> If that's a punishment for us or him
> He who's harassed us all this time
> Then we harassed him this is not like love
> Now finally he's thrown out we threw him out long ago
> Of the possible ways of being human
> & so maybe it's kind that he's now out of time
> With his colleagues because of his manipulations
> I don't like the landlord's hand so much that I am happy but
>> Why's he been so derelict like a lover
>> As to let things go this far?

This sonnet has the steady prose pressure of the Denby poems of the Depression. It is part of Mayer's intelligence that she can modulate from the diction of rent-stabilization to the archaistic sweetness of derelict lovers. The poem is followed by an even more ferocious dream-diary concerning her horror at the world of patriarchy. But the poem has the convincing "sanity" of a John Clare facing a bird's nest. It is a Utopian sonnet of the price of love and money in our time. Mayer's New York City is maximalism.

* * *

For those who want an explicit political poetry, let them turn to Hilton Obenzinger's extremely ambitious work, *New York on Fire*. Obenzinger began as a poet of "The New York School" and was trained by Kenneth Koch and wrote many poems of graceful discontinuity and charm. Some of these (and some terrible early poems of my own) can be found in an anthology he co-edited of Columbia University poetry and prose entitled "The Cinch." What is extraordinary is to see how he has grown and matured and established himself as a vigorous poet of political convictions. His book is beautifully designed, and one might say that its surrealistic convulsive charm is produced most convincingly by the montage of poems and photographs. Obenzinger was working on a species of documentary social history, but the main journalistic task was discontinued, and what he emerged with was a triumphant sequence of poems using devastating fires in New York as a perspective or starting point or pretext, but never without a sense of blazing Realism. The poet gives us a social and private history of a great city by means of this defamiliarizing perspective.

New York on Fire is not only a good political epic, it is a continuation of Walter Benjamin's dream of a book that would be simply quotation and a book that might reveal late capitalism through its objects. Each etching or documentary photograph has the unified thrust of the lyrics. And the lyrics are often nothing more than the encyclopedia's monochrome. Responses to catastrophe yield a sense of social class and caste, and late capital's slouching toward monstrous waste is seen in the "modernism" of a landlord's arson.

Obenzinger's collage poem is one of the most architecturally specific and generous constructions of his generation. It is not without its own ferocious humor. His most inventive linguistic force is seen when he uses an almost undecorated prose diction to gain an intransigent epic tone:

> So when I see the buildings
> all silent—like *Silent Night* except it's
> August—and the flames dancing
> out the window
> I think of Ali in a ball of flame
> leaping over the tracks
> and Futura getting the blame.
> So I saw something—Freak Fire.
> It flashed in my head. It was the good bad thing
> of the fire. It was fresh. I saw it on the buildings
> in big Broadway letters. Fire doing the freak.
> Freak fire that ain't no accident.
> I did a whole-car masterpiece, bright bubble flames
> with Freak Fire jumping over the car.
> I did Freak Fire on all the trains until I became all-city,
> King of the IRT, red orange blue flames on handball courts, any wall
> I even studied the coronas of flames through spectographs
> then made the IRT run from the Bronx to Brooklyn with
> Freak Fire even showing through the buff

> That's how I got my tag.
> And that's how I made the city go up in graffiti flames.
> But there is still one place I got to bomb:
> Yankee Stadium.
> I want to spray Freak Fire
> on all sides of Yankee Stadium.
> If Christo can wrap up whole buildings
> in burlap bags, then I can
> wrap up Yankee Stadium in Freak Fire
> and dedicate it to Futura and Ali.
>
> ("Freak Fire")

This kind of poem as testimony is best when it approaches a complete nakedness. It does not even need "flames dancing." It works toward a zero degree of perfected found poem-object. And in this galaxy of testimonies, Obenzinger brings us back a whole masque of men and women, with an emphasis on labor and sacrifice, as in his masterful rendition of "The Shirtwaist" disaster of 1911: "All the shirtwaists we cut and sew for the Gibson girl, the collar held so close, the long sleeves flouncing up. / I cannot even wish the Gibson girl should fall from so high." The solecisms, the accents, the voices from a vast migration that make up the collage—the politicians call it the gorgeous mosaic—of New York City activate Obenzinger's furious sympathies.

Some may say that it is part of the poem's weakness that it depends upon such a frenzy of design, photograph, and other documentary and typographic design. Actually, the poems, many of them, work with a fine strength alone. But I think it is part of the Benjamin-like strength of this undogmatically "economic" poem to force a marriage of speech and writing, lyric and image. The book demands to be read not just as a choir of voices, but as voices in the context of disastrous circumstances. Each photo is another glimpse of this horrifying context. The little etching of a fireman's hose gives us a shock, as if the privacies of Diderot's encyclopedia were revealing to us, again, the secrets of social history. One might just as well dream of the book of photographs that would not depend upon texts. But the truth is that this imbricated epic of text and picture is a very useful addition to our sense of a poetics. In the Orient, calligraphy bridges the gap between poetry and painting. In New York City, the city of disaster, and a city with a hole in its heart that even the unseen sentimental Ferdinand Braudel has written will never be repaired, a poetry of photography and speech, fact and feeling, marry to produce a humane catalogue of survival.

Multiplicity for Obenzinger is not just an ontological category out of Gilles Deleuze. His poetry includes the voices of mayors, graffiti artists and millionaires. Charlie Chaplin appears weeping before burning towers, and so do minor ministers drowning in isolation, all cruelly and coolly rendered. Obzenzinger's strategy of collage permits his poem to rise beyond the confines of a hedonistic individualism, and the resulting historical narrative shows pluralism in its tragic form of collisions and competing visions.

* * *

The ending of a review might be as conventional as its exergue, and here I pause to remind my readers why I am not so taken with "negative" criticism or the criticism of rebuke or prescription, though every poet practices this within his own art. I have learned from one historian to value journalism but mistrust it when it *evaluates before comprehension*. And I recall being moved myself when, for example, Kenneth Koch in 1962 underlined some of the mad advantages in the collages of John Ashbery. The appreciation of beauties seems simple, but it can be a perturbation of our system and implies its own negativities. After a certain pleasure, Hemingway remarked, there is no going back, and it was this aphorism that Koch used in his special dramatics as a positive critic. I cannot lead most critics, even thirty years later, to appreciate those collages, still deemed nonsensical by many, but if I could, I would not need to make the point by comparison to the deficiencies of other poetries. Criticism need be neither praise nor lament, but it might be an attempt to maximalize critical language itself. And one of the first places might be to delete moralistic rebukes. If I paint flowers, it is not because I am incapable of geometrical abstraction: and if I paint geometrical purities, it is not because I cannot draw. The sonnet does not indicate—at least necessarily—a reformatory program toward other forms. The wars of mimesis and anti-mimesis might accept a kind of pacifist or reconciling treaty. But for those who profit from such wars, a mild pluralism will seem too peaceful.

European friends are always suggesting to me that this form of philosophical or aesthetic pluralism is exactly the American mythology and is useful for the dream of colonizing everything. One thinks of the rebuke of minorities that such a pluralism is one more way to deny their particular cry and diminish its stridency. My own sense is that a pluralist standard of receptivity is still the only way to initiate a drive toward including each individual voice erupting in history and the cry of the oppressed.

What is experienced in America as a mild or moderate or even enervating eclecticism may be appreciated in Eastern Europe, for example, as a wild libertinism. I once spent an amazing day with some of the cultural advisors of Vaclav Havel and while taking one of them to a variety of studios of painters and architects in New York, I realized the immense horror of cultural strangulation. A simple catalogue, another form or style, was cause for this person's jubilation. It is an irony that the poetics of "groups" in America attempt to lead us backward into a reductive line. Unfortunately, most of us know the pain of too much liberty, the by now clichéd indifference to poetry in America that we all mourn, but it would be a more mournful irony if we were to cage ourselves in false working dogmas. The rule is fruitfulness; the standard, a kind of "joy of influence." But perhaps this Shelley-inspired pantheistic dream of poets united in choir is another sentimental delusion.

Our conventional typologies of poetry today seem to me confused. I am often associated with a "New York School" of poetry, but I note that the constant experimentation with form by Kenneth Koch, considered a founding member of that School, is never praised by the poets of the New Formalism. It is bizarre that Koch's mastery of *ottava rima* and the sonnet and sestina form, should be completely overlooked by these practitioners. Meanwhile, Koch functions as a vast example of a comical pluralist whose satirical and encyclopedic work has not been digested by any academy, despite its wide influence. I know that the cubo-futurism of the early New York School has been an influence on the "Language poetries," but one has to agree with Ron Silliman, who recently spoke of the oblivion to which such a fine cubo-futurist poet as Joe Ceravolo has been consigned. Ceravolo, a kind of Reverdy from New Jersey, was amused by the disjunctions between literary groups and saddened by the dogmatics that kept poets artificially separated. The poetry of Silliman, for example, whose work is identified with the Language movement, seems to me a ferocious example of a representational poetics, and his long poem "What" is a scroll-like and acerbic satire on the contemporary landscape and thought. It is personal, urban, political, and "maximal," and while built up in little linguistic aphoristic bits, gives a wide manifesto of America. All this realism should be available, and not only to critics of "language," since the work is so much about immanence and worldliness and not at all a mystical ontology of "Language."

In other words—and this is the theme of Silliman in an essay against dogma and on Lewis Welch and Joe Ceravolo in *The New Sentence* (Roof Books, 1987)—we should be aware of false group typologies as we are of false periodizations. The new conservatives might want to stop berating the great modernists, since they obviously profit from their wake. The example of the dry, daunting Montale (translated by such diverse poets as Charles Wright, Dana Gioia, and Robert Lowell) might lead us to retake our Procrustean programmes.

We need not be paralyzed by our standards, like the man weeping at the gigantic foot of antiquity—the image by Fuseli that Bate chose for the cover of his wise book on "the burden of the past" [*The Burden of the Past and the English Poet* by W. Jackson Bate]—standards which become models of a "joy of influence" that lead us through admiration toward a new excellence. Eliot would be re-read, not as a sterile traditionalist, but as a man alive to the freshest sense of adventure. *The Waste Land* is a surrealist madness and is a useful, musical precursor of our strangest sense of collage. And we can have both Eliot and Stevens, together, we need not continue the stereotyped war between them or between them and Williams. The richest poetry might emerge exactly from the widest and wildest sense of this antitraditional tradition.

Review of *Operation Memory* by David Lehman

In a tumultuous and indelible essay on the Holocaust, David Lehman records not only his own "personal" memories, but those of his mother. He writes the unforgettably horrifying scene of suffering: "They were driven in a truck to an open field, where they dug their own graves and were shot." Trying to write poetry after this reality is, as the philosophers say, impossible, and yet it is our task, not to be abandoned. Elsewhere, forging a poetic, Lehman writes about the "epigrammatic precision" of the sentence hanging over the entrance to Auschwitz. [*Arbeit macht frei*: Work sets you free.] If one wants to understand the fury and indestructibility of Lehman's essentially Jewish poetry, one should consider this sentence as a goal and a limit: "The relation of sign to circumstance, of words to desolate place, is as terrifying as the dry bones of Ezekiel. It is a graver and eerier monument to human vanity than the ruined sculpture of a tyrant...." I read all of Lehman's poetry, his early tempestuous book, *Some Nerve*, with its neglected collage-poem "Baby Burning," and his later volume, *An Alternative to Speech*, as a variety of restrained prophetic denunciation. It is not for nothing that he is the master of the detective story and that he has been able, recently, to find a voice to hunt down and disarticulate what he regards as the bizarre and cowardly scandal surrounding Paul de Man's collaborationist writing (circa 1942). His anthologies on form, and his journalistic work, might be regarded

---

The Poetry Project Newsletter #141, edited by Jerome Sala (April–May 1991).

as attempts to restrain his more essential vatic mode. The effect is that of management of pain and rage through caustic Jewish wit. Such memory-work and grief-work do not set free but bind us more ferociously to a less abstract earth.

This sense of filiation and sacrifice was present early in Lehman's work, as in the lines that moved me in his early piece, "The Kiss": "The love / Of a man for his father becomes / The love of a son for his son." In his new work, *Operation Memory* (Princeton University Press, 1990), he has made the theme of survival his obsessive theme of mourning:

> Our hero, who wasn't always a hero, lives
> In despair but pretends not to care.
> He disagrees with reality. That is his right,
> And he has scars to prove it. Switch off the light
> And he will follow the slowest voluptuous curve
> Between any two stars, elaborating the distance
> Before spanning it in a leap of forgetfulness.

Of course, Auden and Ashbery are the compound ghosts of this learned art. Like a member of the Oulipo group, in love with the manias and mathematics of form in all this formless fury, he turns detective in "Defective Fiction." *Sic semper tyrannis.* He invents an amazing trope of a schoolboy in an Austrian military academy brooding on the square root of minus 1. The irrational in history is thus conjured and oneirically re-drawn. The anti-allegorical topic of immanence is thoughtfully provoked in his eschatological "Four Versions of the End," or let me be clearer: The Jew of the 20th century has become an old friend of annihilation. Their, our, and Lehman's poetry is "awed by the devastation behind us."

There is a lyrical, relenting side to Lehman that has produced beautiful love poems, villanelles, and the fabulously nostalgic "For I Will Consider Your Dog Molly" with its brave use of Jewish themes in Kit Smart's parallelisms:

> For she shook the water off her body, refreshed.
> For you removed the leash from her neck and let her roam freely.
> For she darted off into the brush and speared a small gray
>   moving thing

in the neck.
For this was the work of an instant.
For we looked and behold! the small gray thing was a rat.
For Molly had killed the rat with a single efficient bite, in
   conformance
with Jewish law.

But one sees how the memories of Rosh Hashanah are dealt with, in an efficient scene of retribution. Lehman's best poetry is restless, and his most moving image is that of the sober Noah waiting for a decent sign in a poetics of Return:

—The question is whether the raven will return
After his end-of-the-world adventures, after the storm,

When one by one the masks slip off, and the bride embraces
The guilty son: true to the test remembered and confessed.

A Night Painting of Ron Padgett

Ron Padgett's seriousness is often overlooked, partly because he is a master animator of self-lacerating humor. Most of his readers will know him for the hilarious compressions of his smaller works. In "I will sleep / In my little cup," one of his most memorable examples of opaque zaniness, an off-rhyme and an incongruous anti-grammatical sleep and cup create a little Magrittean essay in personal values. His use of kitsch is not simply Warholian acceptance—though it was inflected by Pop Art and is part of it—but is actually an American inclusiveness which partakes of the democratic antiauthoritarian in Padgett. (See his bias against bias in *Among the Blacks*.) And since his earliest text "Summer Balloons," Padgett has tended to puncture his lyricism with a dissonant wit that never entirely deflates it, in order to say unpretentious but sharp things about the continued shock of (as Walter Benjamin had it) "love at last sight." "Light as Air," a 12-part prose poem in his recent volume *The Big Something* (The Figures, 1990) stands out as a masterful poem of such tones, one in which Padgett creates a truly uncanny darkness.

In "Light as Air," Padgett's sense of unbearable lightness is seen rather exactingly, as when he declares, "I see the light on everything, trees, hills, and clouds, and I do not see the trees, hills, and clouds. I see the light, and it plays over my mind that it is any day, not today, just day." The play *over his mind* is a witty, radiant formulation, and Padgett's is a painterly struggle with generalizing, since this is a poet who hates misty generalizing. His hatred of pretense is immediately seen in the

---

Talisman, A Contemporary Journal of Poetry and Poetics, Number 7, edited by Edward Foster (Fall 1991).

use of "cardboard" language or "chain-link" language, to borrow an analogy from the architecture of the Gehry school. In part 2, he has the trees "swoosh," then later creates an off rhyme within the poem by reiterating, "Slash, slash in the woods." The poem builds up like a Mozart divertimento. Part 3 is a funny anti-commercial for sportswear, in which Padgett suggests that the key to despondency is dressing well: that is, the bright or unbearable surface. Less noted by his readers may be the very theme of melancholy which makes the "lightness" a curious antidote, drug and poison. In part 4, immediately following the entry of this theme of sadness and escapism, the lyric *you* is conjured up: "I look at you sometimes when you're not aware of it. I look at you in those moments the way a stranger might so I can see you better than I usually do." And to make this hymn to an imaginative act of attention not as proud as it could become, he deflates the Romantic defamiliarization with a Brechtian lowness: "And I feel happy just to be looking at you, the way the dog sits at the feet of us, his great gods." This tone annihilates the demagoguery of the poet as seer. Rimbaud's children become businesslike in a way noted by W. H. Auden. Here, Padgett may look as American as Mark Twain, but his self-deprecation is also part of the tradition of the symbolist dandy or *flâneur* since Laforgue, as he wittily continues in a precision that is magical and uncanny: "I sit at the feet of the thing that is you. I look at your feet." He turns his little joke of attention into a bizarre metonymic distortion. The cubo-futurist in Padgett is always slicing away toward a shining fragment.

"Light as Air" continues, in part 5, to evoke and deflate the Rimbaud of *Les Illuminations*, the dancing, flying seer who encompasses all: "I take off my clothes and am in the air.... Air around it all. Air I cannot breathe, because I am also a structure I am moving past, a tomb, a monument, a big nothing." The long sentence is a typical periodicity of Padgett's, as he modulates from the mock-Romantic flying dream to this sense of himself as a Rimbaudian other, to the sense of himself as a kind of architectural irony, a "duck," a simplicity, a double or triple loss of meaning: nothing. Lionel Trilling gained a certain insight into Robert Frost's bucolics by noting the terror and suicidal anguish at its heart. I would not go quite so far with Padgett, except to suggest that it is poetry of immense disappointment, of an almost arrogant disenchantment with himself and others. He pretends now and then to be unpretentious, to be the "AM radio" of a soothing acceptance, but actually there is a jagged, jarring athleticism and aggressivity kept in place with these sharp croppings. The final magic is to make all this aggressive wit, as Freud would note, into something economical and sensuous. In part 6 of "Light as Air," the shift to a silhouetted "he" is an important device of distance: "He is a man of many vectors, that assemble and reassemble.... You must go home and reassemble your rods and cones: night is falling, the soft gray mist of his breath." Here, there is a beautiful balance between the comedy of a Romantic science and the confusion between landscape, consciousness, and the self-reflexive cubism of this assembled and cut sentence. This is far from the image of Padgett as a cartoonist of small proportions, as a maker of fine candies or Robert Herrick to the first generation's Ben Jonson of the New York School of Poetry. What is alarmingly ambitious about "Light as Air" is how it finds a way to establish this fractured landscape and inscape as a poetic problem of some magnitude. It is a kind of healing of the split between Abstract Expressionism and Pop Art in poetry. In part 7, the "Pop" in his imagery makes an intrusive appearance: "I dreamed I had become a tall hamburger piloting a plane going down in a remote jungle waving up at me with inexpensive green cardboard natives ecstatic at the arrival, at last, of their messiah. A radiant hamburger bun top opened above me as I floated softly into their gyrating angular green mist." The typical Padgett maneuver is a dream that announces itself as a possible Romantic expansion, a vision that becomes a worse and worse Disneyland of humiliation and uncanny vulgarity. It's important to note, moreover, that Padgett places this melodrama of Disneyland as a subdominant in the poem, the dominant being the consciousness of an artist who can inflate and deflate this Americana as an arcane dream. Padgett is accused of being an ironic Robert Venturi of complex kitsch, but actually he carefully constructs a box in which, like Joseph Cornell, these different "reaches of the human spirit"—a phrase from Fairfield Porter who loved Cornell boxes and praised them for their contradictions—create a restless critique of all-too-stable kitsch.

Part 8 of this eccentrically multiple "thirteen ways of looking" at air announces itself as another deflation. Padgett says he will "speak only from the heart" but immediately makes a joke about the porters who have carried the *impedimenta* of his rhetoric and creates "a taxi ride" into his personality, or a version of his personality. All of this is a species of parenthetical mania to get to the "nothing" again that forms the "Snow Man" theme ["The Snow Man" by Wallace Stevens] of "Light as Air": "A little mirror, light fog on it clearing quickly." Note the melancholy of the image, Padgett as Lear observing the little breath of his poem's Cordelia, at any rate with the least bombast, the evanescence of things. It is like looking at an X-ray of Jean-Baptiste Siméon Chardin's painting of a boy with bubbles. Padgett's melancholy is the erotics of a middle-class, reasonable perspective. But with less and less faith in reason, and, as Randall Jarrell found in Frost's "Provide, Provide," what is offered as advice is a Lucretian materialism's mild *lack of consolation*.

Padgett is in love with form, can perform sonnets out of single consonants (Zzzzzzz, fourteen times), rhymes brilliantly in translating erotic poems from the French symbolists, and is capable of the musical variations of the pantoum without pretense. But a prose poem like "Light as Air" continues perhaps to be his best vehicle, because prose is the tendency of the Lucretian materialist: the prose of the world, its solidity and its paradoxical uncanny lightness. Padgett needs prose as Jasper Johns needs newspaper in early and late collages: to remind us of the object-ness of the art object, in this case the poem. Can a poem be fantastic, can a poem create a hesitation—answered in the negative by Tzvetan Todorov in his analysis of the supernatural tale. But Padgett uses prose to induce a certain dogmatic slumber in the unsuspecting reader and to charm the wide-awake modernist into thinking that his poem has depth or heaviness, like a window: "Let me recall my hand and fetch them for you. There, now you are creating puffs. But they do dissipate. They form shadow copies of my hand that is moving toward your face." This is a tour of body fragments, parts that remain parts, in a phrase from Jasper Johns. This shadowy prose, inflected by French surrealists, is a realism that points constantly to the surface of the poem. It is at once both window and black mirror. This is the maximal programme of Padgett: pragmatic and oneiric at once.

The long prose poem in Padgett's hands becomes a charming series of repetitions and reversals, with rococo embellishments that might seem decorative to some, but have their own severity. This Mozartean poem begins again and again: "It dawns on me that I'm repeating myself. Another day and there I am, calm outside in the air with my hand returning along its vectors. In this mental clearing the photons are jumping all around the savages.... I reach up and take the light from his face and fold it with the fingers on my hands and it dawns on me that I'm repeating myself." It is not the proud monotony of Stein but this jumpy self-lacerating humor of persistence that makes Padgett's poem so remarkably sad in its awareness.

Padgett's use of shifters is extraordinary and tends to crush any simple iconicity of the poem, leaving behind a kind of trace of a trace. In the Piercean sense, he is a master of the index and its charming ambiguity. Look at what he does with directional uncanniness in part 11 of "Light as Air": "At the end of the light I raise my voice from down there to up here and you are not here." This uncanniness is increased by his use of scientific language as collaged with his colloquial. He continues to harp on the mathematical mania of vectors in his complex diagrams: "Your vectors are heading out away from the voice of my hand and toward what it is pointing to, that bright cloud over there, the one with the burning edges, handsome and lighter than air at last." But what is lighter than air, and why the melancholy "at last?" The cloud is lighter than air, but this burning vision, this Romantic Shelleyesque fire, is one of a lack of meeting, a breakdown of relations between Padgett's "voice of a hand" and his apocalyptic cloud. The shifty shifter of the "you" has become an addressee slipping away in what Willem de Kooning called "a slipping glimpse." Padgett is not celebrating or accepting but is rather giving a startling sense of "love at last sight," and in a fairly chilly and chiliastic mode. Part 12 is a bizarre monument to this eschatological mood: "A cold streak runs through the sky now the color of wet cement that forms the body of the man whose brain is at a height of more miles than can be found on earth." He identifies the flatness of the poem and an absoluteness of emotion: "This emotional absolute zero is like a spine conducting thick fog and thin rain through him, and when the sun's vectors approach his surface they turn and move parallel to it." But what is the *imago hominis* to Padgett, what is his figurative center? "Who is this big cement man? And how do I know whether or not he is the same who came this morning and threw on the power that sent the electricity branching through my heart?"

We reach part 13 of this anticlassical eccentric perspectivist of a poem after that unanswered, perhaps unanswerable question. What is important is that Padgett has been willing to suggest that there is indeed "electricity branching through" a heart, the outmoded heart or center or figurative core contrasting "funnily" —in John Ashbery's language— with the electricity of a powerful "cement man." The "cement man" seems to be a degraded monument somewhat similar to Stevens' "Snow Man." In a poem about lightness, this monumental Claes Oldenburgesque cement man seems to be the comical exteriorized opposite of the whole cloudy nothing which is art's superb operation. The cement man is spectral gravity as opposed to Padgett's love of grace.

What kind of conclusion can we expect from this anti-Aristotelian poet of canny uncanniness? The poem ends with a reiteration of darkness and the poet as a self-contemplative *Schlemiel*: "I sit inside, my right hand touching my head. I look at the floor, the fabrics, the smoke from my mouth." In the mood of Cezanne's *Cardplayers*, all is contemplation and a bizarrely solid humorous game of attention to the everyday. The melancholy grows with a punning on the idea of light, lightness, and the theme of illumination: "It's as if there isn't any light, as if part of things being here is what light they have inseparable from themselves, not visible." The powerful resentment of the poet against transcendental allegories comes with a lashing simplicity: "The table doesn't stand for anything, although it remembers the tree. The table isn't immortal, though it hums a tune of going on forever. The table is in Friday, with me, both of us here in this dark, miserable day, and I have the feeling I'm smiling, though I'm not." This is indeed a conclusion, a stronger one than we might have suspected. The poet of optimism turns out to be the master of a fairly ambivalent misery; the theme of light, as in the impressionism of much of the poem, is made into something melancholy through self-consciousness. In Japanese, the phrase for "light snow" means "perishing beauty." Padgett's burden has indeed been evanescence, how to make of New York School impressionism something solid as the poems of the tradition. (Which poems? What tradition?)

If I were merely underlining the positive beauties of Padgett's poetry, I would point to his erotic translations in "C" magazine, to his devilishly clear renditions of Blaise Cendrars and Raymond Roussel, and to the varieties of lyric from *Great Balls of Fire* through *Triangles in the Afternoon* to the recent *The Big Something*. I would note his mistranslations of Reverdy and his way of finding a place for mistranslation and the sense of mistranslation—the joys of not knowing, the pleasures of a partial plural perspective—in "Tone Arm" and elsewhere. I would point to his beautiful new love poetry, particularly the immensely complex Americana collaged in "Sweet Pea." The question is not one of Padgett's valuing complexity but of his love for a positive *multiplicity*, seen in his longer "crazy" compositions inspired by Apollinaire, Cendrars, Kenneth Koch, and Frank O'Hara, but with his completely individual voice, a voice he has joked about *not being able to lose*. The contagion of his tone of selflaceration and humor is extraordinary as is his evident joy in craftsmanship, seen in his work with children and his stintless solicitude for form in his beautiful *Handbook of Poetic Forms for Teachers and Writers*, where he has continued the tradition of poetic pedagogy in the school system. Translation has furnished one key to his art, the way in which he has become more and more faithful to his sources, but also the way in which he has pragmatically translated French surrealists into something as fresh and dark and miserably American as "Light as Air," his great prose poem. One doesn't want to crush the iridescent butterfly of his art on any critical wheel, but the equal and opposite problem is how often criticism evades the task of appreciating this kind of jubilant, seemingly inappropriately "low" artist. Actually, Padgett comes out of the extremely ambitious innovation of Koch, whose every poem in *Thank You* announced his intention to revitalize form in our day, but without losing the exhilarating force of a new cavalier love poetry. Padgett has carried out this programme of innovation, hatred of false seriousness, and celebration of life's details with a conviction that is all the more incredible because it has had as its constant accompaniment a consciousness of skepticism and vulnerability.

The fate of the so-called second generation of the New York School has been pretty dismal. There has been a critical revaluation of Ashbery and O'Hara, so that many who considered those poets meaningless or trivial have made rhetorical tergiversations to include them as part of the American canon. Koch has been harder for the academy to digest, because of the acute criticality of his comedic means. James Schuyler was at last appreciated as a landscape artist of some wit, but he has not yet been seen as a heartbreaking poet of madness and frangibility. (The *Times* obituary seemed to reduce him to a playful personal poet among snapshots.) What has happened to poets such as Joseph Ceravolo, Padgett and others is a more relentless neglect. They are featured as epigones or disastrous disciples. When critics appreciate the father-figures, the children are made to seem like pygmies. Such is the style of canonization, and perhaps nothing should be made of this in the mode of resentment. This is particularly ironic, however, when the same critics often devote themselves not at all to movement and collaboration in communal style but to individuals and the solitary genius. Actually, Ceravolo is an extraordinary poet whose influential poetic of disjunction has a religious content that is at interesting odds with the other poets of the New York School. The tone of Padgett and his accomplishment have a remarkable unity and consistent sensibility that is identifiable at once and that has its own particular melancholy. (I harp on his darkness because it is neglected.) Padgett disdains false labels and thus, though some of his work could be called "Language" poetry and all of it is "poetry" poetry, he is unwilling to reduce things, and his editing our collaborative anthology, *An Anthology of New York Poets*, made it swerve from any aristocratic ensemble I might have dreamt of to a pretty elastic urban mélange: Ed Sanders, Tom Vietch, Aram Saroyan are examples of the width of his taste. He helped create, moreover, one of the best little magazines of the century: "C." It is comical to underestimate this achievement, after all.

The genius of our time has been in shattered arts of multiplicity. The polystylist painter Lucio Pozzi has had a difficult time being evaluated because he has escaped the signature style of the gallery and swerved from abstraction to figuration and back again in a variety of media. Personal sensibility unified his diverse work, but he was also a severe critic of Romantic notions of personality. Ashbery's recent *Flow Chart* is a stunning blow to critics who would make him seem like a Tory conservative; he maintains his multifoliate rights to the most diverse and anti-authoritarian meditational stream. Koch's poetry is one of our most surprising, because he is a relentless critic of all forms of inflation, and his essentially critical poetry is often masked as an erotic lyricism. Padgett's poetry, which has now been in print for almost thirty years, has been an influence for those decades and is an astounding art of modesty and of imperfection itself. His prose poem, "How to Be Perfect," recently published in Australia, is a cascade of coruscating "perverbs" that mock the degraded idealisms of our day in what seems to be reasonable advice. The poet has praised the paradise of animated cartoons. What he truly loves is the animated paradise of a worldly poetry itself.

John Hejduk, Miroslav Masák, David Shapiro, and President Vaclav Havel at the Jan Palach Memorial dedication ceremony at Prague Castle. September 4, 1991. Courtesy The Irwin S. Chanin School of Architecture Archive, The Cooper Union. Photo: Jaroslav Zastoupi

In Shapiro's 1969 poem "The Funeral of Jan Palach," the funeral is narrated by Palach, the student who had immolated himself to protest the 1968 Soviet invasion of Czechoslovakia. The poem inspired the architect John Hejduk to create a memorial to Palach that included the poem. At the 1991 dedication ceremony of the memorial at Prague Castle, Shapiro read the poem (next page) and gave the speech that follows it. The memorial was permanently installed in Jan Palach Square in 2016.

Poetry and Architecture, Architecture and Poetry

Shapiro began his speech with the poem that inspired the memorial:

The Funeral of Jan Palach

When I entered the first meditation,
I escaped the gravity of the object,
I experienced the emptiness,
And I have been dead a long time.

When I had a voice you could call a voice,
My mother wept to me:
My son, my beloved son,
I never thought this possible,

I'll follow you on foot.
Halfway in mud and slush the microphones picked up.
It was raining on the houses;
It was snowing on the police-cars.

The astronauts were weeping,
Going neither up nor out.
And my own mother was brave enough she looked
And it was alright I was dead.

"The Funeral of Jan Palach" and Shapiro's speech appeared in *BOMB Magazine*, Number 41, (Fall 1992). The poem was first published in *A Man Holding an Acoustic Panel* (The Overlook Press, 1971).

I was in Cambridge, England, in 1969, when I read of the act of Jan Palach, of his amazing words, of his funeral, and of the words of his mother. I read of the march which was so silent the birds could be listened to, and I wrote my little poem in awe of Palach's great courage. For years my friends and I had tried to be courageous against what we thought was an immoral war. [The student protests at Columbia University.] We were timid; some were audacious; we did a little; we were humiliated; perhaps we succeeded, a bit. I had lived through the terrible assassinations, and I recall that I felt honored when a stone struck me at Columbia University after I said that I hoped that what we were doing honored the memory of Martin Luther King.

When I read of the sacrifice of Jan Palach, I was reading of a heroism toward which I had aspired but recoiled. But it is not for everyone to be such a sacrifice; as many have said, it is not even easy to be a disciple of such a hero. Indeed, Palach finally asked others to refrain from a mechanical martyrdom.

Now I feel lucky to have known an architect who draws angels and who refuses to participate. I was more than lucky to have been asked, almost by accident, to meet a Polish cultural advisor of the new Polish government in New York, the painter, Josky Skalnik. And in Mr. Skalnik I met a man with whom I wanted to share this architecture and my poem. He had lived it. He also gave me the honor of introducing me to Mr. Miroslav Masak, who immediately asked to meet Mr. John Hejduk. We were invited to Prague, but we shrank from asking for anything of this inspiring new government. My dream was to give something back to you, the image of Jan Palach, your Torch Number One, as he called himself, the image of your country in resurrection and victory.

Amazing, too, to come in a week of other martyrdoms, other solemn funerals: three in Moscow. When I wrote my poem, I wanted to raise a lament as true as that lover of truth—Jan Hus's phrase—and I am so proud to collaborate with John Hejduk in the Prague of my heroes: Kafka, Rilke, Milena Jesenská, who said: fear nothing, tell the truth. And the children of Terezin who reappear in their drawings.

Each article by Timothy Ash about you [meaning Vaclav Havel, present in the audience] in your "year of the truth" was like a miraculous reward for Palach's act and your innumerable intransigent acts. We read each page of your letters from prison, Mr. President, where you demanded of others elsewhere an "ethical mirror of Palach's act." Czechoslovakia has been for us like George Bataille's image of the sun: it warms us and gets nothing in return. In honor of you, then, and for the people of Czechoslovakia, we thought of bringing you this gift of your own son. Thank you.

Denise Levertov: Among the Keys

I would like to speak of the rhythmical precisions of Denise Levertov, not to expose a metrical mania or pedantry, but to give a sense of the justice of her power. This rhythmic finesse might be said to be the synesthetic component, because here the cadences, wandering caesuras, and musical discontinuities produce a painterliness. It is the oddity of Levertov's work that her most chromatic effects are precisely these tough and anxious shifts of rhythm, and that her polyrhythms, as it were, are more significant than certain aspects of her so-called subject matter. And one might go so far as to underline this cadential mastery as her particular topic and place this musicality as an essential *eros* of the work. I am going to use the poetry selected for the canonic Donald M. Allen anthology [*The New American Poetry* (Grove, 1960)] because it marked for me the repleteness of her work as well as its particularity among other poets.

One is attracted to the dashes and depths of "Beyond the End," and particularly the way the iamb is flouted, a lesson learned from William Carlos Williams, Ezra Pound, and presumably Charles Olson, but here promoted almost to the abstract stage of becoming the "subject matter," not just, in Meyer Schapiro's term, content matter. The process poem much touted in the age of the Abstract Expressionists has, I think, arrived here at some of its most overt propositions:

The 'hewers of wood' & so on; every damn
craftsman has it while he's working

Twentieth Century Literature, Vol. 38, Denise Levertov Issue, edited by William McBrien, Duke University Press, (Autumn 1992).

> but it's not
> a question of work: some
> shine with it, in repose. Maybe it is
> response, the will to respond—('reason
> can give nothing at all/like
> the response to desire') maybe
> a gritting of the teeth, to go
> just that much further, beyond the end
> beyond whatever ends: to begin, to be, to defy.

The passages concerning a poetics have begun to take over the poem itself, very much as the act of staining the canvas had become for Helen Frankenthaler more than a ritual or a carving of shapes, but the act that most proposed the immanent as the naked subject matter of art. I think that this connects "Beyond the End" with those moments in Frank O'Hara's "Second Avenue"—really a book more than a poem, a book dedicated as much to Jackson Pollock as to Vladimir Mayakovsky—when the poetic line in its relations to spilled paint becomes the leading metaphor. Here the subject matter of rhythm becomes an intransigent force:

> It's energy; a spider's thread: not to
> 'go on living' but to quicken, to activate: extend:
>
> It has no grace like that of
> the grass, the humble rhythms, the
> falling and rising of leaf and star;
> it's barely
> a constant. Like salt:
> take it or leave it

In "The Hands" there is another vivid metonymy offered for the act of musical construction. The hands are

> slithering
>   among the keys.

And the "almost painful / movement" of the poem registers Levertov's erotic sense of the "actors at rehearsal," in their demotic costumes, or costumes of the demotic: "common clothes." The whole stage is democratic, flexible and unfixed. But the poem is particularly horrifying because from the beginning the poet has made it clear that the hands are horrible, oneiric, and fragmentary: "Don't forget the crablike / hands, slithering / among the keys." These haunted, uncanny hands are particularly *unheimlich* because of the homely rhythmical maneuvers of the line which slashes them into pieces: parts for the part.

Levertov is the master ironist of this music which "drifts you / off your feet: too easily let off." What would be the possibility of difficulty in this world but nakedly that of "painful / movement"? The enjambments are all ways of insisting on rhythmical breakdowns themselves: "a tension, as of / actors at rehearsal." Robert Creeley was to make this rhythmical indecision into the canonic proposals of anxiety that are, after all, his poetic. In Olson's hands such a consciousness of a rhythmical skepticism has mostly been used for purposes of pedagogy and epic affirmation. Levertov's poetics of difficulty, of painful movement, of slithering hands among the keys becomes, moreover, an urban vision, similar to that which Meyer Schapiro discovered in the intercepting planes of Degas and Pissarro as well as Mondrian.

"Merritt Parkway" is the most obvious neighbor or companion to these abstract pieces of natural and poetic rhythm. Here the effort in abstraction is likened to what Willem de Kooning called the "no-environment" of the city.

>   As if it were
>   forever that they move, that we
>   keep moving—
>
>   ...
>
>   above our six lanes
>   the dreamlike continuum ...
>
>   ...
>
>   passing by, passing
>   the cars that
>   keep moving ahead of
>   us, past us, pressing behind us
>   and
>   over left, those that come
>   toward us shining too brightly

> moving relentlessly
>   in six lanes, gliding
> north & south, speeding with
> a slurred sound—

This early poem, from 1954, seems to me a masterpiece of ambivalence concerning representation. It traffics in the traffic of a poem while continuing to be, after all, a plastic piece of naturalism concerning the deracinations of city and cars. On the one hand Levertov is here closer to the world of Williams' exact observations in baseball games, and his pure horrible products of American lunacy, but she is also already beginning to dissolve all traffic into the unmediated stain of a poetry announcing itself as impure movement. It is perhaps the tumultuous joy of this poem that it succeeds in being, at once, as abstract and colorful as one of Richard Diebenkorn's series based on the urban grid, and also that it is aware of the subject of *the human in trouble*:

> And the people—ourselves
>   the humans from inside the
> cars, apparent
> only at gasoline stops
>   unsure,
>   eyeing each other
>
>   drink coffee hastily at the
>   slot machines & hurry
>   back to the cars
>   vanish
>   into them forever, to
>   keep moving—

The luxury of such a poem is its close positioning, its geometrical congruence, in the device of traffic and the poetic cadences in which this poem makes its shape felt. The theme of movement is part of the sensuality of her "The Way Through," and its wit of tedium vitae: "The water flies in the halfwit's eye / who didn't move fast enough / 'Who do you think I am, a horse?' / but we made it—." The naturalism of this landscape is radically altered by the staggering subjectivity of the end, and its uneconomical luxuries: "Drown us, lose us, / rain, let us loose, so, / to lose ourselves, to career / up the plunge of the hill." The end is unpunctuated ecstasy because the poem has veered so far away from any imagism à la H.D., which it might superficially resemble. The poem is more expansive in its passions, and even more about the "common clothes" of a demotic rhythmic burden: "he backs up / the old car again and CHARGES." Note the capitals.

"The Third Dimension" is interesting in exactly the way it begins to loosen the burden of the sculptural. It looks more like a Spanish song, with the thrilling erotic violence of "They took and / split me open from / scalp to crotch, and / still I'm alive." The rhymes are as funny and absurd as those attempted by early Ashbery as ways of traducing all the positive effect of rhyme: "' … the world's bounty.' Honesty / isn't so simple: / a simple honesty is / nothing but a lie." All sorts of half-rhymes and what John Hollander has called poverty of *rime riche* act upon these lines to thwart any comfortable élan. "The third dimension / hides itself." Particularly in this song of its occlusion, where the volumetrics of cracked stones are immediately dissipated by the sense of "love / cracked me open / and I'm / alive to / tell the tale— but not / honestly." And why does the poet confess that she cannot possibly be honest, sincere, one might add, positivistically a reporter? Because the words, and the rhythms, have changed such a report into song, into "The Peppertrees," into the rhythms that haunt our sense of cadence and conclusion, and lack of conclusion. This unrepaired sense of musical and non-discursive song haunts the "Scenes from the Life of the Peppertrees." Scenes from the life of the "real."

I think still of this poem as one of Levertov's masterpieces, despite the many volumes that have intervened, and despite the fact that one might accuse me of underlining the so-called "anthology" piece in its dusty *gloire*. But I am still dazzled by the freshness of this piece, by the sensuality of those "Cats … stretching in the doorways, / sure of everything." And I think that it is rare that Levertov has permitted herself so constant a humor that does not degenerate into whimsy: "The peppertrees / shiver a little." There is a sequence here that startles with its non-narrative joy in dissemination, from the trees to a cat, to a defenselessly, humorously sleeping anti-hero: "He is good. / Let him sleep." Landscape is animated, but the humor of the pathetic fallacy has become a hilarious device and topic:

> But the third peppertree
> is restless, twitching
> thin leaves in the light
> of an afternoon. After a while
> it walks over and taps
> on the upstairs window with a bunch
> of red berries.   Will he wake?

This little Keatsian ending, which does not exactly solve the problem of whether "he" wakes or sleeps, sleeps or dreams, whether he has been given a reprieve by way of the author, or vice versa, is a charming way of dissolving landscape into inscape, and yet somehow keeping up the more-or-less conventional charms of "a third dimension." Somehow we feel, at the end of the peppertree cadenzas, that this sequence has not accommodated either our rage for the real or our desperate desire to disappear into the relatively irreal. The poem keeps up a steady strain of objects that might be silhouettes of the real, but are, after all, somewhat concealed by sound itself:

> The yellow moon dreamily
> tipping buttons of light
> down among the leaves. Marimba,
> marimba—from beyond the
> black street.
>   Somebody dancing,
> somebody
>   getting the hell
> outta here.

The pleasures and sharks of her fictive world, the Goddess whom she conjures in a fairytale forest, are parts of a scene in which we are plucked "from close rooms" into a power that is elemental, abstract, and removed from the dimensions, or perhaps pulverized within the dimensions, of the real: "I bit on a seed and it spoke on my tongue."

The movement of the sinister sharks is as sullen as this particular craft or art, at its proleptic best: "Dark / the sharp lift of the fins." These hallucinatory movements, these delicate adjustments, are as fresh and final as anything later sought in elegy, politics, or prayer.

David and Lindsay Shapiro by Fairfield Porter. Oil paint on Canvas, 1972. Courtesy of Lindsay Shapiro and the Fairfield Porter Estate. Photo by Matt Flynn. A detail of the painting is on the front cover of this volume.

When Shapiro asked Fairfield Porter to paint a portrait of his wife Lindsay in the summer of 1972, Porter invited the two of them to Great Spruce Head, his family island in Maine, and painted this double portrait. Shapiro's friendship with Fairfield Porter and his wife Anne deepened over the years along with his admiration, not only for Fairfield's painting and writing, but for Anne's poetry. On the next page is his foreword to her first book of poetry. Shapiro's wife Lindsay, an architect by training, is Exhibition Manager of the Smithsonian Institution National Museum of the American Indian.

Living Things: The Poetry of Anne Porter

This is a shocking book, for all its seeming diffidence, economy, and quietness. We are used to poets of skepticism and the subjunctive, from Hardy to Stevens; and we are certainly accustomed to poets of the worldly surface, from Apollinaire to O'Hara. We are perhaps most habituated to the poetry that confesses a separation from the transcendental, and T.S. Eliot himself went so far as to underline how often it is just this that convinces us: the cry of separation. However, we cannot forget how much of modernity is a spiritual art, and that the sacred is what Rimbaud and Mondrian and Le Corbusier thirsted for in their radical work. If we have problems, because so much of the language of belief has grown connotatively encrusted, we wait for the poets who believe enough and can freshen this dialect.

    Anne Porter is one of the rare poets who believes enough, who lives in days and holidays, and who has stunningly found a language to transmit her Franciscan joy in created things. Her diction is as modest as that of William Carlos Williams or of a poet she nurtured as a houseguest for many years, James Schuyler. She has a particular Negative Capability for speaking for the speechless: the poor, the peddler, the homeless, the sick. Her portrait of Anastasia ("My Anastasia") shows how she escapes "Blue Period" sentimentality while she does this, as when she is willing to notice the stain of anti-Semitism in her protagonist. "We were built for heaven, like a boat," she once

---

Foreword to *An Altogether Different Language, Poems 1934–1984* (Zoland Books, 1994). This first volume of Porter's poetry, published when she was 83, was nominated for the National Book Award.

remarked to me, and her poetry has both a child-like flow and a rugged confidence. Her nature-worship might remind one of her Channing family-tradition of New England transcendentalism, but she has a rare willingness to be canonical: "Easter is growing / in the paschal moon / Like a child in its mother" ("In Holy Week"). The poet is certain, not only because a map has been given, but because she is willing to travel without maps, and look, and be amazed.

She takes the side of things, of living things, and of the creator. Is her work a long series of commentaries on scripture? No, because it is observed and biographical: "While the tiny maple leaves are curling like birds' feet round the frost / Through all the whispering to you in buses / As I ride to see grandchildren …" ("The Shortest Days"). From the earliest formal poems to the more recent ones, she gives us a practiced poetry of wonder: "Now the smallest creatures, who do not know they have names …" ("The First of May"), and finds the connections between names and natural things. She is unembarrassed by ordinary, even sordid detail, as in the "sweaty gowns" that stick to the patients in her "Country Hospital." And if one thinks she is merely pious or reticent she finds gigantic depths and tumult, as in "Consider the Lilies of the Sea": "Death sprung open in a depth of sea." Her faith has enlarged her, not the reverse, and her poetry has the grandeur of seeing things "as if for the first time." It is not unusual to be reminded of the Surrealists in this sacred art of the everyday. As when she describes wondrously creature-like poems that "sing / In breaking waves / And rock like wooden cradles"("Living Things").

It's her natural disposition to "pay attention to ultimate reality," words that her husband, Fairfield Porter, who painted her so often alone and with their children, told me should be the conclusion of every sermon. She also knows, like that great painter of "light and repose," that ultimate reality is in everything and not lurking behind it. In her most poignant poem, "For My Son Johnny," she gives us an amazing cadenza of his problems, his humor ("In heaven the angels kid and joke"), and his anxieties. This poem is as well-written as prose and also as song. It has the purity of Apollinaire or Éluard and is filled with the audacious Pop-Art vividness of unembarrassed life. Only a great poet could control this poem of suffering without bathos, and its loving details illuminate for us a whole open house.

Her elegant poem "A Child at the Circus" reminds us that Anne Porter has retained her childhood talent for seeing the world as "one big surprise." She keeps her eyes open on the bus trip in "From Denver to Alburquerque" and spots the graffiti "LOVE IS AMONG US" in the dirty washroom. Like Schuyler, she takes the side of flowers and is "beyond flowers," at once a poet of immanence and exaltation: "No one will see the daylilies / The color of red foxes, / Waist-high coarse-textured lilies." Though some might be misled into thinking this poetry naive, it is gently learned, as when she can suddenly apostrophize the poet and the painter on familiar terms: "Walt Whitman honored you, Jean-Francois Millet ... And I thank you myself." But it is the gratitude, one must say the Franciscan gratitude, that remains, along with praise, her predominant emotional perspective. In thanking Millet for what "no one else could give me," the long-past moment in the moonlit farmyard, she adds: "You saved it for us out of that warm life / Which God has hidden somewhere" ("Farmyard by Moonlight").

These poems are as powerful as secrets, as "secret praise / Which burns in every creature" ("Leavetaking"). They give us the feeling of a complete art, a mature poet, who has the resilient gift of translating seemingly non-verbal, non-sensuous states into sensuous poetry. We accept these "parables of the kingdom," because they are given to us as ordinary and possible perspectives, not obscurities. Though she recognizes irreducible evils, her poetry tends to burst into clarity, as in "A Biography of Flowers," with its microscopy, and the masterful image of dissemination in "The Pear Tree:" "Disclosing every tender filament / Sticky with nectar / Beaded with black pollen." This poetry is so refined that it might be thought of as innocent, but will, like her Sarah in "Another Sarah," become "A wave of living sweetness / A nation of white petals / A dynasty of apples." These last refinements make her an ecstatic exception, an American religious poet of stature who reminds us that the idea of the holy is still possible for us.

This poetry is filled with domesticity and family—the poet raised five children while taking care of countless others, myself included—

but it is also filled with the widest world, from Long Island to Assisi, of material and immaterial spaces and history. Her poetry has digested all variety of traditional influences and seems in this complete volume unmistakable and independent. We are led to the conclusion of Laurance Wieder and others that she is among the superb poets of the sacred in this century, though her subtly assertive work directs praise elsewhere. Fairfield Porter broke the taboos of his age against representing nature and figure, while still loving gesture and color. Anne Porter, with her own sense of liberty and courage, breaks our secular taboo against representing invisible love, while still praising and defining living things in clearest tones.

For Anne Porter, the holy is found in a commitment to Christ the Mediator and his triumph in suffering for a suffering world. However, she gives a constant, almost pantheistic pressure to the theme that the Kingdom of God is within and without, so that her radiant if concise imagism is all in the service of God. This paradox reminds us that while for Pound, a squirrel was just that one squirrel, for Anne Porter, concrete squirrels run into "invisible arks," where "there's no room for us" whose home is "warring disobedient history" ("Oaks and Squirrels"). The concrete is also part of an unruined allegory that harmonizes. It is her oscillation between the literal, symbolic, allegorical, and even anagogic worlds that gives her sparse poetry its strange richness. With the publication of these poems, American poetry is suddenly and substantially enriched.

Van Gogh, Heidegger, Schapiro, Derrida: The Truth in Criticism

> On his most anxious days, he painted the most disquieting objects. How else could he have survived.
>
> Whoever meddles, injects his human deliberation, his wit, his advocacy, his intellectual agility in any way is already disturbing and clouding his activity. Ideally a painter (and generally an artist) should not become conscious of his insights ... That van Gogh's letters are so readable, that they are so rich, basically argues against him.
>
> —Rilke (1907)

May I as a poet be forgiven for making restitution concerning two other poets' mis-readings? If Rilke thought of van Gogh as too meddlesome, Hugo von Hofmannsthal reacted to van Gogh as a painter of pure Being. In May 1901 Hofmannsthal wrote that he felt the soul of van Gogh in his paintings: "The being of every tree, every strip of yellow or greenish field, every fence, every ravine ... lifted itself as though newly born out of the terrible chaos of non-existence, out of the abyss of Non-Being." This poet's sense of animism, however, does not neglect human, emotive meaning: "And in all this one could sense, a heart, the soul of the man who created it."[1] We can sense in the quotations of both Hofmannsthal and Rilke a longing for Being that is perhaps a remnant of the Spinozism in German

---

Van Gogh 100, edited by Joseph D. Masheck. Prepared under the auspices of Hofstra University, (Greenwood Press, 1996). A volume commemorating the 100th anniversary of the death of Vincent van Gogh. Shapiro's essay tackles a famous controversy that arose between Martin Heidegger, Jacques Derrida and Meyer Shapiro about a painting of a pair of shoes by van Gogh.

Romanticism, a pantheism of nature worship on the part, however, of a master of self-portraiture who did not find human passions meddlesome.

To present van Gogh as *either* a painter whose every stroke is one of Being or as one ruined by a meddlesome selfhood is to forget that combination of objectivity and emotion that Meyer Schapiro rightly observes synthesized in *Old Shoes*, whereas, in Heidegger and Jacques Derrida, the self-portrait recedes into the twin abysses of Being and Multiplicity. While the arguments about van Gogh's shoe paintings suggest to at least one colleague "a bottomless pit," in weighing the alternative testimonies we may look for adequacy and tact, fruitfulness and illumination, as when a medical diagnosis takes into account the individual complexities of a case history.

Although we know from Freud how shattered and shattering the case history of a psyche can be, and we look to our critics to provide some close attention to the particular, Heidegger's approach seems to be a mystical reading of the picture as a disclosure of Being that takes no biography, history or context of any kind into account. And Derrida's skepticism is so global that it extends even to Gauguin's letter cited by Schapiro as evidence that van Gogh asserted he had painted his own shoes. Both the mystical and the skeptical readings have an aureate charm, yet both seem blind to the particularities of van Gogh. Schapiro, as a species of restless pluralist, welcomes for scrutiny evidence of all kinds, involved as he has always been in "critical" seeing that discriminates one painting from another and finds meaning in the minutest formal characteristics. Schapiro, a true student of John Dewey and in a sense of William James, has a pragmatic bias toward the concrete. His abstractions suggest tests of falsifiability that one cannot imagine with Heidegger's and Derrida's infinities.

At first the issue seems breathtakingly simple. In 1935 Martin Heidegger, writing a rhapsody on Being, used one of van Gogh's paintings of shoes as an example of the disclosure of the truth of being.[2] It served his purposes to underline the motif as showing the world of the peasant woman, her work, her anxieties, her world, and, even more, how the truth of shoes is revealed in the painting. Schapiro came to question the philosopher, suggesting that the painting, far from being the disclosure of Being or the truth of shoes in general, is a specific, concrete work that in its frontality presents itself as a kind of self-portrait, a piece of van Gogh and not the peasant woman of the philosopher's hallucination. He adduced for this symbolism the sense that van Gogh, grown toward a Parisian self-reflexiveness, was no longer a "peasant painter," and also a confirming anecdote from Gauguin in which van Gogh related that these shoes were a personal relic. In a lengthy meditation on this shoe image, the philosopher of our contemporary skeptical mood suggests that both previous writers are hallucinating presence. Derrida teases both of them, but Schapiro more relentlessly, as being too sure of a symbolic code. He suggests it is not even necessary to see the shoes as a pair. Couldn't these just be detached, uncanny objects, suggesting nothing like a peasant or a self? Derrida goes to great lengths to tease both the mystical and what he regards as the positivistic readings, without considering much historical, biographical or extratextual evidence. The question for Derrida is, How can these two be sure the shoes belong to them? Well, to me, Derrida has gone too far in his eroticization of doubt.

Roman Jakobson's famous schema of aesthetic axes provides a way of evaluating our critics. This involves addresser (or artist), reception or addressee, sensually self-focusing forms, context, code, and physical contact. Jakobson was modulating away from a formalism when he suggested that all these axes were vitally linked: different axes could dominate, and the aesthetic was still the central poetic axis; nevertheless, all the axes are intertwined. With Heidegger, there is a radical deletion of the axis of addresser and addressee. With Derrida, context is deleted, the world in which the artwork is embedded and to which it partly refers.

Derrida despises reference unless it serves the polysemous undecidability be loves. In this he is himself a kind of caricature of Heidegger, whereas Schapiro is a pluralist who positively likes the balance between addresser and addressee; the artwork's sensualism and the artist's psyche; the world, town or country, in which the work is embedded and also its metalinguistics. *Style, artiste et société* is the very title of the French edition of Schapiro's selected essays (1982)—

and the subtitle of his *Theory and Philosophy of Art* (Selected Essays, 4; 1994). Schapiro's criticism comprehends both rapture with forms and solicitude for psychic, social and stylistic conditions and changes. To concentrate on one factor at a time is a useful foregrounding, but to delete one is amputation. In Derrida, meaning proliferates uselessly around no center; in Schapiro, meaning clusters and deepens around the aesthetic pole.

Heidegger's rage against modernity, which Martin Zimmerman has dilated upon, was deep-seated and lasting. His anti-technological zeal and revulsion against Americanism and communism were such that be made no recantation after World War II of his rapport with National Socialism. That in dealing with his beloved poet Friedrich Hölderlin the philosopher deletes Hölderlin's liberalism and the inspiration he took from the French Revolution[3] is a misreading typical of Heidegger, who constantly used texts without context to find in them his sense of disclosures of Being. Friends attested to the fact that cities made Heidegger physically ill;[4] and there are photos of him seemingly masquerading as a Swabian peasant in a summer hut. Zimmerman places this nostalgia in a variety of contexts, including the personal: Heidegger's grandfather was a shoemaker, "his father a part-time cooper and his mother a peasant." His zeal for a peasant "interpretation" of van Gogh should be placed in this context. Relatedly, Heidegger also developed an anti-anthropocentric bias that leads him to underestimate just such self-aware, or personal, choices as Meyer Schapiro emphasizes in his developmental sense of van Gogh. His anti-anthropocentrism leads him constantly to take the addresser, in Jakobson's sense, out of the work of art; his sublime ontology of things leads him to underestimate the artist's expressive presence. Derrida's own refusals to acknowledge presence in texts may be regarded as his precursor's antipathies: both Heidegger and Derrida leave us with a radical lack of specificity where an individual voice may be as a distraction.

It is interesting for Zimmerman to suggest Rilke's misreading of van Gogh and Cezanne as the starting point for Heidegger's meditation on the shoes. In Rilke's letters I notice his initial enthusiasm for a portfolio of forty reproductions after van Gogh—twenty of them, the poet notes, rendered before his going to Paris. Aware of biography, Rilke senses that even with a chair van Gogh is not only interested in fact but in making a spiritual icon out of homely things.[5] In a letter of October 21, 1907, Rilke has what he regards as a great insight into Cezanne and van Gogh: he thinks that that van Gogh, whom he has previously admired for his expressivity, meddles too much, even in his famous letters.[6] Rilke's new focus was an anti-humanistic impersonalism in which colors arrange themselves magically in the painting—a poetics of ontology, as it were. This modernist poetics of impersonality (involving a misreading of Baudelaire and Flaubert) yields a kind of tradition of antihuman hermeneutics. Before, Rilke has a clear sense of van Gogh's anxiety placed in "disquieting objects"; afterward, he often swerves into philosophical cloudiness, and his anti-symbolic misreading of Cezanne, Zimmerman finds, perfectly suits Heidegger's longing for a sublime emptied of the human distortion that he thought traced to a "productionist metaphysics" with the world as raw material.[7]

Heidegger does read van Gogh symbolically, but even the symbolism of the simple world of the Folk gives way to the sense that the true meaning of the work is the disclosing of Being. The student of van Gogh's *Potato Eaters* may contrast this with the vivid expressivity, even in van Gogh's early work, of a concrete sense of poverty and oppression. Van Gogh's religion and politics have to be overlooked if the sublime philosopher looks for autonomous abstraction or the wonder of Being. Heidegger's antihumanism certainly leaves such a work destitute of an addresser, an addressee and the context of social fate so subtly scrutinized by Schapiro.

Heidegger's weakness as a critic is seen in his metaphrasis of a poem by Georg Trakl. Told that in that masterful poem, the author disappears, so that "Language speaks," I can only notice that all the tortured expressionism of Trakl, a haunted man who was a suicide at an early age, is deleted in Heidegger's account. Meter and rhyme, he says, could be analyzed; but they aren't: no wonder Schapiro submits that a real shoe would be as inspiring for Heidegger's analysis as the painting by van Gogh. A line about pain Heidegger calls "startling," but since there is no human self with which to associate the pain, we are left with a pain as empty as van Gogh's shoes. By the way, I'm only a little amazed that Heidegger doesn't pick up, in the poem, on a table set with bread and wine as a peasant meal. He comes close ("Bread and wine are the fruits of heaven and earth.... The things that are called bread and wine are simple things...."), but the Christological in this winter scene is barely hinted at, or the poet's sense of suffering. Heidegger's critique entails a grand refusal of the personal.

Was van Gogh as anti-urbanely reactionary as Heidegger? Derrida seems to insist that the urban interpretation of Schapiro is laughable; but despite van Gogh's often-expressed longings for the country, he did indeed move to Paris, and into the gallery and café world of his brother Theo. There he likes the dandyish Toulouse-Lautrec as well as Seurat and Pissarro, both radicals. Quite unlike Heidegger, with his sacral sense of German as Greek reborn, he loves French naturalist novels—*Germinal*, *Earth*—and paints Zola's books in a still life that once again expresses his self and secret affinities. Van Gogh, who also read English novels, was a cosmopolite. In Paris, he does not indulge in painting nostalgic *sabot* pictures but paints himself more than twenty times; and, whether or not one agrees with Meier-Graefe that his many flower studies are "roses in clogs," he scrutinizes the world around him and his own expressive self. In his newly bright palette is an emphatic acceptance of his new bohemian realm, remote from what Heidegger means by the Folk.

Try to calculate the drastic difference between van Gogh's enthusiasm for contemporary literature and Heidegger's mysticity or Derrida's doubts of presence. Van Gogh joins Baudelaire's and Rimbaud's cry of being of one's epoch and painting the truth of the surround, the context, economic, sexual and urbane. The novels of the Goncourts and Zola are not a congregation of "peasant" novels *tout court*, and van Gogh also had an enthusiasm for the writers' individual styles. The emphasis is on a receptivity to facts and feelings, to the Romantic fact *of* feeling. True, as Derrida suggests, one may find opposing quotations concerning the simple noble life of peasants; but it is important to note in the letters a growing appetite for free modes of self-expression. One should not ignore his religious moods, either, but rather, as in Schapiro's studies, tactfully build up a sense of his tensions and conflicts. Heidigger and Derrida do not yield a sense of this conflicted self, which for the former would be too subjectivist, for the latter, a hallucination of presence.

This controversy reminds one that, yes, there is an outside of a painting: Derrida's sense of nothing outside the text is too global, while Heidegger, because he does not care about the artist's evolving expressivity, has to miss the vital concreteness of the artist whose presence as Jakobsonian addresser is revealed in identification with these bulky, dented shoes. Enraged by the subjective, Heidegger would miss a self-portrait, while Derrida is so unconcerned with concreteness that he equates Heidegger's mysticism with the tact of Schapiro. Yes, Derrida wants to destabilize all sense of the concrete, which is why he insists on turning the shoes into an unpaired and uncanny group. But even that unpairedness would not take away the addresser, with these shoes as "a piece of his own life" (Schapiro). The trouble for Derrida and Heidegger alike is the implicit humanism of van Gogh's work, and Schapiro's underlining of it.

Evidence that van Gogh's own friends understood his work in this way is found in a memoir by Francois Gauzi:

> At the flea market he'd bought an old pair of clumsy, bulky shoes—peddlar's shoes—but clean and freshly shined. They were fine old clonkers, but unexceptional. He put them on one afternoon when it rained and went for a walk along the old city walls. Spotted with mud, they had become interesting.... Vincent faithfully copied his pair of shoes. This idea, which wasn't at all revolutionary, seemed bizarre to some of our atelier friends.[8]

A Derridean might doubt this as an anecdote, or else distinguish between this anecdote and Gauguin's; nevertheless, it suggests the foregrounding, in his contemporaries' eyes, of the self-expression evident in Vincent's still lifes.

Shoes, of course, are an old story, from the *Anolfini* portrait of Jan van Eyck to the single (real) shoe of *High School Days*, by Jasper Johns. And a modern painter may well use the shoe or any other handy thing as a metaphorical equivalent to his psyche, thanks in part to van Gogh's victory over a more ideologically conservative symbolic code.

One might also think of Morandi's "family groups" of still-life objects, in which, too, some legacy of van Gogh's expressiveness is found—and further proof of the repleteness of Schapiro's method.

Disclosure of self may well perturb the artist. Van Gogh had his own need to conceal himself, and Schapiro subtly discerns how often he used the "peasant theme" to hide: "His decision to be a peasant painter was itself an attempt to master the difficulties of his person; it excluded the excitement, the complexities and the passionateness which were sources of anguish to him."[9] Remarkable with Schapiro, however, versus Heidegger and Derrida, is the negative capability of identifying with van Gogh's turmoil, and the ability to find in such formal elements as his perspective schemes emotional features. To the philosophers, this is an expressionist fallacy. Actually, it illuminates the decisions of van Gogh and grants the pictures a lived space. It also serves to distinguish one painter from another: for example, Schapiro discriminates between Cézanne's contemplative spirit and his reduction of the intensity of perspective, and van Gogh's exaggeration of the extremities of space.[10] To Heidegger, van Gogh, Hölderlin, Trakl all seem reduced in a sequence of Priests of Being. To Derrida, all authors announce dissemination and. slippage and multiplicity. But to Schapiro, there is distinction and difference.

Derrida thinks restlessly about whether the shoes are pairs, and he regards both philosopher and critic as trapped by the sense of the pair. But why not look, like Graetz, at the enormous number of pairs and pairings throughout van Gogh's work.[11] A pair of books—his father's Bible and his own diminutive copy of *Joie de vivre*, the pairing of the two chair paintings and—poignantly, as Graetz discovers—pairs of pillows in his solitary bedroom, a room prepared for a companion. Pairing in van Gogh is an important psychic component, even an obsession; which Graetz rightly stresses in the symbiosis with Theo. Both Graetz and Schapiro are correct in finding a personal, symbolic, physiognomic character in the shoes.

I do not see this as mere expressionist pathos, for all that van Gogh spoke of worshipping sorrow, since he tended to balance that with the study of patience and resignation. Schapiro's sense that his imagery represents the attaining of a free self would be derided as mere subjectivity by a Heideggerian committed to avoiding the personal, or by a deconstructor used to thinking of the self as a logocentric hallucination. But why not think of this self as an achievement of *sophrosyne*, much more Greek than expressionist, a self put together like a sturdy chair or battered shoe. Self-portraiture here is an essay, a test of reality, a symbolic investigation, part of a representational project scorned by the anti-mimetic Derrida (though one notes that Derrida still signs his books, giving them the illusion of presence). Schapiro teases Heidegger as Theodor Adorno did, for the "jargon of authenticity"; but we might want to tease Derrida for a "jargon of inauthenticity."

The most tolerant vision of Derrida might be as chief philosopher of multiplicity, of a Heraclitean flux, and of the undecidability of interpretation. His vision of art as an inexhaustible polysemy makes van Gogh's painting into just another specimen. The shoes might be two left pairs, two right pairs; they may be made for a monster, or for a limper; they are the castoffs of a ragpicker; and there are other possibilities. Derrida's reading, of course, is never limited by the biographical or social. Indeed, the readings of van Gogh's "Shoes" seem purposely, and with some infantilism, ingenious. Never are they even tested. For example, one might be delighted to see Derrida work out the Bosch-like possibility of the monster, or the Walter Benjamin-like possibility of the shoes being about the unsalable—a ragpicker's shoes from Paris. Derrida never acknowledges what Schapiro has called "the fatalities of social being." The polysemy of his and lesser hands becomes a kind of private kabbalistic free association.

Schapiro makes a simple quotation from the novelist Knut Hamsun about finding oneself in one's own shoes. Derrida gives it a limitlessly polysemous misreading of uncanny possibilities that would have defied Rimbaud:

> ...Hamsun writes "They (my shoes) affected me like the ghost of my other I—a living part of my own self." To conclude from this, as he seems to do and as Schapiro in any case hastens to decide, that "my other I" is myself, is *I*, and especially that its ghost is *I*, you really have to have your fingers stuck in your own ears. What

is "my ghost"? What does the phrase "the ghost of my other I" say? My other I, is that myself or an other I, an other who says "I"? Or a "myself" which is itself only divided by the phantom of its double? ... —But then what about the haunting of these shoes? *Are* they a ghost (a piece of a ghost, a phantom member)? In that case, are they the ghost of van Gogh *or* the ghost of the *other I* of van Gogh, and what does the *other I* mean then? Or else, *without being* a ghost themselves, do they *have* the ghost, are they the propitious place for having, bringing back, taking, or keeping the ghost, and which one? His own or the ghost of the (detachable) other?[12]

Derrida makes Heidegger seem positively commonsensical. This infinite misreading is laughable and eristic. A simple identification is smeared into infinity.

Derrida is complacent in recontextualizing our critics as two projectors. Is it fair to equate the Heidegger who drifted into National Socialism with Meyer Schapiro, who skeptically punctured his cloudy abstractions? If Zimmerman is right to recontextualize him as a voice of the antiauthoritarian 1968 movement, we may see Derrida lashing out against two enormous father figures with an enormous "anxiety of influence." He has himself an anti-metaphysics which descends from Heidegger, to whom he carefully makes restitution by suggesting that Schapiro has unfairly lifted quotations piecemeal or fragmentarily from "The Origin of a Work of Art." Yet he makes almost no effort to look at Schapiro's larger, cathedral-like oeuvre. He reduces to a humanist-cum-positivist this Schapiro who has made the subtlest contributions to a skeptical use of psychoanalysis, to a dialectical use of sociology in his medieval studies and also to a semiology whose method has more "doubt" than Derrida's. Derrida gives us a caricature of both Schapiro and van Gogh, who is turned into a master of the postmodern undecidable, a floating Magritte of infinite multiplicity—of multiplicity that itself becomes a mad monism. Of course, such proliferation of meanings delights the Derridean. Well, Meyer Schapiro is also a master of multiple meanings, but he tries to discover ones that will be adequate to the object.

Note that Schapiro does not dismiss the peasant painter in van Gogh. His studies are full of a sense of van Gogh's identification with the poor, but he discriminates his religious empathy with an ideology of being. He compares the effort of the artist with that of the peasant, but he sees in his shoes "a concern with the fatalities of his social being."[13] Again unlike his critics, he discriminates between the unworn sabots on a table and these shoes of a "self-conscious contemplating wearer, one whom he discovers in Hamsun's expressive phrase "Something of my own nature had gone over into these shoes; they affected me, like a ghost of my other I." He also defends van Gogh from charges of subjectivism in Rilke's sense, and Heidegger's, with an amazingly just sentence: "They are not less objectively rendered for being seen as if endowed with his feelings and reverie about himself." (Ironically, Shapiro's fuller sense of an objectivity that includes thing and emotion would have saved Rilke from some of the bathos of his philosophical poems.) Schapiro's forte is his identification with the artist and his chosen forms. When he wants to, Derrida too can have a passionate sense of self, though elsewhere he makes it seem as if Schapiro's sense of van Gogh, like Heidegger's, is only passionate self-projection.

Seeing van Gogh in these shoes: why is it such a taboo for both Derrida and Heidegger? Derrida speaks of van Gogh's self-portraiture lightly, then veers away; but van Gogh unflinchingly produced study after study of the figure of himself. And Meyer Schapiro's book on van Gogh, with its delineation of the development of van Gogh from "peasant painter" to a painter of the self, illuminates so much of the evidence. (Interestingly, it was Meyer Schapiro who defended de Kooning's *Woman I* to the artist himself as a complete expression.) So we can understand how much of himself is in van Gogh's famous empty "Chairs," in which he takes the sentimental English illustration tradition and gives us in a ferociously free and intimate new symbolic code his wild self-abnegation in a sturdy chair and his frenzied admiration for Gauguin in a phallic candle. Schapiro's physiognomic sense of the object explains the chairs, and more.

Is it possible that Heidegger has associated the shoes of van Gogh with the peasant woman of an earlier period; and is it possible that this is part of the pathos of the philosopher remembering with some loss of acuity an exhibition in which "peasant paintings" of the early period hung with the shoe pictures? It is certainly possible that van Gogh modulated from his obsessive "sabot" paintings, metonymically reproducing his own shoes with a new sense of his nomadic self. He was thus not far at all from the English illustration tradition, in which Dickens' empty chair was limned as a reliquary of the master.

At least one Dutch observer suggests to me that in the Fogg Art Museum version there may easily be male and female shoes among the six shoes limned. Graetz and Sweetman have seen "family" symbolism in the shoes; with van Gogh presenting his dependency on Theo as brother.[14] Sweetman thinks this is a logical outcome of Theo's seizures in Paris and Vincent's anguish concerning his brother's troubles. Neither Graetz nor Sweetman, however, would delete the sense of the personal and the self-expressive in these shoes. Schapiro's suggestion, confirmed by Gauguin's anecdote that van Gogh had kept the shoes as relics of a pilgrimage, is the maximal argument: it explains the formal syntax of the shoes as a kind of "I"; it fits the shoes with the Parisian self-portraits; it reveals the evolution of van Gogh and his new sense of expressive self; it accords with memoirs by Gauguin and also Lautrec's biographer. Schapiro's argument has its limits, but Heidegger's faith in Being and Derrida's doubt have no limits.

One creates a kind of anthology of portraiture for shoes; and as Joseph Masheck finds an extraordinary self-reference, a Flaubert letter of December 13, 1846,[15] I would like to adduce a poet whom van Gogh might well have read in Paris, Arthur Rimbaud. This poéte maudit wrote of his bohemian wanderings in a style that is tense with naturalism and symbolist ferocity:

> When rhyming in the midst of
>   fantastic shadows,
> Like lyres I pulled on the laces
> Of my wounded shoes, a foot
>   next to my heart.[16]

What Heidegger and Derrida forget is this sense of the bohemian in van Gogh, especially in the Paris period but also before. Van Gogh, like Rimbaud, is observant and self-observant. And the fact must remain legalistically, despite Derrida's doubts, that van Gogh did indeed reside in Paris, was "a man of the town and city," in Schapiro's phrase. Records of Vincent's rage for walking 100 miles and more suggest that the shoes symbolize more van Gogh's battered and pilgrim spirit than the peasant toil evoked by Heidegger. Derrida might be more convincing with his theme of multiplicity and polysemy if he had at least accepted a sense of symbolist self-portraiture among other possibilities.

Some theories may not foreground the human, but it is an inescapable part of art. I think it useful to consider, also, the antihumanism and anti-existentialism inherent in Derrida's position. Recently Yve-Alain Bois, underlining the rage against metaphor, against symbolism, in the paintings of Robert Ryman, quoted Robbe-Grillet, the novelist of the 1950s most concerned with the escape from metaphor, a passage that is illuminating in our debate. If one listens carefully to what Bois calls the vehement and negative assertion in Robbe-Grillet, one can catch some of the meanings of this debate and sense how contemporary Derrida's misreading really is:

> The man grasps his hammer (or a stone he has chosen) and strikes the stake he wishes to drive in. While he is using it, thus, the hammer (or stone) is merely form and matter: its weight, its striking surface, its other end for grasping. The man, then, puts down the tool in front of him; if he has no further need of it, the hammer is, merely a thing among things, apart from its use, it has no signification.[17]

Bois states it clearly: Robbe-Grillet and Roland Barthes were enemies of "the bards of the tragic," and such hatred of pathos and the anthropocentric, such rage against humanism, is likewise central to Derrida's perturbations. But the tragic symbolist sense is not misread by Schapiro as an anti-metaphysics of the new novel or as a mysticity of Being. Van Gogh's letters are filled with metaphors and metaphorical readings, as Jan Bialostocki pointed out (in 1965). Van Gogh loves metaphor and symbol as our contemporary Ryman loves the literal (and one should remember that even the word "literal is a metaphor!).

What good can come of a criticism that finds a fashionable absence everywhere? Derrida is at ease with Jabès, Artaud, Nietzsche. He is not fitted to find much in more stable sources. This has been the problem with deconstructive criticism: its zeitgeist is so peculiarly ours that it is not much more than a surrealism of negativity that "explains," or is at least fitted to, the age of Johns and the poet John Ashbery. But when deconstruction takes up other eras, other minds, it becomes a kind of blood sport in which the specimen is reduced to neo-Nietzschean bits. Each text of the West—now architecture, now painting—is submitted to the uncontrollable adventures of a global or totalizing negativity. The shoes of van Gogh are made to become a meaningless escapade or cadenza of discontinuities. Derrida never has to read the three volumes of van Gogh letters and find the slightest problem with the avowals made therein. Schapiro, on the other hand, may be accused of finding the human everywhere, but note that it is a human with so many shades of difference. Derrida's work is written in one color and needs to be: it is all one passionate doubt. It is sad that Derrida never seems to have developed a taste for this positive infinity, the magnanimity of the great and restless, Herzen-like pluralist. His work will be seen as a comical self-portrait of the dandy-philosopher of the day.

When a deconstructivist psychiatrist appears, who neglects to look for epilepsy or cyclical schizophrenia in yourself or your child exhibiting some of van Gogh's symptomatic behaviors, then you will notice the limits of skepticism. I would like to suggest that hermeneutics of Meyer Schapiro's radiant sort is part of the intellectual health of our city, and that his method permits a check, a limit, of verifiability and falsifiability. Joe Masheck said recently in talking with me that Schapiro and Heidegger had had a *conversation*; but the skepticism and groundlessness of Derrida permits little or no response. A doctor does not hallucinate or appropriate a patient's symptoms just because his diagnosis entails tactful empathy. Meyer Schapiro, like the philosopher Ernest Nagel, believes in an ever-corrigible sense of truth. A radical sense of truthlessness pervades Derrida's work, which one finds difficult to equate with the religious positivity of van Gogh and his desperate empathetic zeal, his passion for the human.

The death of the author has its comical corollaries. The translator and art critic Guy Davenport is reported to narrate his incredulity that van Gogh ever existed. Rob Kenner has told me of being spellbound as Davenport recites the long list of evidence that Vincent van Gogh is a fiction. For examples: the lack of photographic documentation of this presumably fairly sociable Dutchman; the fact that the letters of this Dutchman are mostly in French; the fact that correspondence disappears at exactly the moment of his entry to Paris; and so on. I would add that the death of Theo, as uncanny partner to van Gogh's supposed suicide, might read as a Borgesian device to get rid of both protagonists. Davenport's joke is a parody of certain skeptical critics. The paintings are hardly interpreted, simply offered up in nihilist readings without tact in a fashionably inhumane retort to the Romantic idea of the artist. The danger is that all sense of factuality is discouraged, and the critic becomes a cynic rather than participating in what Meyer Schapiro has called critical seeing.

What are the issues in interpreting these paintings? One might want to say that the main hermeneutic problem is the burden of synthesizing extratextual knowledge with the sensuality of the artistic object. Derrida, famous for saying that there is no *hors-texte*, seems to retreat before evidence, as when his essay deletes the Gauguin reference to van Gogh's ascription of the personal to his shoes. Schapiro has always promoted a sense of the political and the psychoanalytic in relation to formal or autotelic concerns in art. Heidegger explicitly forswore the biographical approach, as when he says that Trakl's personality does not concern him. The Aristotelian might say there is little hope for anything but a nondialogue here, between a skeptic, a humanist-pluralist, and a mystic of ontics.

However, I think, at least in my own biased, humanistic pluralism, that the competing claims can be judged as more or less satisfactory approaches to the beloved object. If van Gogh's painting in its inexhaustible repleteness is our object, it seems fairly clear that Heidegger's ontological approach does indeed, in Schapiro's phrase, do too much and too little. Think of what Heidegger leaves out: not only the artist's personality but his milieu; his formal, constructive work; the specificity of the object; the tradition of Dutch still life; the reception of the work etc., etc. At least one has to credit Derrida with taking the time to question the certainty of what for him is a positivistic approach. Symbolism in van Gogh was an issue before him, but Derrida raised the stakes in insisting on a kind of convulsive nihilism.

Schapiro's approach restores, I think, a sense of the sensual specific object and a proper materialism of life and milieu. His work leaves open critical possibilities and "communal seeing." Constructive rather than destructive, he lets us see. Indeed, Meyer Schapiro's criticism approaches what for me is a kind of ideal of receptivity. He has always been open to the uncanonic. He is a model of critical seeing and restless tolerance, and his criticism matches the inexhaustibility and repleteness of the artwork.

Only a painter with a sense of the achievement of a self could say that his café was a place where a person might destroy himself, and only a painter who cared about humanity could say he tried to express its terrible passions in red and green colors. These passions and this sense of self should not be expunged by a philosopher of Being, nor by one of Undecidability. It is the art historian Meyer Schapiro, however, strangely, who has the intersemiotic translation and discovers the fury of van Gogh in perspective projections and a self in a pair of shoes.

Schapiro has observed in a "Post-Scriptum" (1981) to the van Gogh essay that Heidegger left a marginal note (between 1960 and 76) saying that he could not be clear about to whom the shoes belonged.[18] Schapiro noted wittily that perhaps a doubt had occurred to the philosopher but that he nevertheless wished to reaffirm his interpretation even if the shoes were van Gogh's personal possessions. The clinging to the interpretation despite doubts is a last and bizarre underscoring of the tenacity of the mystic philosopher of Being. One now wonders what certainties or evidence might move Jacques Derrida to admit to a personal symbolism. There was no mention of Derrida's skepticism in the terse original "Post-Scriptum," but more than one participant in the Columbia seminar at which Derrida originally launched his attack recalls that after the interminable polylogue, the art historian said, "I am a student of John Dewey, and I believe in the truth."

Endnotes

1. Susan Alyson Stein, ed., *Van Gogh: A Retrospective* (New York: Park Lane, 1986), 313–14.

2. Heidegger's "The Origin of the Work of Art" can be found in his *Poetry, Language, Thought*, ed. and trans. Albert Hofstadter (New York: Harper and Row, 1971), 17–78.

3. M. E. Zimmerman, *Heidegger's Confrontation with Modernity* (Bloomington: Indiana University Press, 1990), 114.

4. Zimmerman, *Heidegger's Confrontation*, 210.

5. Rainer Maria Rilke, *Letters on Cézanne*, ed. C. Rilke, trans. Joel Agee (New York: Fromm International, 1985), 67, speaking of a poem by Baudelaire and likening it to Flaubert's victory over subjectivity.

6. Rilke, *Letters*, 75. The other letter quoted here as epigraph dates from October 4 of the same year.

7. Zimmerman, *Heidegger's Confrontation*, 239.

8. François Gauzi as cited in Stein, *Van Gogh*, 72.

9. Meyer Schapiro, *Van Gogh* (New York: Abrams, n.d.) 28.

10. Schapiro, *Van Gogh*, 29.

11. H. R. Graetz, *The Symbolic Language of Vincent van Gogh* (New York: McGraw-Hill, 1963).

12. Jacques Derrida, *The Truth in Painting* (1978), trans. G. Bennington and I. McLeod (Chicago: University of Chicago Press, 1987), 373.

13. Meyer Schapiro, "The Still Life as a Personal Object: A Note on Heidegger and van Gogh," in *The Reach of the Mind: Essays in Memory of Kurt Goldstein*, ed. Marianne L. Simmel (New York: Springer, 1968), 208; this essay now repr. in Schapiro, *Theory and Philosophy of Art: Style, Artists and Society* (Selected Papers, 4) New York: Braziller, 1994), 135–42.

14. Graet, *Symbolic Language*; David Sweetman, *Van Gogh: His Life and Art* (New York: Crown, 1990).

15. See Schapiro's "Further Notes on Heidegger and van Gogh," in his *Theory and Philosophy of Art*, 143–51.

16. Arthur Rimbaud, "Ma Bohème," in Angel Flores, ed., *An Anthology of French Poetry from Nerval to Valéry in English Translation* (Garden City, NY: Doubleday, 1958), 350–51, here translated by the present writer.

17. From Alain Robbe-Grillet, *Nature, humanism, tragédie* (1958), in *Pour un nouveau roman*, 2nd ed. Paris: Gallimard, 1967), as quoted by Yve-Alain Bois, *Surprise and Equanimity* (New York: Pace Gallery, 1990).

18. Schapiro, "Post-Scriptum," in *Style, artiste et société* (Paris: Gallimard, 1982), 359–60; see now, "Further Notes," 150.

Pluralist Music: An Interview by Joanna Fuhrman

All of David Shapiro's writing is simultaneously earnest and explosive. To read a David Shapiro poem is to enter a space in which "emotion" is as abstract as theory and an "idea" is as visceral and tender as the best pop song. This interview was conducted at the café in the Cooper Hewitt Museum on a sweltering August Monday, drinking decaffeinated diet cola. JF

Joanna Fuhrman: How has your idea of what poetry can do changed since you were young?

David Shapiro: Poetry was very important in my family. My uncle had published sonnets in *The New York Times*. My grandmother was very literary. My mother read something like a book a day and loved to read to me. One of the great influences on my life was my father constantly memorizing Virgil, Shakespeare, Milton, and he had me do the same, as soon as I could speak. Music was also important in my family, so my idea was that poetry was this musical/theatrical thing. What a Russian called "the articulatory dance of the speech organs," I associated with songs. So when I was about nine writing a song with words, something about an irradiated man, I realized I just had written a poem, and I started to write poetry an hour or two a day, like violin practice. One of the things I tended to do was to fall in love with a poet—for example I would memorize *The Waste Land*, in 1958 or so, then try to write like that. I went through a Beckett period where I wrote a lot of bad plays. I fell in love with Theodore Roethke, and if he would use the

---

Rain Taxi, edited by Eric Lorberer (Fall 2002).

word "tendril," I would use the word "tendril." It got to the point where I would memorize their voices—I had a lot of the Caedmon records—just like one would a concerto. I kept being influenced by different people. The French Symbolists one year were very important to me, and then they were important to me forever.

I was about 12 or 13 when the Donald Allen anthology came out and I memorized that too. I was called the "Beat Prophet" in eighth grade. I would go to parties and recite "Howl."

My ideas of poetry changed very rapidly between the ages of 9 and 15 in the sense that a different poet would be a different universe. I liked the big golden voice of Dylan Thomas. Kenneth Koch read my poetry to me, when I was fifteen, in a very quiet voice—I liked that. I had considered the poem very fortissimo, a little bit like D. H. Lawrence but also with Dylan Thomas in mind. When he read it very quietly, I liked that. He also showed me new work by John Ashbery, *The Tennis Court Oath*. In was in July or August of 1962, and I thought it was fairly ugly: "To employ her / construction ball / Morning fed on the / light blue wood / of the mouth," and so on. Then I came upon sections which were more melodic, and I had a big conversion to the idea that he was floating melody inside static. Lines like: "I must say I / suddenly / she left the room, oval tear tonelessly fell" or "I moved up // glove / the field."

And I thought, oh, he's using the word "I" like it's any other word in the dictionary. That's interesting. It reminded me of a Raushenberg collage and suddenly I fell in love with it. I was converted by *The Tennis Court Oath*, and I still love Cubo-Futurist style. I liked a lot of the lowness and the cheapness of the words. Allen Ginsberg said to me, "But can you memorize it," and after I recited a lot of it, he said, "Oh it's like Alexander Pope." I didn't think it was like Pope, but I liked its elegance. I loved lines like: "Over Mount Hymettus / And sudden day unbuttoned her blouse" and I know Kenneth liked that line too. I liked what was very fresh about it; it seemed to be draining all the sentimentality I loved in Theodore Roethke out of poetry. It was definitely something new. I feel like I had good taste in that sense, for a fifteen-year-old, but I must say my taste has continually changed. The difference between me and other New York Poets is that I never gave up my love of what I already loved. I'm still a person who can see what is good in Eliot, Stevens, etc. I don't feel like I renounced earlier ideas of poetry. I like the idea of something synthetic or pluralist.

My idea of poetry now is pretty endless. I know people who just like Ted Berrigan's *Sonnets*; they just like one kind of thing. Particularly because of music I tend to not think in that way. I like John Cage, and I like Eliot Carter. They don't like each other. I once said to Eliot Carter, "What do you think of John Cage?" He said, "No, I don't really think so." And the same thing happened when I asked Cage, "Don't you like Carter?" "No." "What about the 'Polyrhythms'?" "Not really." They hated each other, but I think poetry can *combine* these different things. I like a sonnet and I like shattering a sonnet. I like *The Tennis Court Oath*, but I also like *Some Trees*. This puts me in a bad position because you might say I therefore lack certain purities.

JF: What about your own work—how do you think it has changed?

DS: When I was young, my work was very expressionistic, sort of like my brain. Obsessive and expressionistic. Like anyone else I felt like I had to drain that. Ron Padgett once mocked me—I had written a poem when I was fourteen called "We are gentle" and he said, "We are gentiles," and Ted Berrigan called it, "We are jungles."

Ted once said to my sister, "The difference between your brother and me is that he writes, 'I am on a beach,' and I write 'I am on a beach ball,'" but that doesn't seem to be very fair. The truth is that like everyone else I wanted my poetry to be as tough as this tabletop [he taps on it]—I wanted it to be cold and tough like Formica. When I was seventeen Marianne Moore said about my poetry, "He is not stark enough. He is an accomplished man and artist, but he is not stark enough. I too lack dynamite." They used some of that blurb, but I used to brood on "adequate starkness." I liked the severity of Jasper Johns' newspaperese period. On the other hand, I wrote books like *Man Holding an Acoustic Panel* in a science/hardware kind of interrupted style. I constantly was changing from one style to another. One thing I liked was the melancholy of Johns' smallest light bulbs. I wanted a poetry, and I think I still do, that would be as melancholy, dense, and severe as that. I wanted a poem that would somehow emit that kind of darkness. I also wanted poems that would go from one tempo to another. I loved Mozart's divertimenti, and I liked the fact there would be one movement, another movement, another movement, but they would form a unity.

I like the poems of Ashbery like "The Skaters" and "Europe" that you might say have one style but are also very multiple. My best poems attempt that. I also wanted a poem that was more Lucretian, that would *explain*. What I loved about "The Skaters" was that it seemed so vast. I asked Kenneth what "The Skaters" was about before I had read it, and he said it was not about anything, it was a whole philosophy of life.

Still, I also love writing smaller poems that are like watercolors. I like the immediacy of Cézanne going out with just red, blue and green. I recently wrote a poem where I just used a Ryokan index of first lines and changed the nouns—it's like a little watercolor. And sometimes I feel I am really getting someplace in my collages. I hope they lead to a new impersonality, but not Eliotic. I am not a confessional poet, but there's enough in me of Jewish guilt to make a lot of my poems more naturalistic than what other people might find. Someone once said there was very little sex in my poems and I said, "What else is there?"

When I am writing a long poem, I think about how not to merely intimate. I want something more like an epic, but I found I'm not as good at that. Kenneth Koch once said "Write an epic poem about the history of music"—I haven't been able to. That generation was very good at the long poem: Kenneth, John, Frank. My best long poems are sequences, and I actually get sad when people ask, "Why hasn't he written a long poem?" I really do regard my sequences as a long poem. I've keyed them so that one part follows the next like a divertimento. Or I think of them as panels of paintings that go together. But people don't always read it like that. I think that's a problem with my work. I sometimes print them as separate poems, so people just see them as separate poems. Eliot did that with *Four Quartets*, but no one thinks of them like that. If the seams show, maybe that is a problem. I love the idea of Keats that you wander in a very long poem, and I wanted an entire book like *To an Idea* to be one suicidal fairly depressed poem—though in it there are different kinds of things.

When I give poetry readings it is very hard because I tend to see them as little encore pieces and don't play the concerto. Or I am very worried about boring people with an adagio. Charles Bernstein said, "What's wrong with boring people?" But as a violinist, I hate to see the woman in furs yawning, as I once saw when I was giving a concert at the Brooklyn Academy of Music. I was playing "Gypsy Airs," by Sarasate, and it's very hard and very flashy and the woman in furs was yawning and I thought, "Ok, I am giving up music." But I haven't given up music because poetry is music, and I don't care about parts of the audience falling asleep.

But I always liked the idea that poetry doesn't need to be performed; my greatest moments in poetry have been quietly reading. Like when I had the forty pages of "The Skaters," when I was 16—it was written on crinkly paper from Paris, and every page seemed more beautiful than the last. Every line seemed up to the level of the last. When I was finished with that experience, I really felt very great poetry had been written in our time.

JF: You mentioned the Donald Allen anthology. How do you think the state of American poetry has changed since that moment?

DS: I was saying to my wife, it's canonic to praise that anthology and I've committed an anthology too, as they say. But it is interesting. One thing I liked about the Allen anthology is it gave a lot of information that was hard to find. I had heard of John Ashbery because I was reading things like the *Partisan Review*. Kenneth had a very bizarre early essay putting down a lot of minor poets which ended by quoting and praising a section of "Europe."

But I will say, Kenneth wasn't very well represented in that anthology. Frank O'Hara was. One of the reasons I wanted to attend the Wagner Writer's Conference when I was fourteen and fifteen was that I wanted to meet Frank O'Hara. I knew his poems by heart. I loved "Ode to Michael Goldberg ('s Birth and Other Births)." It was a very great poem. The beat generation was sort of known already. I fell under the spell of Charles Olson for a while—I loved "The Kingfishers." I really loved his variations on Rimbaud. Also, there were people in there who weren't such great poets and that was very useful to see too. It was very clear that Olson and Duncan were better than x, y, and z. It was clear "Howl" really did something compared to others. It was harder to say how good Jimmy Schuyler was, but there were some very beautiful poems: "Their scallop shell of quiet / is the *S.S. United States* / It is not so quiet and they / are a medium-size couple / who when they fold each other up / well, thrill. That's their story." I remember memorizing that. It's a very pretty little piece, and John's poem "How much longer will I be able to inhabit the divine sepulcher / Of life, my great love?" So that was a very good anthology because it contained differences; people like Frank did not like Charles Olson very much. I think that's been one of the best anthologies because Donald Allen was not dogmatically inclined toward one.

The weaknesses of anthologies are obvious. I know an Italian scholar who said his father would never have an encyclopedia in their house. But then there's Diderot's great encyclopedia. The eleventh edition of the *Encyclopedia Britannica* is so beautiful. It has Donald Tovey's articles on music, Whitehead on math. My father used to buy them all the time and I would give them away just for the illustrations. There are moments when a good anthology is useful. The Bible is an anthology. But I am always impressed by how many people were lit up by the Donald Allen anthology. I think that's because it has these four swathes. It's funny that it didn't connect them. It did connect them against a certain kind of poetry. It was very clear to people like my friend John Ciardi, who I knew in my youth, that they were not in it. Likewise, Richard Wilbur, who is a terrific translator of Molière in rhyme, represented a version of gentility that was not included. Though I love tennis, I remember an anthology with a picture of him playing tennis and it said, "What does a poet look like? He could look like this," and I thought "Oh, no."

JF: So, what about the state of poetry now?

DS: The hardest thing for me was feeling that the Language school had, as a group, somehow "disappeared" certain New York poets. I put it this way once to Charles Bernstein, which my son thought was too turbulent a way to put it and he made me call Charles up to apologize, which I did. But I still sometimes feel that a lot of us get no credit for what we did between '62 and '80.

For example, an academic who will remain nameless once told me she'd never seen "C" magazine and had never read Joseph Ceravolo's poetry, and this was after she praised people who were using the same techniques but much later. In art history, we don't praise you if you do a drip painting today because we have a sense Jackson Pollock did it in the winter of '47.

I thought someone like Joe Ceravolo never really was given his due. Or someone like Dick Gallup, who had an amazing poem in "C" magazine called "Life in Darkness." Now if it was published, people might say, "Very interesting poem in the style of, let's say, Bruce Andrews," but that's not really fair. There are a lot of ways in which the last twenty years created a labeling, or "branding"—horrible word—of certain formal innovations that weren't really innovations. A tremendous amount had been done by John and Frank and Kenneth, yes, but also by Ron Padgett and Ted Berrigan and others, and somehow there was an inclination to overlook it. When I mention this to some of the "Language" poets, they say they felt like we were already known, so they had to start their own team. At any rate, language and experiment are not magazines or precincts. No one owns language.

So when you say what's happening now in 2002, I still think it is a useful period. You can feel in your generation that people are not willing to buy a party line. I guess Americans really don't like popes. And the New York School really had a tremendous sense of being a male team, though with some women in it. I am still apologetic for having left out Barbara Guest from the anthology—a turbulent decision—but I am happy that there are twenty poets who had hardly been published before.

This is a much looser period. Maybe like the '70s in art. It's much harder to write minor imitations of Clark Coolidge and call it an innovation, and so there are less claims that lines like "Clump Peach Ounce" are dazzling. Clark's geology is so singular: each word a stone. I might seem like an embittered poet. Maybe Zukosfsky felt like this at the end of this life. But I think there would be a lot of information out if people had, for example, all of Ted Berrigan's "C" magazine printed together. It's really amazing that people have gotten away with an ahistorical take in an American culture that fetishizes history. It's not because of a war of style, it's simply that in a mood of generosity I wouldn't want to overlook the gifts of certain people. I still feel like people don't know what Ashbery's "Tennis Court Oath" is, or Ceravolo's poetry or Clark Coolidge's. I think a lot of things are buried that are very good.

But it is always a good time to be alive. It's good the way someone like Barbara Guest can be partially rescued by younger poets who saw what she was doing with stained language and syntactical disruption. But still, why wasn't Joe Ceravolo's book *The Green Lake Is Awake* launched with greater flair? Joe was remarkable for a flawless Reverdy thing, and though he was a student of Koch, he went beyond that in many ways. We edited only a partial aspect of his work, because Kenneth wanted a perfect book. I wanted everything. It would have been better if Joe had been represented by a 500-page book. We still really need that to know his range.

The other thing is I think almost anyone like me who wasn't making a claim to a certain kind of technical problematic was disappeared by a kind of taboo against certain subjects. And I think we lost a lot because Frank O'Hara was much more of a pluralistic acceptor. He liked my poetry, Frank Lima's poetry. He said to me about his "Ode to James Dean," "Don't you think it's sentimental? Kenneth thinks so." And I said "No, I love it." But then, we entered a period in which poetry became less and less. I once asked Meyer Schapiro why neo-expressionism was catching on and he said, "People want more meat." And he didn't mean it just as a put down. And it's true poetry can be lovely in its reductions. Ron Padgett could make the finest candies, like a Robert Herrick. On the other hand, he himself will sometimes write a very different kind of composition. It's very important to realize that poetry can be like a honey that's sweeter, richer, but also a protein. Kenneth Burke called it "equipment for living." I love Clark Coolidge not just for his smaller poems, but for the whole *Crystal Text*. So you can like a rock or a watercolor, but you can also like a whole geological stratum or a mountain.

Here I am using a kind of shorthand. All of these assertions would have to be made very particular. I do want to say though it is impossible to get away from the idea of groups. We are either alone or not alone. I didn't invent the English language. "Even your dreams are social," as Meyer Schapiro suggested, critiquing the surrealists. And I understand that. It is wrong for me to put down any group of poets who push themselves forward in different ways, that's just what young people do in a jungle.

But I think there should be more of the joys of influence than the anxieties of influence. The saddest thing in poetry is where you have what I regard as male competition. Neo-Nietzschean noble rivalry is one thing, but it becomes very male, in which one person wins and one loses. Tennis: which is not poetry. Then there's the Swedenborgian "the more angels the more room." Meyer Schapiro, if he praised Jackson Pollock, would praise someone doing an equal and opposite kind of work. He liked the underdog. Sometimes I think there's an irresponsibility which certain scientists know—if a scientist doesn't footnote a work on penicillin, it's considered a lack of generosity. Meyer Schapiro said the love of footnotes was a love of generosity.

JF: How did you meet Kenneth Koch?

DS: When I was a kid, I was probably over-professionalized; I was sending out my poems to bad magazines and loving that. And I had heard that Frank O'Hara was coming as a guest to the Wagner's Writing Conference. One of my ninth-grade teachers said, "You are really not old enough for this, but I heard you liked poetry." My sister's friend said, "This is ridiculous. The conference is supposed to be for teachers." But I thought, well, you never know. So I sent them poems, and Willard Moss accepted me, saying "there will also be this Puerto Rican juvenile delinquent who is nineteen and just out of jail, who has written poems like, "I am going to beat you out of your lunch money again for my drugs and evening fix."

When I went to Wagner, I met Kenneth. I hadn't liked his poems that much in the Allen anthology, except for "Fresh Air," but I didn't tell him that. He was dressed in a white suit. Very elegantly, he said, "Oh, I see you like Rilke and you also like the form of questions." Of course, I immediately liked him a great deal. I realized he wasn't just a satirist. We got along. Then I met the "Puerto Rican jailbird" Frank Lima who became almost within a second one of my best friends for life. We still talk to each other about once a day, and I just edited his selected poems. He was just out of jail, but he was very gentle and very brave. He was a boxer, very disciplined. He loved language. He became a very close friend of Frank O'Hara. Lima still impresses me every day.

Joe Ceravolo was there also, and he was little depressive and a little older. He loved to talk about the poetics of engineering. That moment was like the Donald Allen anthology. Edward Albee was there too. Kenneth said to me, "If you don't beat that guy in tennis, I'll flunk you." I said, "Why don't you like that guy?" And he said, "Oh, he's the kind of guy who knows what the weather is going to be like the next day."

I met a lot of different people. There was a whole swathe of academic people there who would say, "But Professor Koch, Frank Lima's poems are disgusting." And Kenneth defended them wonderfully, saying, "Perhaps, but after having read them, I can no longer think of English literature without them." Kenneth could be wonderfully brave. In the hospital, I lied and told him he wasn't missing much when he wanted to go out and get some fresh air and he said, "Oh yes, I am."

JF: For twenty years you have taught at Cooper Union. Could we end by talking a little about your experiences there?

DS: I was very lucky. This mad dean, John Hejduk, my best friend for twenty years, believed architects should be thinkers, not greedy connivers, and that they should learn from poetry. So bizarrely enough, though I have always taught children and believed in it long before other people did, I began to teach young architects. I saw them as structuralists of the imagination. I taught them not just to write a sestina, but then to build a house in the form of a sestina, or to build a house in the conditions of a villanelle, or to build a pantoum house.

Teaching architects at Cooper has been very important to me. It was the first completely drenching experience I had after teaching with Kenneth at Columbia, but Cooper was more widely open. When you went into Cooper Union, you might meet a doctor, a surgeon, a poet, an anthropologist. I invited Israeli novelists and French philosophers. We were all interested in analogies—to see if you could get some immortal energy from these different fields and make your architecture as fresh as a surgical cut or your poetry as fresh as a spare cage.

So for many years John Hejduk was scorned. It was hard to get through the accreditation processes. He had to make the school very strong in practical ways so they could do this other thing. Most architecture said we destroyed architecture. A lot of people felt like it was a wonderland: enter here and give up everything but the imagination. John felt a drawing was just as great as a building. He gave Emily Dickinson's poetry as the best thing ever done in America to the president of Romania.

It is very unusual for a non-mediocrity to land on top, for a genius of creativity to be able to do the bureaucratic work of creating a school where the faculty and the students could meet at a place of thought. He used to say he'd done better than Black Mountain; there's just person after person who after this experience has changed the vocabulary of architecture. Now architecture with literature is taught all over the world.

I wrote a poem that has a line "Blessed is the school," and people asked, "What school are you talking about. Is that David Shapiro's mad academicism?" But actually, its kind of anti-academic. To me school became Cooper Union, a very special place of freedom and thought.

I Loved You Once by Pushkin

I wish I had a copy
of Pushkin's poem
"I loved you once"
which is said to achieve
the intended effect—
"wistful resignation
half-concealing half
revealing a still
smoldering passion"
"without having recourse
to figures of speech."
O it would be clear to you then
there could be such a thing—
I would leave you a copy.

—David Shapiro, *A Burning Interior* (The Overlook Press, 2002).

The Story of the Tower of Babel

I feel more and more that we must not judge of God from this world, it's just a study that didn't come off. What do you do with a study that has gone wrong? It's only a master who can make such a blunder ...
—Van Gogh, *Letters*

Unless the Lord builds the house, its builders labor in vain....
—Psalm 127

We do not customarily pray in the direction of the Tower of Babel. It is, perhaps, more of a tradition among secularists, modernists, and Spinozists like myself. We find ourselves praying to what we see: the artist Brueghel and his bright painterly burrow; and we pray in our personal noncollective way in the direction of the starry chaos of Proust and Kafka's inner and outer burrow. We pray and don't pray; we find it impossible to pray; we take our place carrying the holes of the philosophers and poets. The hole is the tradition. Otherwise, some pray to Rimbaud and give up in the great tradition of personal silence.

Emmanuel Levinas, the contemporary French Jewish philosopher, rebukes us and suggests that like Spinoza, we may simply not have had good enough Hebrew teachers. Otherwise, we might more fully partake of his parable in which two arks are carried. In one a man lies who has accomplished the law contained inside the other. But for us, too often, the arks have become coffins. So then, at least, we acknowledge the power of the stories, and if not the whole narrative, the jokes, and if

---

Genesis: As It Is Written, edited by David Rosenberg (Harper San Francisco/ New York, 1996).

not the jokes, the endless dispute, and if not the dispute, the horrible artfulness of those who would destroy us and the endlessness of our dispute. After all, the dispute is our Tower. "A strong tower against the enemy."

In the midst of Fritz Lang's dazzling and infantile film classic, *Metropolis*, lies an uncanny tower within a tower and midrash, or rabbinical commentary, from the purist Maria. She recounts to her protofascist audience the Babel story, in which the elite planners grind into dust such lumpen who construct it. She, the simpleminded Mediator of this film beloved of Hitler, concludes that the story demands a mediation between architectural mind and the vascular hand of the herd that builds. After the pyramids, a new Passover! The more grisly element of Metropolis remains within its film-noir mists: a vision of the shocking city as Moloch into which we are poured like so much nutritious cement. And Lang's response to Hitler resonates ironically. Invited to head the German film industry, the artist fled in the night with visions of an unmediated Babel. Dispersal, centripetal flower, kept him alive for the classic *Contempt* and other film-making integrities.

Isn't dispersal worse than death, and isn't such a scattering better than death? All the commentaries agree to disagree. The story must be placed next to Noah's destroyed contemporaries. Noah's generation was butchered in a stormy allegory for its disunity in murderous internecine corruption. Meanwhile, the Babel Tower was built with urbane or imperial unity. A unity that was only punishable by multiplicity, of course. Even the modern Hebrew poet Bialik speaks of the two essential movements of the Jewish people as dispersal and homecoming. And further, the Babel story speaks of the essential concentrate of "civilization" as either a profound mistake or monstrous excess. A Blakean reading, for instance, will permit the Tower always to be more interesting than the sin of building it. After the covenant, we hardly expect a rainbow behind this Ziggurat, but we are compelled to see the story as a uniquely horrifying addendum to the Rainbow. A covenant of peace with man is immediately followed by a story of immense penology. The Tower appeals as an invasive prong with the requisite sense of an Antagonist. If the Tower is not built to last, it is at the least scaled with seven Assyrian rungs to Paradise. Mies Van der Rohe, the modern architect par excellence, would have approved.

When I was a boy of ten or so, my uncle gave me a book on modern art that included an illustration of Mies' Glass Tower project. The transparent splendor of this futuristic folly struck me, and his abstractions became my obsession, yielding an image of eternity. It is always suggestive to remember the paradox that architecture is a private, tragic, and fragile art. Books may last longer than buildings, and Shelley's "Ozymandias" is part of the correct commentary on the hubris of place and the Jewish denunciation of such a spectral architecture. Babel horrifies with the connotations of ceaseless metropolitan work and its naked assertion that architecture may dominate time. The Babel fable italicizes the fragility of all human construction, as if it were all an Assyrian astrology. The majesty of the Babel story is its naked condensation. It is a teaching story, and the rabbis have understandably loved it, as in the great commentary that lost brick would cause more tears in Babel than a fallen worker.

Is it language that rises or falls here? Architecture is married to poetry in our story, and no commentator can escape this sacred synthesis. The rise of the city of arrogance is the end of language without puns. The Hebrew language should have been the sufficient blueprint of a perfect world. The apple of language rots upon touch and disintegrates at the foot of the Tower. The perfect language is murdered by multiplicity. Here, Jewish wisdom is most divided. On the one hand, the commentaries teach us that the scattering is good and brings Jewish wisdom into the many worlds of history. But it is also the world of babble indeed, the multiple shifting perspectives of an exile in horror and falsity. Architecture rises as the somber specter of such fallen man, fallen tongues, and the exile of mistranslating. It is for this reason that a critic like George Steiner emphasized in lectures I heard in Cambridge in the late 1960s that the true moderns were bilingual and exiled essentially to that condition of multiplicity. We live in the condition of the collage at the end of *The Waste Land*, and only the macaronic cadenzas of the Wake bring us the proper sense of the inner and outer exile of our lives. The happiest view is that such multiplicity, autumn coloration, is not functional but a happy scandal of abundance. God scatters us into his abundance, on a wave of language. Here, I think of Roman Jakobson, of whom it was said that he shouted for help, when struck by a car, in forty-seven languages. Poetry may be this cry for help in forty-seven languages. The Flood of languages produces an odd covenant. We may find, with Steiner, that language "after Babel" will henceforth be the master of the nations.

* * *

Ricky Small, my best pal, and I would meet in 1959 with Tzionah Ben Tzvi in my house in Newark to have tutorials for our Bar Mitzvahs. I was going to a Hebrew school, Bet Yeled, that emphasized a lot of singing of Zionist songs and Hebrew "as a living language." On violin I was learning the Hebrew Melody by Achron with the cadenza by Auer for a concert after the Bar Mitzvah, to compensate for my lack of a voice. Achron had known my grandfather, and it was reported also that the jazzy accompaniment to the Melody was influenced by their taste for Harlem forays.

My grandfather, one of the golden Chazzanim (cantors), had died praying in1954 at the local Young Israel. I brooded and was told this was the best death. A few years ago, researching his career and finding a scrapbook given to him after a decade in South Africa, I found an interview with him under the headline: "I Want to Die Singing." I was always hypnotized by his voice, at table or on the old 78s, a sweet tenor with a coloratura falsetto. The doctors, I was told, had warned against such embellishment: it could darken the voice. It was a way to produce the sense of forbidden instruments in a synagogue.

* * *

After the story of Noah in Genesis comes the building of the great cities. The names shock us like a noise, and I hear these names the way I saw the Assyrian reliefs at the Metropolitan Museum last year. The Assyrian works were as sophisticated and severe as a horrible Pop mural, crammed with bleeding lions. Babylon, Erech, Accad, Calneh. Names that have crumbled more times than an obelisk or a late Romantic. Nineveh, Calah, Babel. The refined and beautiful small writing of the Assyrians was strangely elegant as any hanging garden beside a ziggurat—and reproducible in cunning seals. The great cities in the nude of their names strode past us.

We begin with a dream of sacred unity: God and his people are one (at least, they speak the same transparent language). The city emerges from an enormous migration, physical and spiritual. We are given with naturalistic economy the materialism of their means: "Come, let us make bricks and burn them hard." It is possible that the Tower was no larger than a department store in today's Manhattan, but the urge was the irresistible conquest of a starry summit. "A tower with its top in the sky." Who can resist the appeal of this structure? There is hardly an interior, just the desolate summit for a Babylonian astronomy. There is nothing wrong with the architect, but collaborative projects like this communal science are intrinsically flawed. Our fable will yield the adventures of history after this astrological assault.

And even God must "come down" to look. There is something grandly theatrical in this descent after the naming of the great cities. Perhaps even the supernal Draughtsman is silently jealous of the little humanist science below with its cognitive invasion of the sky. It is after the time of the intercourse between angels and man. It is a time after the obliteration of Noah's corrupt generation. Now God pronounces, but only to himself or angels, that this rebellion will leave "nothing out of their reach." And so the urbanists have forced the Deity out of his refuge. The Tower has reached those clouds that occluded his Unity.

I was always struck in my youth by the first great and seemingly absurd question—"Where are you?"—asked of Adam in the profanation of his vows. A riddling question in Eden, since the Architect sees every locus in the forest and may pierce every shameful mind. But the Tower of Babel is another epitome of a shamelessness that almost works. The scattering begins with a tidal wave of language. Word and object are divided for the philosophers, and home itself is disseminated into the nations. With this story, we have a kind of parenthesis in the covenant. Does it look forward to the worst in our century? The rabbis have noted that technology and civilization itself are implicated, as the great project occasions a never-ending punishment.

It is hard for us not to look at this as a little fairy tale in the Russian mode of "It was and it was not." Jakobson has said that modernity itself is the palpability that emerges in the division of sign and object in such a space of crushed realism. This fable—part cartoon and part anti-imperial document—is filled economically with a great and concentrated mistrust in palpability. And the scandal is that the Tower is a success. It still exists and is very like Rome or London or New York. Gigantism shouldn't bother us any more than the bewildering smallest brick. We were driven out to become geologists and businessmen, gunrunners and silent, disillusioned carriers of dictionaries. Multiplicity is indeed both our curse and blessing and the true Dark Tower: Time, in which we place our indestructible lack of serenity.

My son Daniel writes his own midrash: "The people were angry at God for making them stop working on their religious spirit the Tower of Babel. Their work was over and their thoughts of seeing God were gone too. It's sad how God didn't want to show himself to the world. He probably thought the world wasn't ready. The Tower of Babel if it was still made would show the world how close mankind got to God." This commentary is not far from certain Talmudic perspectives, and it is also close to the naturalistic echo of Babylonian "gates to God," where a romantic science could have been practiced.

* * *

One wants an encyclopedia of the images of *tohu bohu*—of confusion, chaos—and our best art may be nothing but the illustration of that majestic, essential word. Since my earliest Hebrew classes, after the comic-book Bibles and the childhood vision of God glimpsed in the Atlantic Ocean as a destroyer and a voice, this word has appealed to me as a burden and a dissertation. First chaos, then the world. I have always kept on my desk, next to the red folio and the blue dictionaries, the Bible given to me by my grandmother with the pathos of her inscription that I return to it as to a perfect language. *Tohu bohu* made its entrance into the French language, but I see it as something more astonishing than formlessness.

To speak, to confuse, to approach a false Paradise: this is the triple pun of our story. The lost original was either a ziggurat for the purposes of worshiping Marduk and the stars, a parable concerning city and language, or a combination of elegy and fable to denounce Empire and its bituminous ashes. The scholars are almost right—Man and God do not speak to each other in these fables. But they do not always understand the triple meaning of this separation: one from the other, ourselves from ourselves, the others from the One. We have lost the words to speak of such lost unities. We are saved only when confounded in a community of exile, and we will enlighten others only by striving to resurrect a truer architecture and an imperfect, more natural poetry: a gate to the unconfused earth.

Conversation with Michael Goldberg

David Shapiro: Michael, there has been an almost infinite series of definitions, de-definitions and redefinitions of so-called Abstract Expressionism. Do you now have a way of typifying it or calculating its coherence for yourself? How does one make one definition for a phenomenon that embraces, say, Still and Rothko, de Kooning and Guston?

Michael Goldberg: I always thought that the definition—it was an attempt to loosely group a postwar phenomenon in American painting—had very little to do with the actual painters grouped under the rubric. It was just a convenient term to encapsulate the whole spectrum of postwar American painting. There were really two divisions in the period we're talking about—some people were interested in immediacy and energy and some people were interested in the sublime. That is the way I see the differences.

DS: Much philosophical ink has been spilled about gesture in art. Do you agree with Suzanne Langer—that art creates symbolic forms for feeling? Is the gesture in your early work an analogue for emotion? And at any rate, how does the ideal criticism of your work calculate this emotion?

MG: It's very much like semiotics, you know, that anyone is free to interpret the texts as they want to. My chopped liver might be somebody

---

Michael Goldberg: Goldberg Variations by David Shapiro, Jeremy Gilbert-Rolfe, and Elisabetta Longari (Edizioni Primaprint, 1997). Text in Italian and English.

else's smoked herring. I thought that gestures were almost a way to relate energy to emotion—my own emotion. In other words, it wasn't a facsimile for emotion, it had emotional connotation. Energy is the visual rapidity of the hand. The clear indication would be Lichtenstein's brushstroke paintings: facsimiles of an emotion, the real core of what Pop Art is.

DS: Michael, thinking back to the period of the late '40s and '50s, can you suggest whether the political moods of the period affected your work, and in what ways? Someone has suggested that Jasper Johns' paranoid structures reflected the Eisenhower-McCarthy period of suspicion and dread. Others might suggest that your works bear the burden of your own post-war—and traumatized—sense. Did your work as a parachutist have an infiltrating inflection in your work? Some see the present moment as a *fin-de-siècle* and the '50s as one of the optimisms of the victorious Empire. What is your sense of that now?

MG: I don't know whether you are talking about politics or art politics. Most of the people I knew were vaguely apolitical. Those who had been in the war were so glad it was over. In terms of art politics, you had the feeling there was so little opportunity to exhibit anyway that everyone was in the same glorious boat, and it was very exciting. Actually, we're talking about the beginning of the Cold War era, and I was vaguely aware that Russia was right: a fantasy. We're much more political now. I feel that I am so strongly involved with making order out of chaos that what I am working with is a much more universal material.

DS: Fairfield Porter talked of what he learned from de Kooning, of the painterly surface that attracted him early to de Kooning's work, yet one also hears of the dichotomy between de Kooning's Dutch and learned facilities and Pollock's American themes and procedures. Could you discuss now what you think of this problem, both the American formulation and the de Kooning influence?

MG: I always thought that de Kooning represented a synthesis with the earlier abstractions of Kandinsky and Picasso. And as such, technically one could lift whole sections of the work and proceed from there. Whereas Pollock, whom I thought of as the most important

American painter of the time, was involved with such a closed technical system that you couldn't lift anything from him except his attitude. I was always influenced by Titian and Velasquez. I wasn't running away from anything. I didn't have to be a super-American painter. I thought that most of the European painters of that period were full of shit. The work was too pretty; they were still trying to make a painting, and I wasn't really trying to make a painting.

DS: You have made jazz one of the analogues of your art; one of its influences. Jazz is little understood or analyzed by musicologists, even today, and its influence on performance poetics is just beginning to be explored. How does the improvisational characteristics of jazz suggest your own work? Did you always paint to music? Is it the complexity of jazz that one loves, its ferocity, its ethnic meanings, its subversive political undertone, or its sexual vitality? Is jazz still as important to you?

MG: Yes, jazz is still as important to me, and I don't think that there's a parallel between what I do and music. I think it's much more interwoven in my being. Actually, without a profound understanding on my part, I also think that trying to come to terms with the black experience of music (jazz) has made me a much more rounded person. I think probably Duke Ellington or Louis Armstrong or Charlie Parker have continued to be strong influences on my life and my creative life. I think that Duke Ellington is probably the major American composer of our time—with no qualifications.

DS: You were a close friend of the poet Frank O'Hara and accomplished, among other things, some significant collaborations with him. Can you describe what you think of his work in this period, how you might have thought of it differently then? And did his own poetic work influence you, or do you agree with the more traditional observation that the painters presided over the poets in the period of 1945–1960, with the poets learning their technique from the painters?

MG: Frank wrote with this extraordinary immediacy and clarity, and also there was a quality of sharing that Frank seemed to care about an incredible amount. I found that he illuminated all kinds of human attitudes, I suppose that kind of added to my life. And still does. We were all vaguely self-destructive, we all thought we would live forever. I think "To the Harbormaster" is probably my favorite poem of his.

DS: By 1961–1962, many critics have suggested a vast divide between the emerging "Pop" artists and those who had seriously digested abstraction and its intransigent attitudes. How did you receive the humor or parodistic tones of Pop Art? You once joked about your disdain for some of the "real" material in early Pop artists, such as the hangers in Johns' collages. What is your sense now of the tone of your work as compared to Rauschenberg and Johns.

MG: But you know, I never thought that Johns or Rauschenberg were as involved in Pop as Larry Rivers. One might call these people proto-Pop artists; Jasper had this painting hanging in the backroom of Leo Castelli's and it had this hanger hanging off this peg. And I lifted the hanger off the peg, mainly relating to it as an artifact. Somebody said, "That's part of the work." As if I didn't know. So I put it back. Chuckling.

I don't think that Pop Art is concerned with the human condition. And I never have thought so. I thought very little of Andy [Warhol], but at the same time, Andy forced all of us to look at art in a different way and that's not given to many people to do. And I always thought that Andy was the purest disciple of Duchamp or an inheritor of Duchamp.

DS: Jeremy Gilbert-Rolfe has made some useful suggestions concerning the universals that are always part of abstract art. We also know from Joseph Masheck's research how much the cruciform has affected the Western tradition of verticality. How much should we associate an early work of yours like "Georgica Association," for example, with the universal spirit of landscape? How much of your own work, for instance, might be said to be an "essentializing" from scape and figure? How much of scape and figure was taboo in this period?

MG: I've always admired the landscape abstractions of Kandinsky (1909–1915), and I've always been influenced by the moralistic objectivity of Mondrian—but in answer to this question, I never particularly related that idea to my work. At the time you're talking about I was trying to reduce the explicit visual material that I was concerned with and make the paintings that much more impenetrable.

DS: Your work influenced me by the mid-1960s because of its energy, its dynamic compositional sense and its strategy of enormous scale. Frank Stella once said of himself that he couldn't succeed with small paintings. How did you come by your decisions of scale? Jim Dine said he would love to have the billboards between one city and another. How much was urban scale the chief metaphor of this scale? In relation to this, was mural-sized Mexican work an analogue, as in the case of Siqueiros' influence on Pollock?

MG: I don't know the answer to that question, either. I was always interested in vaguely large-scale work until I moved into this studio (222 Bowery) where the ceilings are 25 feet high. Onward and upward. The Mexican artists didn't influence my work at all. I was impressed by their expressionistic social fervor, but they certainly didn't influence me at all. I thought that Pollock was always much more creative on a large scale. You could follow the line out to a greater degree or the complexity of the lines intersecting to a greater degree: more information.

DS: It has been said of Pollock that it is his chief achievement to have dissolved the line-color antithesis, and to have achieved mural-sized scale without a corresponding loss of intimism. How were your color decisions made in your early work, and would you see great changes in your palette over the years. Since you are a lover of paper, I would also be interested in any remarks concerning the classic and perhaps nonsensical division between color and linearity.

MG: I've never been able to make a great separation between drawing and painting as such. I've always been able to use what the hell I wanted to: whether it's color, whether it's mass, whether it's line or form or lack of any one of those. These things have not been my chief considerations. I've become a more exuberant painter. Metallic colors I started using around 1972 or 1973 using black bronze powders and gradually started using other different colored bronze powders. They had a very subtle inflection, enabling me to reduce the means I was using to gain a much more universal image.

DS: A brilliant aperçu of Frank O'Hara was that in our century there have essentially been two movements: cubism for aesthetic technique and surrealism on behalf of revolutionary new content. Can you say how your own work engulfed both Picasso and Breton? What was surrealism for you in the forties and fifties? How would you differentiate your own form of gesturality from surrealist automatism? Does Masson ever interest you?

MG: I grew up reading Lautréamont, Jarry, Baudelaire, de Nerval, and so I was very prepared to accept all these possibilities of surrealism. And my early paintings were surreal in the sense that they were narrative. The War kicked narrative painting out of my being. And so my relation to surrealism was only as a viewer and not as a participant. I met Matta and liked him enormously. For me, surrealism was a literary movement; as a pictorial movement, the only ones who had interest were Max Ernst or Masson and Masson doesn't influence me particularly.

DS: Mondrian once said that he was the true surrealist. For all your biomorphism and cadenzas of improvisation, an early work of yours such as "Sea Spray Inn," 1960, has a geometric burden of several uncalculated but determined stripes. How do these stripes relate to the kind of geometrical painting that was starting up in the country as the same time?

MG: They don't relate at all. Mondrian also said that he was the only real expressionist, so you can say everything. He probably said he was the only real cubist, though I don't know about that. They all refer to a painting of Baldini of a young woman in a striped black and white summer gown; pattern involves repetition, and I am not involved in repetition. I want to establish a kind of structure that people cannot feel secure about. The stripes are all contained but their relationship to each other is, at best, insecure.

DS: I think that many critics take an attitude toward early work, especially your own early work, that it is locked in a debate with your elders. This agonistic philosophy sees you wrestling with Pollock, Still, de Kooning and Rothko and judges the work on a kind of victory or not over them. Another philosophical or critical schema can be adduced, on the "joys" of influence, that suggests that your early work is not so much agonistic with the older generation as collaborative with them. Which schema is closer to your sense of the truth now?

MG: I think the second. I was using territory that had been opened up and hopefully bringing my own sensibility to it. I was a follower admittedly; the Oedipal thing I did not feel. One of the things that has always interested me is that in the late '40s and early '50s there was no distinction in terms of age because the rewards were so limited and, consequently, everyone was accessible to everyone else. There just wasn't an oedipal situation; The Fathers you didn't think of as fathers, they were more like older friends. I think that Bill's [Willem de Kooning] entire output up until 1970 was partially concerned with disguising the mastery of his hand. And my whole work has been concerned with trying to gain mastery of hand.

DS: Going back to the sense of drawing, could drawing in the early period have been preparatory, considering the improvisational nature of most of the paintings? What, then, was the role of drawing and how has it evolved for you?

MG: Drawing was like doing warm-up exercises. I had done life-studies at the Art Students League and in Hofmann's classes there was always a model. I think of drawing as a much more precise and descriptive activity. It is much more immediate and much more throw-awayable. Ingres was a great draughtsman; I like him for his apparent purity, and Cezanne for his apparent clumsiness. I've tried watercolors, but not really.

DS: Franz Kline has been said by some to be unjustly neglected in our day. Reviewing some of your early paintings makes one sense that you were one of the few to have early on understood his enormous challenge in calligraphy and color. What do you think now of Kline, and how important are the coloristic aspects of his work as well as the gestural? Elaine de Kooning once suggested to me that she and Bill had shown Kline the way out of his early figurative conservations by employing an enlarger and showing him the abstract possibilities of scale changes; does this seem to you a possible translation of your own work of this period: enlargements of detail out of an urban post-impressionism?

MG: Of my own work, no, it is not an enlargement. I love Franz Kline's work and I love Franz. And I would find the work today as vital as it ever was. I don't know how Franz would relate it to his work, but he was a great admirer of the painting of Turner. I don't think color was that important to him. Franz was extraordinarily outgoing, a raconteur full of jokes and very American, yet he never really talked about other people's paintings. The immediacy of all the paintings we're talking about has been leeched into the historical process. No one who thinks that Bleckner or Salle is extraordinary would want to look at Franz Kline. There's a new show of Julian Schnabel at Pace downtown and they are very flaccid, empty paintings that employ an attitude of gestural activity without being able to activate the empty spaces of these huge canvasses. And I found a huge relation between these huge paintings and Franz Kline but without an understanding of the way in which Franz could activate the empty spaces in the canvas. So more is given of the look than the core, a look or appearance. But also much of today's art is about appearance.

DS: You are now a well-known pedagogue at the School of Visual Arts, and I have observed your tactful criticism in life-drawing classes. How much did your early teachers affect your style of teaching and painting? I am, like anyone else, particularly interested in whether Hofmann's famous classes exerted any pull over you, and in what direction. We are obviously interested in whether Hofmann's theories of surface and perspective changes meant anything to your early paintings.

MG: Hofmann, for me, was not a particularly terrific teacher. A good deal of the time I didn't understand what the hell he was talking about. But Hofmann and his school created an aura that what we were doing was highly professional, and a love of art was the general atmosphere. I didn't go to the one in town but to the one on Eighth Street. His example is not something that I use in any way in my teaching, save for that area of professionalism and love of art. I met Miles Forst, John Grillo, Jan Mueller and Milton Resnick. I've liked some of his (Hofmann's) paintings enormously. I also met Larry Rivers and Jane Freilicher there. Sometimes you worked from a model and sometimes you didn't.

DS: Looking at your most recent paintings, we are interested in their supposed continuity and discontinuity with the early work. Do you now know how to characterize the differential between the work of the last fifteen years, say, and your early work? Is the development Darwinian and toward complexity and toughness, or would you say there are other ways to indicate the variation and growth?

MG: I am dealing with very much the same content as I was 25 or 30 years ago, hopefully at a more mature or higher level. The artist feels he or she is always right; I'm waiting for the big kick in the ass where I tell myself it's all full of shit. I've taken both Greenberg and Rosenberg seriously, but it hasn't affected my work. I found it provocative. I found Leo Steinberg very provocative. I don't read criticism to tell me how to do it or to find out what it's all about.

DS: A political-gender question arises in terms of the perceived masculinist ethos of the Abstract Expressionist period; Rita Reinhardt once told me a story about Clement Greenberg being enthusiastic about a black painting in Reinhardt's studio until he was told it was painted by Rita. How much of the energy and dynamism of your work do you suppose has as part of its ethos or mythos the ideal of sexual man? How does the feminist cause affect your work, particularly in light of your relationship with the sculptor-painter Lynn Umlauf? [Umlauf was Goldberg's wife.]

MG: I suppose I do feel that it is as much my problem as any woman's, but to a different degree. At the same time, I also don't feel that I've solved the question of what being a man is in our society, and it's not that I'm ambivalent about my maleness so much as I'm uncertain as to what my role is.

DS: Perhaps we can continue with the question of woman by asking you what you thought then, or think now, of the question of the figure in de Kooning's "Woman"; did that challenge or interest you? What do you think of the painter Joan Mitchell's work then, and now, and what was the nature of its influence "with" you? I am interested in whether the figurative is seen by you as betrayal, that is, when certain abstractionists in this era re-introduce the figure.

MG: I myself have experienced that point when I could no longer push abstraction any further, and I had to resort to a kind of figuration.

Figuration is a sort of restorative activity and I really like de Kooning's figure painting very much. They did not seem like compromises. The way he was doing them, they were never finished. *Woman I*—I saw that in a dozen different states.

He had this studio on 4th Avenue between 10th and 11th Street and my studio was on 10th Street between 3rd and 4th Avenue. So I went over often to see the *Woman*. Don't forget that all the artists I knew at the time were vaguely constipated. The favorite refrain of the period was "Ain't it hard, gee ain't it hard!" The person who shouted the loudest was Milton Resnick. Certainly, de Kooning shared that sentiment. It was true. One of the problems Bill had with Pollock's painting was that he thought they were too easy; he was close to Jack Tworkov; I liked Tworkov's work a lot at that time: the fluidity and the classical formal qualities he was involved with. I liked, and continue to like, Joan Mitchell's painting very much. I always wished that she could have expanded landscape abstractions into a much more truly abstract painting. I think they are very beautiful, but I never thought she pushed them far enough.

DS: Jazz is serial; jazz may be thought to bear what Jeremy Gilbert-Rolfe might call the topic of multiplicity itself. How much would you think of your turbulent work, say, *The Keep*, as having within itself this topic of the multiple. How much did you think of your work of this period as serial? I am interested in sequences at this time, for example, in the poetry of O'Hara and his Odes. Can we think of your own long or large works as being comparable to his long multiply organized works? How did his colloquialism affect you? What would be colloquial in your work?

MG: To answer that, I never made a conscious break from one group of paintings. They were steps along the way. I would think of all the works as autobiographical—presenting some aspect of myself that I was trying to come to grips with and discover. I find that Derrida is a luxury that visual artists can do without. Even T.S. Eliot couldn't do it; I'd like to make my paintings less personal but not impersonal. Mantegna is very often a decorator.

DS: You have referred to abstract landscapes and New York, or urban abstractions. New York is perhaps the chief poetic topic of the 20th century and perhaps the capital of the 20th century, for all the resentments against it and the resentments against the idea of the capital. Can you characterize for us what these terms may still mean to you? And how much "Broadway Boogie Woogie," in a sense, remains or is the topic of your urban painting? Is New York City, and now Italy in the summer, the secret or open challenge of these works? Is it the eclecticism of New York you love, its impurity, or what de Kooning called the "melodrama of impurity?"

MG: New York is my home (laughing). I think in order to be a painter in New York, you have to find some means of isolating yourself. I always had the image of the painter badly sunburnt. You sit around picking off your dead skin until you get to the core of your being. And it's much more exciting, or stimulating, knowing that there are millions of agitated assholes outside than in some gorgeous retreat.

DS: Michael, William Rubin has been criticized for seeing a few apotheoses in the history of modernism: late Cezanne, Picasso's cubism, Pollock and the expressionists, and certain aspects of Stella's abstraction. How much is left out of the Museum's narrative of modernism, and what would you now see as neglected in the most typical narratives? For example, are there neglected artists—one thinks of Pavia, Vicente, Nakian—that you would underline as deleted or "disappeared" from the usual narratives of the museum?

MG: Millions. In the same way that one had to coin group definitions that lump all kinds of artists together, the museums, by the nature of the people who run them, have had to establish a hierarchy. And an awful lot of people get left out of consciousness like de Kooning, Kline, etc., but how much do young people know even of Gorky? There are too many.

DS: The stigmata of the "second-generation" Abstract Expressionists has been vast. You are often characterized as floundering or befouled by the influence of the Master Heroes of the first generation, so-called. Is there any way to rescue now the sense of your generation—say yourself,

Leslie, Mitchell and others—from this stigma and taboo. What would be your own opinion of the best way to make such a rescue operation or to salvage the true sense of the integrity of that generation. It seems as if only recently have we been able to get a clearer sense of the enormous accomplishments of your generation. Is it "Pop" and "Minimalism" that mostly obscured the achievement or linear history itself?

MG: I think that's a dead issue.

DS: Carter Ratcliff has praised John Ashbery for his extreme, perhaps surrealistic, insight that Pollock's painting was important, not for formal reasons, but for its extremism, for the fact that it seemed to be an eternal challenge to the possibilities of painting. Do your early paintings seem now more or most interested in this ferocity or extremism, this gesture of radicalism or would you say that Donald Judd is right, that Pollock and yourself, for example, are constructors more than their critics know, of controlled paintings with the topic of turbulence.

MG: I would like to say that Donald Judd has spent an entire career finding ways to buttress his lack of daring. And since Donald Judd doesn't know how to look—everything he says about painting is sadly suspicious. At the time, Ashbery's statement seemed true, because you couldn't take from Pollock; the content and technique were closed expressions. I would think that my early paintings were never as implacable as I would have liked them to be. There was too much either/or in them. It reminds me of the way I've always felt about Lester Young—chorus after chorus, each slightly different. There's this built-in variance in them and that's the way I feel about my early work.

DS: You have learned a lot from your time in Italy and your new paintings often bear the marks of a Renaissance allusion. But do these early works swerve completely from any classic or neo-classic equilibrium? And how deliberate was that then? Is there any possibility of reading back into paintings such as *Raunch Hill*, 1960, and *The Keep*, 1958, any lessons from classical painting? How important were, by the way, in this period the admonitions of Cezanne against mere impressionism? Is your new work trying to make something solid and hard as the art of the museums out of earlier, more impressionistic paintings of flux?

MG: Art comes out of art, and in most instances doesn't spring full-blown from the head of Zeus. The classical references have been used and made my own. They exist; I don't deny it. I could be more specific, but that's not important now. A lot of my classical references were almost contemporary, meaning Clyfford Still, meaning Picasso. The time sense in the paintings early and late is dissimilar. The paintings were speedier then.

DS: In what I think is the most inspired reading of your recent work, Gilbert-Rolfe has spoken of the vertigo induced by your patterning and "melting" your deferrals and disjunctions; and the jazzy way in which unanchored verticals work in your particular kind of shallow space, which he sees as derived from the Analytic Cubism. I would like to know how much of this vertiginous use of patterning, melting, landscape abstraction without horizon line you learned as a response to Cubism. Also, can we say that the "performance" aspect of this space, which the critic adduces as "another way" of reading the art of Goldberg, is the provocation of eternal readings and mis-readings? How much of this art agrees with Paul Valery, that modern art resided in making the viewer or reader feel tricked and managed, as if he had been asleep all his life?

MG: It always seems to me that there is no definitive reading of contemporary art. I love Valery's statement and I wish to Christ I had said it. I don't think that the work I'm doing today is in response to Cubism, but at the same time, it's potentially anti-cubist because of its lack of formal structure. But I'd be hard pressed to tell you what it is. It's easy to talk about what it isn't. It's not futurist, it's not Pop, it's not minimal, it's not X, Y or Z.

DS: Meyer Schapiro once suggested to me that the audience for neo-expressionism in the '80s was a swerve from minimalism, because people "wanted more meat." How much is our compacted and vertiginous space a maximalism, a complex that is a conscious swerve from reduction. We know that de Kooning once said that he was made sick by Kierkegaard's "Purity of heart is to will one thing," and we know his polemic against Mondrian's putative Platonism. How attracted are you to the notion that your own impurity is a de-Platonizing, a materialist aesthetic based on multiplicity and doubt? Emerson said there was only this world. Do you accept this almost Judaic formulation of the immanent? Did anything of your Jewish upbringing emphasize this-worldness? Do you think this is the only world?

MC: No!

DS: You survived the War. The War produced in its wake the enormous knowledge of the American empire and also the horrifying disclosure of the Holocaust. I do not accept some of the more trivial emphasis on post-modernism, and your own work seems both radical and profoundly conservative to me. But could you see your work, this early work particularly, as a response to the dislocations of that great War. How much is this an overly contextual reading? How much of your own work remains a challenge to Adorno's famous dictum: No poetry after Auschwitz. Is there painting "after," and is this the kind of turbulent, vertiginous painting that we were likely, if not to expect, then to desire or need? How much, Michael, were you conscious of in your efforts to create an adequate painting after the horrors of war.

MG: I see myself as an unreconstructed modernist. Because I do think that art can change the world. And the horrors that mankind inflicts on itself no longer surprise me, neither does the extent to which it's capable of these horrors. It's just that I want to be sure that I'm not capable of giving in to any of these horrors.

DS: Two things I have learned from you, aside from the love of paint and paper, surface and improvisatory attack, are your love of "implacable form"—your own phrase—and your sense that painting's structure is "incommensurate" with literature or linguistic structure. In your vertiginous paintings, despite your rapport with surreal automatism and poet-friends, and despite collaborations with O'Hara, myself and Giorno, voluntary and involuntary collaborations, your painting suggests that you are "post-structuralist" in bias even in your earliest works. It is for this that Gilbert-Rolfe has had to use such a phrase as "melting" to describe your discontinuities. Again, how would you distinguish your kind of form-giving from the more stable painting that surrounds us and that surrounded me as a young adult. How much was this destabilization simply a heritage of Abstract Expressionism. and how much of it would you distinguish as your own (neo-Nietzschean) contribution?

MG: We've both been engaged working under what I would consider a false assumption, that art is important to the society in which we live. It is important to you and me and other small groups that inhabit this globe. But its effectiveness, as I assume the bulk of this question is directed, is at best severely limited.

Frank Lima: The Poetry of Everyday Life and the Tradition of American Darkness

to Elaine de Kooning

Frank Lima's poetry is a poetry of everyday life, but only a poet of enormous strength and fearlessness is capable of describing the everyday. One might say that the life Lima describes is so exceptional that it cannot or should not be placed under the idea of the everyday. But I think his inventory of traumata in childhood, of drugs and dangers, of incarceration and release, of his triumphs as a man, a father and husband, a cook, a translator, an artist—this inventory in its inclusiveness of urban space is exactly what the French thinker Lefebre meant by the production of the everyday. Lefebre suggested that the real philosophy of modern life could be accomplished by the description of a single day. Lima, learning from poets as various as Villon, Neruda, O'Hara, Lowell, and Corbière, emerges with a mixture of day and dream that is a maximal realism and rendering of his more than a half-century of living. It's a story of survival and, crowned by his compassion, much more than any facile listing of a victim's horrors. He concludes this volume with extraordinary poems of religious depth and poems that create a public, even vatic voice—poems for all victims,

---

American Poetry Review, Vol. 26, No. 1, edited by David Bonanno (January-February 1997). Reprinted as the foreword to Frank Lima's *Inventory: New and Selected Poems*, edited by David Shapiro (Hard Press, Inc, 1997), and in Lima's *Incidents of Travel in Poetry: New and Selected Poems*, edited by Garrett Caples and Julien Poirier (City Lights, 2015).

for a Hasidic youth, for those bombed in Oklahoma, for an older mortal prophet, and for his own children glimpsed in their fragility and resilience.

This development toward poems of wisdom is an unexpected delight and a sign of his status as a major poet. When I met him in 1962 Frank Lima had already written extraordinarily sensuous descriptions of the street and the body, and he had already conquered any timidity in poems that shocked everyone, concerning incest, drugs, and violence. Instead of pursuing this as a single reductive mode, Lima accepted influences and worlds that made him larger and richer. He harbored a disdain, he once told me, for Beat poets who wanted to return to a poverty he wanted to transcend. He was always willing to look backward and even with nostalgia he studied, but he had a ferocious way of engulfing new experiences. After the first volume, and early poems that are as poignantly particular and sharp as prison slang, he learned from Frank O'Hara and wrote poems that sweep us into abstractions and stories that are mythical and urbane and humorous. He had always had this humor, as in his eerie comparison of a lover to a judge of the criminal courts, but the poems now accepted and assimilated a disjunctive poetics of the New York School. He loved this tough art of welding disparate poetic worlds and dedicated his own art to that of David Smith's heraldic and monumental sculpture.

He has never stopped learning, never stopped being a student of himself, language, and the city. He became a master chef, cooking having always been one of his talents, received a master's degree from Columbia with the same earnestness that had led him to study Villon in his teen years even while in rehabilitation, and he has now become the master of a magical-realist style that I identify with Marquez as much as with Neruda. Strangely, he has turned a prose fragment into a dazzling lyrical-narrative autobiographical sequence. In the future, we may expect more from this novelistic mode that includes amazing cinematic sequences, for example, a horrifying scene in which he observes his father drunk and near death in a park. Lima, a New York surrealist, completely seizes the rage and detachment and strangeness of this vision. It is something he accomplishes from his earliest work, but now it is not just snapshot photography at its best—no small achievement itself—but a masque-like architecture of great scale, where the instants add up to a whole social vision.

After our first amazing meeting, I was touched by what Kenneth Koch called, in his introduction to the first chapbook of his poems, his courage and his honesty about pleasure and poverty. These early poems are still luminous achievements, and there can be no anthology of the last fifty years of poetry that does not include something of these extraordinary poems without a loss. No poem that I know of speaks like "Mom I'm All Screwed Up" about childhood torments and its ferocious intimacies. No city poems about Spanish Harlem have ever yielded the completely convincing tones of these early works. They are fast, furious, and alive with the musical grace found in this sudden bit of landscape and church music from "Abuela's Wake":

> *Dios te salve Maria*
> *Dios te salve Maria*
>
> outside
>   the snow-mouth of December tinked on the windows

"Pudgy" rises to the sweetest and most serious sensuality in "O my chocolate princess I / lay in bed / smelling of Lifebuoy soap and toothpaste / light a stogie and watch the smoke / unshoe ghost-nude thoughts." This is a poetry of a young man with great insight into the body's possibilities, but it is important to realize that he didn't stop with this kind of expressiveness. He went to school with the "ordinariness" of the New York School and the empiricism of his great friend and mentor, Frank O'Hara, and always learned too from the perfected finesse of Kenneth Koch. With such a different vision, it is hard to believe that he could synthesize these elements and sublate them into his turbulent scenes: "where the fish bring light to the sun / waiting for the weakness of a dreamer." But that is exactly the task of his middle-period lyrics and prose in which he mixes hedonism, picturesque whimsy, and his particular form of honesty, emerging with extraordinarily strange tales of the ordinary as in his "1/2 Sonnet," or his suddenly violent "Plena" or "Postcard" or "Patchouli." If his usual forte and dramatic instrument was naturalist description, he had now expanded his palette to include something as large and "anthropologically" vast as his "Cuauhtemoc": "I always bring captives here / and let the grapevine choke them."

The snapshot aesthetic of Robert Frank is thus given a funny and more intense inflection when it collides with the possibilities of a kind of historical or historicized surrealism. The search for the marvelous should not be mere and should not cut poetry off from its worldliness: "The face of poetry is an expressive cut of meat that gives us a glimpse of truth." Lima has a tremendous, almost compulsive need for truth-telling, and one remembers that Paul Goodman once suggested that poets did not write novels, not because of a lack of imagination, but because they had a compulsion to avoid fiction in a love of wild truth. This is why Lima's New York School use of symbolism and surrealism never led him away from his solid sense of thing and fact, boundless body and private streets. If anything, he reminds us that the surrealists at their best—one thinks of the Aragon that Benjamin loved in *Paysan de Paris*—were a final if seemingly superstitious stroke of realism in its extremity. Lima's works—like Schwitters' Merz constructions—are towers of the convoluted debris of everyday life and not reduced ejaculations or cries of protest. This is what Koch admired early on in their lack of moralism, and it is to his credit that even in this sense, Lima has been able to develop, so that strangely his new moral-religious odes are willing to add to his snapshots of the marvelous in the everyday a new cognitive dimension. His integrity in developing this moral dimension might be said to occur in poems in which he is more parent than son, more citizen than nomad.

Thus, I find Lima's journey from the poems of prison, drug-addiction, and the frenzy of sexuality to his new poems and autobiographical narratives to be a triumph of what Erik Erikson used to speak of as the antinomy of wisdom and bitterness. In these poems, again and again, his early toughness is matched by a gentle largeness of generosity and something elegiac that seems necessary and not politically pretentious. He can write about the "shadow of the twentieth century" because he feels it, in Keatsian negative capability, "on my liver," and thus his ode to the Cedar Bar poets is as personal as the most personist of O'Hara. I think any critic will want to praise the imaginative vividness, syncretism, and "publicness" of these new orchestral poems. It is enough to tell the truth, though O'Hara used to joke that that was all that was necessary, and form was as simple as a good fit in clothes, but the truth slant as in Dickinson is the proper opaque for a master like Lima of what I have called the tradition of American darkness.

I have always admired Lima's Whitmanesque wit and wisdom, and I recall that he once laughed back at an older poet who had told students at Columbia that they needed more solitude. "I've been in solitary and I don't need more solitude." I like his human and humorous poems, and in his late poems, like "Father's Day," he creates his own apotheosis and dissemination: "I have seen the seeds in our seeds / Become an army of paper children ... An imperfect father gives his / Children a drawing of an old Sun." He can be as gently attenuated as a Valery Larbaud in his food poems ("Ode to Julia Child"), but these are just his most recent scherzi. The new magnitude in his work is seen in his homage to an ancient Mexico and to the tenderness of poets: "Allen will be taken from us / to the slaughterhouse of dear God." Somehow, I trust his Jewish and his Catholic poems, his poems of an unbearable ethnicity, and his poems of a soaring universalism. Isaiah Berlin has taught us to dream less and less of a homogenized world of unconflicted happiness. Lima is a tragic pluralist, who knows what it's like to be almost run over in social collisions. He has gone from a poem as subtle and slangy as "In Memory of Eugene Perez" to a poem as sustained and furious as his "Oklahoma America." I have always enjoyed the way Frank Lima disdained poets who too greedily used their origins to gain a false publicity. He has an amazing lack of self-pity, both in his poems and in his presentation of himself, but I do pity those who neglect his voice and wise rage. I think Lima's story and his fabulous dark insistence is one of the most remarkable American triumphs. We have witnessed, in these thirty-five years, along with his friend, that amazing cubo-futurist Joe Ceravolo, the creation of a mature American poetry of everyday darkness.

Frank Lima could have stopped when he had finished his Rimbaldian poems of the street, rough and physical and full of caricature. He could have also accepted complaisantly his re-formulation of the New York School and stopped as a poet with a control of surrealism and urbane fancy. He has refused to stop, and his poetry today has the rare public-private synthesis that counts, and a supernatural naturalism that underlines him, in an M. H. Abrams sense, as a late Romantic. He finds in the turbulent darkness of New York and America his mythology, his Alps, his truth.

Some Notes Toward Twombly: A Man Without a Boat, or A Boat for Everybody

Only the mast broke it for me.
Then the boat died ...
I spent the nights inside
A shelter of wood and embraced the shadows.
    —*The Tale of the Shipwrecked Sailor* (Twelfth Dynasty)

I sailed the divine boat of Thoth upon ...
I equipped the barque, [called] Shining-in-Truth
of the Lord of Abydos, with a chapel ...
I led the way of the god to his tomb ...
I conveyed him into the barque [called]
The Great, when it bore his beauty;
I gladdened the heart of the eastern highlands;
I ... ed the rejoicing in the western highlands. When they
saw the beauty of the sacred barge, as it landed at Abydos ...
    —Breasted, Ancient Records of Egypt

O sounding-poles of Horus, O wings of Thoth,
ferry me across, do not leave me boatless.
    —quoted in Dilwyn Jones, *Boats*

I, even I, am he who knoweth the roads
Through the sky, and the wind thereof is my body.
Manus animam pinxit
My pen is in my hand
    —Ezra Pound, *De Aegypto*

David Shapiro

1.

It's not for nothing that this "Egyptian" painter, Cy Twombly, recently chose to pay homage to *The Fighting "Temeraire" Tugged to Her Last Berth to Be Broken Up* (1838) of Turner. The sun, steam, and smoke of Turner's catastrophic sunlight partly reigns over Twombly's *Coronation of Sesostris* (2000) and gives him an analogy and a demon. In Turner, the old ship dies an amazing death next to the tugboat of the modern. In Twombly, there is this loud dizzying music of the departure of the gods, as in tercets by the poet Patricia Waters [the poem incorporated by Twombly into the 6th panel]. In Twombly, there is also a voyage from a white moderate morning to the highest flames to the lightless Field of Reeds at the end. In Twombly and Turner both, a boat like a locomotive is a crowd, demography, and a physiognomy. As in no other painter, Twombly's alizarin can become a wild color for a stalk, a person, an oar, or a blossoming mast. These are the colors of a shipwreck or a ship dying, as in Turner. And all the *non-finito* from Dubuffet and all the child-speech of Twombly's calligraphy in extremis cannot take away the immensity of this new sublime. In these gorgeous dissolutions of the self, the soul boat, the soul house, Twombly lets us drift in the sun. Oars become human, but uncanny, personages of light. The painting lives out this doubled, haunted world, essentially one of reflection, like Monet's. It's not for nothing that Monet used Turner, and that Twombly himself has referred to this room of barges as *Waterlilies*. Here the essential homage is to light, and each of the ten paintings creates an enjambment in which the circle of morning to evening, world to underworld, is enacted like a priestly processional, without a break.

2.

Twombly has taken the Egyptian theme out of the vitrine and curiosa and cabinet and set it into our most poignant private space. He has already accomplished this in his masterful sculpture of 1985 entitled

---

Cy Twombly: *Coronation of Sesostris* (Gagosian Gallery, 2000). The catalogue for an exhibition at the Gagosian Gallery. The entire ten-painting cycle can be viewed at: https://gagosian.com/exhibitions/2018/cy-twombly-coronation-of-sesostris/

Winter's Passage, a ghostly funerary barge, with mast tilted at what David Sylvester has subtly read as both acute and obtuse, each angle changing the tempo of the sculpture. In other "barque" sculptures of 1992, Twombly has rendered the poetry of the "model boat" in a kind of fleshy plaster deprived of any extraneous detail, pulsating like de Kooning's women. These are presented with none of the overdetailing one sometimes finds in the Egyptological galleries, where the cloth is still apparent on the figures four millennia later, and each thread of the oarlocks is restored. Twombly has always known how to give, as in the curt funerary block on *Winter's Passage*, the ultimate geometry of these toys, toys for broken adults, Baudelairean caricatures in answer to the question of the symbolist: When shall we sail for happiness?

3.

In a trialogue with Francesco Clemente and Richard Serra in *Res*, Brice Marden emphasized his delight in the scroll-like opening of Twombly's work, whether it implies a Chinese or an Egyptian reading. As a matter of fact, the *Coronation* is a panorama that invites polysemic readings. The Egyptologist Bob Brier, my neighbor in Riverdale, instructed me that Egyptian hieroglyphs are always read "in the direction of the bird's mouth," but implied no canonic left-right readings. Brier is one of those who is obsessed by ancient transport and is making a model of the Khufu boat: 155 feet and ready for the Nile in a few years. The lure of Twombly's panorama is not historicist but is a quiet contemporary mistranslation of the solar voyages of the god. In each of the ten paintings we are given a transcription of myth, poetry, and the path of the contemporary mind. Wittgenstein has a wonderful sentence: "Perhaps the best image of the human soul is the human body." To which this painting seems to answer: Perhaps the best images of the human soul are signs and the poetry of language itself. This is the ultimate and elegant refinement of Twombly's insistence.

4.

The *Coronation* or Solar Voyage is a kind of march from the morning. It begins with a gigantic crayon sun as helplessly infantine as one could imagine, with an unimaginable audacity. Twombly has described doing these early paintings as an almost automatic dry marking. The sun is put on wheels in the second passage, and the title emerges as a powerful equivalent for these signs of the god or king. The announcement of Sesostris is as bold as the pharaoh described as a military genius by Herodotus. Herodotus notes that Sesostris set up crude genitalia as signs when he conquered a city. This is the kind of Ozymandias-like poetry that we find in these Romantic panels. But "something besides" always remains. In the third panel, Twombly gives us not only the melancholy poetry of an erased apothegm: "Eros, weaver ... Eros, bitter and sweet ... Eros, bringer of Pain." The artist is not sure of the author, but his intuition about its triple power is fine. But the childhood of the sun has been transformed into a violent mixture of red and yellow with the most adult streaming of painterly chromaticism. Motherwell, scholar of automatism, once joked to a mother that her child could do something once, but not forever. Here, the melancholy narrator gives us a flux and flow of color worthy of Ruskin's adulations. And again, we return to a sun that has turned into a gigantic relic of itself. In the next three panels, the barges appear in all their grandiose carmine and alizarin glory. They are heraldic, triumphant, and blazing with mixed colors from purple to gold.

Nothing could be more Venetian than these Egyptian relics of the living and the dead. The oars exude long shadows that drip into the bottom of the panels. Those aboard could be, as one finds in a mortuary model at the Metropolitan Museum of Art, New York, looking at their lotuses and munching on their lunches. Here all is excess, all is regal wit. The saddest lesson is imposed by a poem of departure and explanatory wit on the hesitations and departures of the gods. But Twombly is a master of the nominalist, and it is only the names that remain. It is significant that Twombly told me that he loved the sound and look of Sesostris as a name, and he took the word "god" out of Waters' poem as a reticence.

5.

It is a clue to the *reticentia* and limits of concealment in Twombly that he is willing to give such commentary as Waters' lyric provides about a high music and the sounds of the (gods) departing in our own bodies. This poem is draped by an explosion of more than twenty clusters of dark alzarin, which the artist told me he considers as red flowers, and flowers they become. These clusters are themselves also abstract symbols of a high remorse, like fireworks in Turner. The poem introduces his greatest triumph, the doubled boats of panel seven, before the whole sequence becomes drier, empty, and blackened as an underworld.

The seventh panel is perhaps the explosive center of this centerless divertimento of the dead. Here Twombly shows his absolute command of light, as the barges themselves dissolve in solar spots and flares. In this panel, the flesh of light is consummately done. Some will see Turner, some Moreau or Monet, but the immediacy of this decorative fleet is a coup de théâtre. It has been prepared for, but it is still a shocking *subito sforzando* in this musicalist parade. One realizes that all these graffiti are more pentimento than hitherto subscribed. The shadows of color lying beneath mist and ghostly streamers subside.

In the last few panels, gold is only a memory. And bright dark barges consume the enormous spaces with swift purple marks, as if to conclude the ceremony hastily. The driest penultimate painting gives a Greek poem of farewell: "leaving Paphos ringed with waves." The calligraphy itself breaks into waves. Water is the medium, but the last panel concludes with something sculptural, Egyptian indeed, and resolutely geometric as a shrine ramp of Sesostris I: the blackened purple of a royal enigma. Above, as from Shelley, these words are again stamped: "Eros, weaver of myth; Eros, sweet and bitter; Eros, bringer of pain." The rained upon memorial ends, but the panel of paintings is circular and must recommence with the simple sun. A solar wedding, a solar coronation, and a funeral: an Egyptian movie of a tremendous representative force. Ten coronations and a funeral end with our complex knowledge of a lack of forgiveness in Eliotic profusion. Twombly has remarked to me that the whole ends with a bump like a train. But the dark, Degas-like shape in the last panel is more like a significant dark shrine, in which all allusions of an open art are compacted. How much Twombly learned in the winters he kept in Egypt is here lightly confirmed. It's an art as open and intelligent as his own speech.

6.

Twombly has given us rare pleasures and permissions, like the permission John Ashbery said Henri Michaux gave certain poets, permission in the sense of an army leave. Twombly does what Valery Larbaud once said was the genius of some American poetry, not so much difficulties surmounted as *easinesses found*. For those of us who look to painting to give us the anti-dogmatic pleasures of the seething surface, Twombly has responded with a lifetime of an allusive and melancholy art. I think the new sequence stands with the best of his work. It is as simple as a chiseled Sapphic line; it is as layered and humorous as the Archilochus he quotes; and it is woven like a text, like a myth, bittersweet and painful as the fragments of a fragmentary, poetic "open field," as the best of the Black Mountain school: Olson and Creeley.

7.

Freud in one of his most skeptical stories speaks of the three insults to mankind. The first insult is Copernican: we are not at the center of our solar system. The second grave humiliation is Darwinian, which leveled us with the animals. The third, Freud mordantly but grandiosely asseverates, is his own insult: that man is not the master of his own house. These insults are indeed the very basis of Twombly's art, and I believe that as a maximal artist he transforms them into The Three Compliments.

In Twombly's art, we are given back the sun and the sun boat and the great Ptolemaic myths, and we enjoy the process of watching ourselves in this decentering mirror. Man in Twombly is a child and a bit of a representing ape or monkey, and the pleasures of graffiti are the pleasures of playing the child. Only an adult can regress to the state of the child, and only a wide-awake mind can pretend to be dreaming. The sequence *Coronation of Sesostris* is as mad and mediated as any transitional object, any doll, any mortuary fiction. The third great compliment that Twombly pays us is that we are indeed happy to be the passive guests in our shattered house. "Shattered as the fruit-dish of Cezanne." We do not long for an idiotic unity, like the regressive conservators of our day. Nor do we run in the street and shout "Viva Multiplicity," as Deleuze warned us was insufficient. Twombly breaks our heart with the imitation of the Palmer Method of a child, with the wild sun and animality that we deserve. We are no longer unhappy, as we study the nostalgias, or, at least, we have only an ordinary unhappiness. We are happy with these insults or compliments to our new state, better than "hysterical misery," the dark alternative of Freud. Off to the side, brooding on the decentered myths; off with the animals and ourselves no better in clearest ecology; and shattered like a ten-part painting in which all we know is what we have lost and how the gods have left us. The *Coronation of Sesostris* is the richest response to Freud's great fictions, that we are now happy in our unbalance between worlds of control and Eros. The barge is funerary, but the elegant solution (as in Wallace Stevens) is our Paradise of the imperfect: civilization is the prize and price.

8.

There is an anxiety expressed by our critics that we have lost a sense of the past, that we have ruptured all traditions, and that what we have left is shapeless "postmodernity," that hateful word. But in Twombly we actually have a learned painter and a learned painting, fresh, but knowing freshness a long time, as Stevens has said. We have a painter who connects us to the best in our traditions of painting, from Egypt to Greece to the Heraclitean flux of Turner and the catastrophes of expressionism. Here is a Virgilian sequence, which is full of a twilight observed and self-reflexive, self-telescoping light, and here is a melancholy secondariness that speaks of the epics that have been and the epics to come. We do not have this work praised by our conservators of culture, but if they would, they might find here what Eliot meant by a work of art that does not give us novelty but a true rearrangement of the tradition.

The melancholy of our time is that we do not applaud sufficiently these grandeurs of the mind. Twombly's art is one of our most civilized and civilizing possessions, and it is in his *periplum*, his voyage of rediscovery and deletion, that the reader, viewer, and student of painting finds a new regard for calligraphy, a new assessment of the illustrative, a ferocious new color sense, and a monument to legibility and the canon of light. And always in him, as in our best poets, is a study of Lucretian uncertainty, a passionate hesitation before assuming dogmas, and therefore I call this painting a radiant pluralistic art. This art is one of the American meditative triumphs, like the sequences of Stevens or Ashbery, collages where parody itself is effaced, because there is no single simple target except torpor. The opposite of painting, as of poetry, is stupidity; and the only way in is a slow reading, where the canonic speed-reading of our day is suicide. These paintings release their charm slowly like radioactivity. But the sequence itself is replete and shows a drive toward a beauty of inexhaustibility.

9.

The Twombly paintings remind one of the strange machinations of Egyptian myth. The myth, like that of our own culture, was a "civilizing love of death," but one so refined that it becomes, after all, a civilizing love of pleasure and the joy of having a body. The paintings call to mind the phrase for the poorest Egyptian: a man without a boat. Each man, we think in our American sense, may be a king, but the king here is indeed Everyman with a boat, a funeral barque of magnificence and scale that is, by itself, the sun in its journey. Christo once satirized modern democracy by insisting that kings, in their representative function, were extremely democratic, much more so than our distortions of plurality. The king is for everyone.

The joy of the Egyptian Sesostris is partly based on the comedy of a Lieutenant Kije—there may never have been a Sesostris at all, just a collage of a variety of kingly doings in the XIIth Dynasty. A famously assassinated king, Sesostris I is also associated by Breasted with inscriptions and admonitions that may be sacred hoaxes, the way Twombly paints a kind of profane comedy of quotation, allusion, appropriation, and desire. What could be a finer humor than Twombly's joy in graffiti of desire celebrating a pharaonic monster—an almost fictive one—who, as Herodotus contends, was an obscene artist in his conquests. Just as Lieutenant Kije was a character transformed out of a misreading, so these paintings stand for the colossal strangeness of a past that is a glorious net of contending myths, lies, and velleities.

10.

Egyptian myth has a sun god riding through the sky and into the netherworld through the threatening night. Twombly's paintings do indeed initiate and enact such an arc. We find the sun of morning in the first passage. Titles emerge like those of certain Egyptian written panels, and the whole continues through the day until it sinks into the tenth panel of a Franz Kline-like sculptural darkness. The whole is, therefore, an example of the family narrative, which Trilling said our generation has squandered in ruthless searches for self-realization. Only after such a crucifixion by causality can one say, the critic asserts, "It is finished."

Twombly begins with what seems the most minimal assertion of the sun voyage to the underworld. With the minimum of incidents, he wrests the maximum of light and adventure. The paintings are *malerisch* in the extreme, and, as a matter of fact, are untranslatable, implacable in their wide force and form. They derive their highest pleasures by way of making color and light as flesh the heroic center of each exposition. The repetition of barque and sun, with an accompaniment of language itself, is a masterstroke of reduction and maximalism. This is demanding painting, for all of its gorgeous distributions. It is "funereal and witty," as Frank O'Hara once paradoxically praised. But the dry wit of exposing a solar funeral in ten cinematic passages is uncanny and affirmative. There is repetition, there is moreover persistence, and the whole reiterates like the melody in John Cage's famous *String Quartet* and *Six Violin Pieces* of 1950. One is dazzled by these quiet repetitions, as if one were seeing nothing but the tracing of a hieroglyph, itself a tracing from an arche-mold.

The exceptional strength in which Twombly breaks his solar imagery into a refulgence of imbricated colors begs us to rethink what we consider imagery in painting. He has always been a master of almost imageless calligraphy. But these reiterated barges with their rudimentary oars—or are they persons, or are they both—underline the length Twombly will go in order to ruin the expectations of a horizon or a "thing." For him, the poetic thing, as in his sculptures that disturb me like Mondrian's cubist trees, are dissolutions of the usual thing.

They are indeed wit at the funeral of imagery. And they reestablish, like O'Hara's own pragmatic kinetic poetry, the fresh immediacy, which is, in our own day, one of the possibilities of painting. It may seem here as if the theoretical-moral component has been dismissed, as what Northrop calls impressionism's stance—but Twombly reinserts all seemingly deleted moral-theoretical work in his commentary through poetry: "Eros, bitter and sweet; Eros, bringer of pain." To anyone who reads as well as sees, Twombly's work emerges as the marriage of Duchamp and Cezanne, marriage of eye and mind, marriage of sun, person, barge, and symbolism. His work for me is as full as that of Olson's escapades into American history with the personal Maximus, or Creeley's dazzlingly dry lyricism of anxiety. Each Twombly, Barthes used to say, sizzles, and it is the heat of these vast canvases that remain to stain them.

11.

Twombly avoids what Meyer Schapiro called "the kitsch of abstraction" in our time. He makes it impossible, moreover, to have a too neat *iconomachia* between the figure and the nonobjective. He has always maintained a vigilance for the flower, the stalk, the sensuous nudity of the name, and he has refused to give up his rights to these while answering also with elongated passages of the purest largesse of light. I think that this painting therefore heals a horrifying split in our culture of painting and is the most significant resource. He has never seemed to be part of the militant fashions; and his poetry of the plural, abstract and figurative at once, has sidled up to none of the working dogmas of the day.

12.

The neo-Egyptian in our culture is often itself a kitsch that Twombly doesn't share. Since Napoleon, the taste for things Egyptian may be a kind of fear of change and a taking sides with what seems eternal in that paranoid geometric culture. Plato has always seemed like one of the first philosophically to prefer the Egyptian stasis to what seemed the pornography of his day. But Twombly does not use Egypt as the eternal, nor does he use it, like Norman Mailer in *Ancient Evenings*, to give off the Orientalist snake charmer of exoticism among the erotic myths. Twombly's Egypt, like his Greece, is closer to a meditation on relic, reliquary, and the shadows of our own time. In this sense, we must agree with those who have found in him no antiquarian. And Twombly's quotations are not those that Proust says should be avoided like expensive price tags.

Twombly is always a painter of modern life, and we have even his monochromes as part of the dungarees of our day. Moreover, his calligraphy is always there to depose any bombastic rhetoric. He undercuts all arrogance with the child's point of view, as if Proust's pedants and snobs were to recite all their *perverbs* with the tongue of the child. Everything here is narrated by Klee's uncertain humans, who know that they do not know. This is an Egypt closer to Pound's *Love Poems*, where the drastically lyrical is offered as one mask among many. As pastoral is always an urbane form, so Twombly's Egypt is always, in a sense, the abyss of America. This is not travelogue, this is the truest mistranslation, macaronic too, as when Pound tilts in his Egyptian translation to give a sudden passage in Latin. The great sequences of our time have these multilingual, "macaronic rhymes," where Greek and English rhyme, where the graffiti of our day meet Greek gods and Egyptian kings. Egypt, walk down any street.

13.

Six drawings are as grand and peremptory as any painting. This is the Twombly who gave me one of the greatest pleasures by simplicity of "bachelorhood of the sign," in his *Six Latin Writers and Poets*. In those prints, he offered names that became physiognomies and the physiognomic that became a whole style in a proper name. The *animus* of these explosive drawings is an orchestral fury that raises the tremulous in those drawings to a brassy triumph. Six drawings, each of the sun. Like William Carlos Williams, who began a poem with the reiterated: "The stain of love is upon the world / yellow, yellow, yellow," Twombly reiterates in each of these drawings a gigantic yellow, the yellow that in Egypt symbolized woman's flesh. And it's a yellow that he can derange with fog, as in his second drawing. It's a yellow undermined and embittered and slightly loopy with line. And in the fourth drawing, it's a yellow that remains only as a completely eccentric smudge, while the sun has become a tangle of scarlet. It's yellow and red in a sunburst, and in the sixth, it's a little Klee-like graphesis of green above a diminishing outline. These six drawings are a very stately, plump way to initiate a procession of paintings. They already bear the atomic design of the larger strophes.

Ben Jonson liked to write his poems out first in prose. Twombly doesn't have the luxury of the academic. He writes his out in these compacted glyphs. Whoever wants to find the painterly equivalent of madrigals need look no further. These are resolute irresolutions, and they go a long way to clearing the air of cant. Pound said he learned a lot—saving us years of learning—when Ford Madox Ford rolled on the ground in laughter against too high a rhetoric. Compared to the false rhetoric of the sensationalists of our time, no matter how seemingly vivified with irony, these loving sun boats come as a shock of lyrical humility.

14.

Two fragments of Pound could stand watch over these paintings of light. "The sunset grand couturier" and "The light there almost solid." The first gives us that sense in Twombly of pure delight in the vagrancies of lines of color, and the second dramatically resolves for us the "substantial light" that Sylvester finds. And we find it as early as the monochromatic sculptures: compacted light. These are essays, personal essays on restless life in public scale. We can never forget the last dark panel, where a hat shape, perhaps out of Degas, stands like an intercepting plane in Mondrian. Here words lock together, another form of intercepting imagery, what Schapiro found common in Impressionism and Mondrian. All this darkness, this dark time, this time of *no longer and not yet*, is a time of mental travel. Just as in Turner's Petworth interior are strange, smoky corridors, full of the subjunctive—burning interiors—so Twombly gives us burning and intercepting passages of a wild calligraphy.

15.

Twombly himself is a weaver and unweaver, of course. He weaves in these macaronic paintings Egypt, Greece, and America. He makes a multimedia piece in wet acrylic, oils, and sudden crayons and pencil: a textual painting. The title comes on like a cinema of the most public proportions, and Twombly has tears for things. In his secondary epic, everything keeps changing: oars, blossoms, and boat. The journey ends like an elegiac distortion in Hölderlin: "The heroes are dead, and the islands of love are disfigured." But the disfigurement is a witty end. The disfigurement in Twombly is always a rotation of puns like a rotating Anemic Cinema in Duchamp. But as Brice Marden noted in the *Res* magazine colloquium, Twombly modulates from the word as answer to the image, here the open sea of the canvas finally yields us an image simple as death. Sartre joked: "I am about to do the one natural thing in my life—I will die." Twombly's smudges of blood and legibility give us the essential place and topic of light, created for the flesh that dies.

Flesh and light are puns in Hebrew and in Cy Twombly's art, but the sun darkens us paradoxically. It lightens the lightless world of our deaths. Identity itself is the darkest riddle—boat equals sun, sun equals boat, god equals all, man is a solar riddle. That is the coronation, the bittersweet coronation of Eros. The anonymous lines are close to Auden's indelible lament: "Sad is Eros, builder of cities." How powerful that these paintings and drawings delete horizon, that we are smashed into them as into Monet's waters, that we journey across the sky with this trepidation of impasse and destabilization. In his color (like Antony for Egypt) Twombly is dolphin-like in his delights. His sunset is not just a couturier but a fiery symbol of a high Romance that almost embarrasses us, as Ricks has it of Keats, embarrassed by sensualism. In a white moderate morning at the end of endings, we begin as in a fold, and we end in a radical underworld morning. Whether the Egyptians or Americans enjoyed life, the symbols we have are of a cosmological wealth. We are buried with our cars, as they were with their boats. What a painter Twombly is, to make a circle weep, to make the hero of his very physical mental journey, an outline of an archaic glyph that means nothing to almost all. Frank O'Hara summed up this collusion with refraction: "Maybe they're wounds but maybe they're rubies / each painful as the sun." John Cage always said that those who loved music preferred the softest sounds. That is a good practical reason to praise the soft refulgence of this luminist of our late empire.

16.

Egyptian art is a paradox, almost like American art, which I usually find Assyrian: militant, cruel, boastful, enormously in love with bigness and emptiness. Egyptians, said Thomas McEvilley, didn't even have a notion of art, of our Greek aesthetics. But then I wonder: Why the love poems? Are they only functional fertility songs? Twombly, at any rate, is a refiner. I have learned much about the impossibility of the word "primitive" from the anthropologist Francesco Pellizzi, a great admirer of Twombly, who speaks of the primitive, so-called, as refining cultures, and loves to speak of America and New York as an "empty center" and the truer primitive. But here I must say that in our own barbarism, we are most lucky to have the refinements of Twombly, who links god and man, as Heschel said the prophets do, and whose tentative tremolos of the child have become our resource and refuge, however temporary, in the ten stations of light, above and below, within and without, in what Gilbert-Rolfe might call the contradictions of immanence. It is not behind everything, it is everything, as another lover of the sun, Fairfield Porter, told me on a white, moderate morning, on the beach at Southampton, where a religion of the sun seems almost self-evident.

Shapiro with his son Daniel. Photo by Rudy Burckhardt. © 2025 Estate of Rudy Burckhardt / Artists Rights Society (ARS), New York.

"Poetry is at the center of Shapiro's work," writes the poet Rodger Kamenetz, "not poetry simply as a formal activity, but as a way of thinking and a way of feeling, and even of being." This clearly included the upbringing of his son Daniel, with and for whom he wrote many poems. In a *New York Quarterly* interview (p. 253), Shapiro spoke of how, as he walked Daniel to school in the morning, they would "write in the air, as it were. Haikus, tankas. I remember teaching him Homer by teaching him how to sing dactylic hexameter."

A Book of Glass

On the table, a book of glass.
In the book only a few pages with no words
But scratched in a diamond-point pencil to pieces in diagonal
Spirals, light triangles; and a French curve fractures lines to elisions.

The last pages are simplest. They can be read backward and
    thoroughly.
Each page bends a bit like ludicrous plastic.
He who wrote it was very ambitious, fed up, and finished.
He had been teaching the insides and outsides of things

To children, teaching the art of Rembrandt to them.
His two wives were beautiful and Death begins
As a beggar beside them. What is an abstract *persona*?
A painter visits but he prefers to look at perfume in vials.

And I see a book in glass—the words go off
In wild loops without words. I should
Wake and render them! In bed, Mother says each child
Will receive the book of etchings, but the book will be incomplete,
    after all.

But I will make the book of glass.

    —David Shapiro, *House (Blown Apart)* (The Overlook Press, 1988).

New York Quarterly Craft Interview
by Malachi Black

NYQ: Much of your work is haunted by music. Would you tell us how music has affected and influenced your work?

David Shapiro: Poetry may aspire to music but indeed is and isn't music already. My greatest influence has been being born a violinist. A violin was literally put in my crib, and I came from a family of musicians. My father didn't believe in cartoons and comic books for kids, I was always amazed when my neighbors had cream cheese toast and ginger ale and could read what they wanted to. I was pretty much a trained monkey on stage, but luckily, I was one of those who for a long time thought that what I was doing was fine.

The violin is often given the 19th-century repertoire, but my family had a string quartet. My father was an amateur (but very determined) sculptor, dermatologist, and musician. He found nothing greater than playing quartets every Friday. For 30 years or so, about 30 people would come over to our house and play chamber music of different kinds—till the morning, practically. Our religion was chamber music.

Also, we knew an amazing composer, and we did push into the 20th century. That didn't mean that we played Elliott Carter at home, but we played Bartok, Ravel, and at least Jewish things like Shostakovich. Then I began to compose, and I was very influenced by Elliott Carter.

New York Quarterly, No. 65, edited by Raymond Hammond (2009). Part of the *New York Quarterly* series of "craft interviews with outstanding American poets."

My mother said to me once, "It sounds like a family argument." But I liked the idea of the instruments in polyrhythms. In my poetry, I've tried to build up a certain chamber music, to make poetry as multiple as a chamber work. We're talking about late Beethoven, late Bartok, early Elliott Carter, and later John Cage (from the 1950s). Those were standards in my mind.

We often wonder whether the greatest violinists could do nothing but imitate the voice. The human voice, my mother always said, was the greatest instrument. Poetry to me, at any rate, comes out of all the music in my family. My grandfather was a great cantor. In Jewish circles in the teens of this country, he began to record his voice. But he was known even at seventeen to have an amazing voice with a *coloratura flautando*, so that he could suddenly sound like a flute. The voice in Jewish circles was used to imitate the instruments that couldn't be brought into the synagogue. So this becomes a kind of endless play.

Not only was there music in my family, but also a constant sense of politics and of leftist politics. My parents were very involved in trying to integrate Newark, New Jersey. The constant theme of my mother—who had lived in South Africa for ten years, where her father sang in Johannesburg—was justice. And many of my earliest poems, from age nine, were about slums, injustice, racism, etc. Those are not poems that you'd necessarily find in my *Collected*, but they are perhaps what became over time—in *A Man Holding an Acoustic Panel*—poems that lived in the wastelands of the political left-wing direction.

When I think of the greatness of certain political writers—one thinks of Brecht—I see something almost impossibly crude and raw and astonishingly musical and political at the same time. That's something that's in my mind now as I write; it's not merely to come up with something *jolie*. I believe in uncontrollable beauty, and I believe in the subversive aspects of beauty. I believe, with Jeremy Gilbert-Roth, that beauty is an uncontrollable element in late capitalism.

In my own work, I see a kind of struggle between Mozart as a standard and someone like Martin Luther King as a standard. And can they be brought together? I don't know. There's been an attempt in my work to do that. My father used to tease me: "You lack the common touch." But at the end of his life, he was reading both *Finnegans Wake* and Proust, and we both believed in that sense of Proust with his double. On the one hand, Proust is amazing music—those great sentences, each made line of his style. But on the other hand, he is a great early *Dreyfusard* and was very proud of it. Proust's every page, almost, is a lance against "ignorance," and I think it's one of the great volumes of assault against novelty, not what some people think is sort of drowning in novelty. The critique of social envy and the kaleidoscope of social envy. As I get older, I notice two things: the starry chaos above and the starless chaos within; Kafka and Proust.

NYQ: You've said a great deal about the idea of poetry as a form of chaos or as an ordering chaos in your book on Ashbery. There, you describe Ashbery as a "Lucretian poet in the minimally explanatory mode," and characterize poetry as "an unpretentious emptiness." Do these statements apply at all to your own poems?

DS: Well, I certainly remember very clearly my conversion to John Ashbery. I had seen a little essay by Kenneth Koch in *The Partisan Review* saying that there was this new telegraphic style:

> I moved up
>
> > glove
> the field

(John Ashbery, "Europe")

At the time I was in love with Theodore Roethke and certain other very lyrical romantic poets, and I thought that John sounded a little noisy. But in the Donald Allen anthology, I fell in love with him again for "How Much Longer Will I Be Able to Inhabit the Divine Sepulcher …" When I met Kenneth Koch in 1962, he wanted to convert me to John Ashbery, and he gave me *The Tennis Court Oath*. And I still remember at night reading:

> I must say I
> suddenly

> she left the room, oval tear tonelessly fell.

(John Ashbery, "Europe")

I thought it was a little filled with static, but then when I read:

> You girl
> the sea in waves.

(John Ashbery, "America")

I thought, "Oh, it's like a melody that's floated up in this static." I, by the way, don't believe completely in the legitimacy of my insight. But at age 15, I did have this great tergiversation or conversion experience in which I believed that John was using the "I" like any other word in the dictionary. I thought, "*That's* interesting." All the discontinuity added up to something that I'd seen in Rauschenberg—I'd already seen Rauschenberg's work—and I loved the multiplicity in John. So there started a long time of my life in which I defended him.

I was very proud to help him publish *Rivers and Mountains*. My editor at the time, Arthur A. Cohen, a Jewish theologian, should get a lot of credit for publishing Ashbery and others. He felt that John was chaotic and "meaningless." I defended John and was able to convince Arthur, at least a bit, that this was not absurd. Another editor, when John wrote *Three Poems*, said to me: "He contributes more to the absurdity of the universe than explains it."

One of the notions of art, said Meyer Schapiro, is that there's a kind of kitsch of abstraction in which people will choose a random bad picture as opposed to a Mondrian because they presume that modern art is merely disordered. What's amazing about John—who once turned to me and said, "Maybe it's time to become coherent again"—is his ability to be elegant and multiple at the same time. I think for some people it became very important to establish that John had certain themes. And yes, he does, self-laceration being one. It appeared almost too much in my book [*John Ashbery, An Introduction*]. But the difficulty that many people had with him is like a difficulty in Cubism. Cubism had its enemies (that's the title of a great book: *Cubism and Its Enemies*), but I think in terms of Cubism and its discontents, there are many critics still who find *The Tennis Court Oath* to be impossibly experimental and would banish it. I know that John does a little bit of this banishing himself in his *Selected Poems*. Like Picasso and Cubism, John learned so much from doing the collages, like "Europe" in *The Tennis Court Oath*, that, no matter what he does, it's informed by the lessons of that Cubism.

I sometimes think of John as a kind of Picasso, but that doesn't mean that his neoclassicism has displaced what he learned in Cubism, just as Picasso's sweetest "neoclassicism"—the so-called "return to order"—still tremendously accepts disorder. I see it as the negative capability that Keats was talking about, the kind of capability within sound itself, organization, structure. All of these things are difficult in poetry because poetry has such a pragmatic view. It may be, Meyer Schapiro once told me, that it was easier for people to engineer formal changes in painting because painting does not necessarily have an everyday pragmatic sense of itself. Poetry is always competing with speech, you might say; it is and it is not speech. And Jakobson said that it's very hard for people to accept abstraction if the brain was organized visually to see the enemy or to see food sources. Many people are looking at an abstract work of art as if it doesn't have the face, as if it doesn't have the psychological face, doesn't have the horizon.

Sociologically, there's a great deal of frustration with the "New York School" poets, which includes me as a kind of mascot early (since I met them in 1962). My idea was to see perhaps how much noise and sound *à la* Cage one could put into poetry while having an effective melody.

NYQ: And somehow that noise, that sound becomes part of the music, a situation you describe in your poem "Cheap Elegy for John" in *A Burning Interior*.

DS: Right, I wasn't religious about chance in the way that would have pleased John Cage. He once said, I think in '65, that I wasn't really going in the direction of chance. I felt that I was using as much chance as I could. I remember when Kenneth Koch found titles by opening a book at random and pointing. I thought that was wonderful. Also, when I was in Paris, I saw a violinist put down his violin, pick up a green umbrella, open the green umbrella, close the green umbrella, and then pick up his violin and play. And I thought that was extraordinarily musical. That's the dance of everyday walk in Merce Cunningham, which was a great influence on me, the idea that we maintain dance but in the most colloquial form.

I spent a lot of time dragging my poetry down a bit—what Koch called the art of sinking. Kenneth Koch loved similes, as in Pasternak, that are drawn from everyday life. "It was hot as the top level of a Turkish bath." Or: "You came by, took my life down from the shelf, and blew the dust away." Or: "Kisses on the breast, like water from a pitcher."

NYQ: What would you define as other important influences on your life and work?

DS: I spent a tremendous amount of time imitating Jackson Pollock and de Kooning in the basement. I was lucky enough to have seen and been converted to Jasper Johns' work very early on, when it appeared on the cover of *ARTnews*. Somehow, I saw it, and I thought that his *Target with Plaster Casts* was just a change in the universe.

You have to remember, too, that I was constantly memorizing Shakespeare, Milton, and Blake as a young violinist. I went from that to memorizing every single poem I could see in certain anthologies. I had a very good library in the Newark Public Library, and I decided to read every single book of poetry in their poetry collection (a lot of it being very bad poetry). But I was very influenced by every poet I read. I went through a period of imitating Dylan Thomas until I could hardly tell my poems from his. Then I went through a period of imitating Yeats and T.S. Eliot. I tried to memorize Eliot's *Waste Land* and a lot of it I still have by memory. I certainly can recite "The Burial of the Dead" for you. I asked Kenneth Koch during an oral exam if he'd like to hear me recite it. He said, "No! No!"

Other things influenced me as well. I was always reading the great Russians, and reading Tolstoy was a change in my life. In England for two years in college, [Cambridge University, where he earned his M.A.], I was able to see a lot of Chekhov. He became after a while my favorite artist: the idea of the mixed style, where you didn't know whether you were laughing or crying at any given moment. I loved the pauses in Chekhov and in Beckett.

When I look back, I think that one of the problems for me was not to become a mere ventriloquist. On the one hand, I paid homage when I imitated others, but finally I realized that one of the most interesting things was to seize, as in quoting. The Israeli poet David Avedon once said to me, "Well, you only quote to agree. What about the quoting against the quote, as it were?" I thought that was very smart.

As a violinist, I had been mostly taught a repertoire that's fairly hackneyed—except for the Bach and accompaniment, which was the sort of thing that is a bible of severity. I still think of poetry as an unaccompanied sonata. But as one becomes older, there is no reason (says Auden) to write poetry unless it's true, beautiful, and also yourself alone. And I think it happens, but, as every teacher knows, it happens in a slow way. It really took me from age five to age nine, and then I wrote about two hours a day, like a violinist—sometimes all day, with a kind of hypergraphia, one might say, I was mad to cover a hundred pages. Somehow, I loved the idea of writing a book. A sort of visionary book was inside me as an idea. When I was fifteen, my friends hated when I called them up saying, "I just wrote a book— would you listen?"

In this way, I learned poetry, though very often before I could comprehend it. My mother would tease me when I memorized *The Waste Land*, "Do you really understand what you're saying?" And to some extent, I felt that I did. *C'est le ton qui fait la musique.* It's the tone that makes the music.

But the best thing that happened to me was when I became conscious enough of picking up other people's tones to be a little skeptical of that. I learned from playing the violin to try to create one's own tone, not merely to imitate Casals or Heifetz—and, usually, one knows the great violinists within three bars, just as one knows a really good line of John Ashbery within about six words. I was very impressed, not by empty technique in violin playing, but the people like Szigeti, Menuhin, and others, who risked scratching and playing badly but had invented their own shape.

Jasper Johns told me about the moment when he decided he was not *going to be* an artist but *was* an artist. He also destroyed a tremendous amount of his early work—as much as he could. I tried to tease him once by saying that of course no one is original, and I noticed that it was still very important for him to have destroyed a great deal of imitative work, and to know that he had become himself at a certain moment.

When I look at my poetry, I think that there was something that I was doing after about, oh, 1960—part of my self is really inside my poetry. This may seem very expressionist to the generation of language poets who are brought up to feel that that's an absurd claim, but I must say I began like many others, although more in childhood than in adolescence. I had certain advantages and disadvantages of being a person who was mostly inchoate. I was trying to carve out my own kingdom, as a psychiatrist once said to me, by leaving music.

Incidentally, I once met E. M. Forster at Cambridge, and I told him that I had "given up music." He said, as a rebuke, very slowly and wisely; "I fail to see how anyone can give up music."

NYQ: Would you talk about the role of experimentation in your work?

DS: There are many poets that I think aren't interested in something I'm interested in, which is the explosion of two words, the juxtaposition that the Surrealists talked about, and the "mild surprise" that John Ashbery used to talk about. Koch used to say, "Put a surprise or two in every line."

The problem of course is that an aesthetics of transgression gets to be impossibly non-transgressive. How do you create surprise? If you have five surprise parties every day, you lose a little bit of the tang of the surprise party. This was a constant problem in aesthetics in the twentieth century, and it's why a lot of conservative aestheticians like to talk about the death of the *avant-garde*. Experiment and the liveliness of poets cannot die. It's much more likely that poetry—not to sound like Bob Dylan—will be busy being born, rather than busy dying.

If there's a new country, there's a new poetry. I was astonished when an anthropologist once said to me that he'd gone to a place where there was no poetry. And I said, "No poetry?!" He said, "Yes, there's no poetry." And I said, "Are there songs?" He said, "Thousands of songs, of course." I said, "Are the songs without words?" He said, "No. They have words." I said, "Well, clearly then, there's poetry." He said, "No. There is no poetry."

When I was 16, Howard Nemerov said to my mother, "I'm worried about what David does." She said, "What are you worried about, Howard?" And he said, "Well, what he does is not poetry." And then my mother, in a great Wittgensteinian defense, said, "Then what is it, Howard?" That stopped him. It took him so long to understand my work that after about ten years, he wrote to me saying that he was beginning to "get it," that it was parataxis.

But to reduce myself to a prestidigitator of devices is to do something that John Ashbery didn't like when he thought I was reducing him to a precise palette of certain innovation. I do know when I see sestinas, villanelles, and pantoums praised in the work of, for example, Paul Muldoon, that someone else was freshening up those forms in a special way in the '50s, like John.

At any rate, I think a lot of us have to struggle—and there is a struggle. Brancusi talked about how very hard it is to live and grow next to some of the great oaks. Kenneth Koch once said to me that he had grown up not admiring any living poets. Of course, this wasn't really true, because he had Auden and Stevens, but it's true that a particular problem that I may have had meeting certain strong poets when I was 15 was that I felt a joy of influence and an erotics of influence—not to sound like Harold Bloom's *Anxiety of Influence* theory. I loved imitating, and I loved parodying, finally. And I think I got more information through loving different poetries than other people have when they think that they're simply isolating themselves.

Someone said it's easy to be a Zen monk on a mountaintop; harder to be a Zen monk within work. And I think it's harder to be a poet in this urban situation, but it's the only way that there could be a renaissance. One can't imagine Shakespeare without Marlowe; one really can't imagine Keats without his dialectical reproach against Wordsworth's egoism.

NYQ: Do you think that to some extent in your work the repetition of phrases and images and ideas is an effort to establish an imprint of the self? It's not uncommon for snow to appear in a David Shapiro poem, or hands, or different colors, even violins.

DS: Well, I sometimes feel that it's terrible to have so much snow in my work. Now that global warming is becoming a reality, however, maybe it will have a political aspect. I once saw a book that was called *The Economic Significance of Snow*. I turned to a physicist and said, "I've never thought of the economic significance of snow." And he said, "You haven't, David? You haven't thought of the economic significance of snow?"

I've thought of snow almost as a Christo—snow as covering up, veiling, simplifying. It was also a way to get away from school, so snow in my youth was also a holiday. It's a little bit of a little bit of nature that gets done, for example, in New Jersey.

But let me just say that there are motifs in my work that I've had to drop due to sentimentality. Frank O'Hara once said to me, "There are a lot of seagulls in your poems. Why?" I was 15, and I knew it was a reproach. I said, "They're images of freedom, don't you think?" And he said, "Huh. Why are there so many?" I said, "Well, *you* have an image: 'and one alone will speak of being / born in pain / and he will be the wings of an extraordinary liberty.'" But he teased me in letters by signing them, "Yours in shaking seagulls." And I never mentioned a seagull again for about 20 years.

John Ashbery wrote to me in those years saying that the real subject matter of poetry was what happens. He liked my poetry because of the recurrences, as in Proust. And slowly but surely, I have come to agree with some aestheticians that repetition is the heart of all art. Repetition not just of motifs, but repetition of sounds, for example, that makes such a scientist of Keats. One feels in Roman Jakobson's work on vowels that, simply put, poetry has this wild element. Dante even speaks of words as hairy.

I'm very interested in textures, rhythms, and repetitions. One of the reasons that I'm still linked to architects is that they know that a building is not just built religion; they know it's not simply ejaculatory—they *build*. And many of them have loved really reading poetry—Rimbaud, Baudelaire, Mayakovsky, Pasternak, Frank O'Hara,

Wallace Stevens, John Ashbery. At Cooper Union, I've done a lot of teaching of repetition, but I think what one learns about repetition, as with parallelism in Hebrew poetry, is that it's always persistent, as Gertrude Stein said. "A rose" is one thing. "A rose is a rose" is another thing. "A rose is a rose is a rose" is an example of a repetition that finally is chillingly funny and strangely beautiful.

A lot of my work is not just to make these repetitions or parallelisms, but to invert them, to strangle them, to inflect them. We're dealing with repetitions, but we're also dealing with a repetition that counts. Otherwise, it would be very easy just to take a time signature—4/4, common time—and feel that all one has to do is "da DUM ba DUM ba DUM." In Donne, late Shakespeare, and Wyatt's great "They Flee from Me," there's always a tension in which rhythm becomes alive.

I used to love John Giorno's doubling, but, as with anaphora, repetition can become repetitive. One really has to watch out. I've noticed in my work the kind of thing that Allen Ginsberg was picking up from the Bible, Whitman, and other key thinkers of repetition. But even in "Howl," one has to be very careful to change a lot between the lines and inside the lines. Otherwise, the "who" becomes, at a certain moment, reflective, automatic, and one knows that Ginsberg himself had to drop aspects of that in any later poem. Some of his better poems, like "A Supermarket in California," have enough repetition, but sort of a mechanical anaphora.

I'm always trying to release myself from automatic continuities and discontinuities. And it's not so easy. I've learned from Chinese poetry and sometimes Rimbaud, who is up there in my starry firmament as my standard, because he was a dazzling Latinist who knew how to write in every possible form. He imitated the first Romantics, the second Romantics, the Parnassians—he imitated everything. But, at a certain moment (it may have taken him a few years), he becomes this dazzling, disdainful creator of that new thing: the prose poem.

A lot of my life has been lived under the rubric of prose—trying to make my poetry as well written as Pound, but also as well written as scientific prose, and as well written as Flaubert. Fairfield Porter said a very wise thing about John Ashbery: "He writes poetry as if he could also write a good business letter." I sometimes worry that in a way my poetry isn't prosy enough. I'm sure it's one of the reasons the younger New York poets thought I wasn't grungy enough. I've tried to learn from Guston's second phase—cartoonish, simple. To a student who was spending too much time in being pretty, he said, "I'll show you how to make a clock," and made a very simple circle, two arrows, some numbers. "That's the way to make a clock."

Because of a book I helped edit, *Uncontrollable Beauty*, I'm often linked to a kind of Paterian stance. That wasn't what I was trying to do. I tried to create a book that would show a lot of opposition to beauty, skepticism about beauty. Meyer Schapiro thought that beauty was a hypothesis. He was constantly showing imperfections. When Barnett Newman liked a painting and thought it was "perfect," Meyer said, "Would it interest you to know that a few inches were lopped off in the 19th century?" Some people seem to think that I have a Catherine Deneuve complex, that I'm looking for an aesthetic of easy symmetry. But what I was actually trying to do throughout that book, if anyone reads it, is to set up essays that show how tortured the whole notion is. So when an ex-student of mine said, "Poets babbling of beauty—there I draw the line, although I can accept wounded beauty," I felt like saying, "Duh! Of course, I'm talking about wounded beauty."

At any rate, I'm very influenced by the moment in 1906 or so when it is said Pablo Picasso took a trip to the Museum of Natural History and decided that a mask is not pretty or beautiful, but magical and powerful. A lot of the things that I truly love dislocate usual ideas of beauty. When Jasper Johns did a very dark, huge work called *Diver* it was almost utterly stained with melancholy. I heard someone depose him as "related to the 19th century and Symbolism." Well, we *are* late Symbolists. But I don't use that as a way of deposing or lamenting someone. I think it's very powerful that we are still in relationship to the greatest visionary Romantics. Hölderlin is John Ashbery's favorite poet, and mine.

Cubism and Surrealism, said Frank O'Hara, divide the world. And they do divide the world for me. I can't imagine my poetry without thinking of the dislocations of the Cubists or the oneiric, hallucinatory, and convulsive in Surrealism. That's one of the ways in which I'm canonically out of Novalis's *Pollen and Fragments*.

NYQ: Let's discuss your career as an educator. You've been a very committed pedagogue for much of your life and have often collaborated with young people—perhaps most notably with your son. How has working with young people changed you, if at all?

DS: Teaching has taught me a great deal. Over the years, I've taught (whatever that can mean) poetry and now, I've been very happy to teach as an art historian for about 25 years. I love doing very close readings. And I've had very good students—Luc Sante, Jim Jarmusch, Phil Klein. I've also been teaching architects a kind of "City and Poetry" course at Cooper Union in a special seminar for the last 25 years. I've learned from all of the arts and the dynamic spin of all of the arts.

When my sister Debrah was born, I was often put in charge of her. I taught her the violin. When I said something was "sharp," she'd say, "How do you know?" I found that to be an amazing moment in teaching. How do you establish for the student—except by dictatorship—that you know when something is sharp or flat? The violin, of course, is an instrument of intonation.

Kenneth Koch laughed at me when I began to teach little kids, because he couldn't quite believe—at that moment—that there was a lot of aesthetic dignity in children's work. Later, I helped him teach kids in Bedford-Stuyvesant. I really always loved to do it. He was very interested in creating formulae that you couldn't lose with, and I think that was brilliant. I was interested in having kids do something that Tolstoy did with peasants, that is, tell their stories. In my collaborations with them, these stories became poems, and poems became stories. I sometimes couldn't tell where my work started and their work ended, and vice versa, but giving kids autonomy was primary. I happen to like playing duets, and some poems became very close to being duets. I published some of them in *A Man Holding an Acoustic Panel*.

Fairfield Porter once said, "Teaching is a great sin. What can I teach?" I thought this was very funny, because in a year or two he had taught me so much about painting that I thought of him as one of my great teachers. He once said that he would teach me foreshortening, and I stayed up all day like a night student waiting for what he would say. We sat down, and he said, "Now draw what you see." And I said, "Is that all?" He said, "Yes, draw what you see."

Of course, as in gymnastics, one can give little exercises. "I used to be, and now I am" was one of Kenneth's favorite exercises. (I finally said, "I used to be a blank, and now I am a blank.") I think that even great athletes learn a lot from push-ups, sit-ups, and stretching exercises, so I think it's very useful to practice, even all day. But one learns in teaching not to end with stretching—not to end with gymnastics, but with dance. And it may be that it takes a tremendous amount of time at the bar, a tremendous amount of time playing scales or arpeggios. I very often teach so that it goes from the smallest thing to the largest. I will begin by teaching tiny exercises of similes and metaphors and little games of epithets and perhaps, with certain people, metrical games. My son and I would walk to school, and we would write in the air, as it were. Haikus, tankas. I remember teaching him Homer by teaching him how to sing dactylic hexameter. If one gets used to these things, one can rhyme while walking.

Kenneth Koch loved to rhyme improvisatorially, and so did Allen Ginsberg. But when that's over, and you've spent ten years imitating every poet who ever lived, I say read Ezra Pound's *ABC of Reading* and everything it says to read, and then read everything it says not to read. That's a pretty good reading list. And after all this reading, which is like paradise, you are at the beginning of being able to do an architecture that is one's own. One's own shelter, one's own refuge.

I'm sure that some people think that I am hobbled by learning, but I'm much more hobbled by ignorance, it seems to me. One doesn't know how much one needs to know. But re-reading James Shapiro's book on 1599, one understands how complex the plays of Shakespeare are, embedded in their context.

I also think that poets need to work a great deal. Jasper Johns once said, "You write a lot, but publish a little." That's the way. I love the severity of Jasper, and I also love the way he doesn't want to teach. He actually is one of the great teachers. I've learned more from him than from almost any other human being. And what does he teach? Well, as you watch him work and develop and change, you get a tremendous sense of his highest standards—the discipline that you feel in his constantly *not* abandoning motifs. I compare him to a jealous lover in Deleuze's sense of Proust, that you keep working for the traces of this thing. I once asked Jasper what he thought of Morandi, and he said, "I find him repetitive." I said, "People actually think that of you." He said, "I know, but I really do find Morandi repetitive."

I do feel that Jasper's ability to keep burgeoning and finding new motifs without giving up motifs—and the way he went from what seemed like a non-psychological or anti-psychological mode to other modes—is an example of courage. And I do think devotion is very important. One thing one can learn from teaching, like regularity in psychoanalysis (which John Ashbery said was the only thing he learned from psychoanalysis), is that showing up on time, as Woody Allen said, is part of genius. Often, a poet must write uninspired work to get to something that is inspired. John now says that he's invented a mode in which he doesn't have to revise a lot. But it took him 20 to 30 years to really get to the point where the rhetoric flows in that amazing way.

You know, my standards are Wallace Stevens, Bach—they're very high standards. Arthur A. Cohen once said of Judaism: "It may not be true, but it gives you very high standards, at the least." "It's not up to you to abandon the task," says a rabbi. "It's not up to you to finish your work or to abandon it."

Poets write for many different reasons. Montale said that he felt that his poetry had reached its destination when it was read by Mayakovsky. I thought that was odd, because I never thought of Montale as courting Mayakovsky, but I know that when I was 15 and I thought John Ashbery was reading me—that sometimes seemed sufficient. Delmore Schwartz said to Meyer Schapiro—though most of their correspondence is lost, unfortunately—that he would rather have the response of Meyer Schapiro than anyone except perhaps the Eliot of the '20s.

For a long time, when I wrote a book, I liked Kenneth Koch's idea that a book could be sent to anyone. You can send a book to Catherine

Deneuve, you can also send it to Schweitzer, you could send it to Whitehead (if they're alive). One does transmit one's work to many different people. I knew that Meyer Schapiro would be one of the first people to whom I would send my poems. He cared about things that were of concern to me. He knew when I was alluding to Luria, the neurophysiologist. But it wasn't just references; it was a sense that poetry matters.

One of the things I realize now about why I was so close to John Hejduk was that he cared about poetry more than most poets do. When the Romanian president came to Cooper Union, Hejduk gave him what he said was "the best thing that America has to offer." It was the collected poems of Emily Dickinson. I gave the leader a stone, because he was a geologist, but John was giving him perhaps the very best thing that America has to offer.

NYQ: Would you talk a little bit about your process? You've mentioned that you produce considerably more than you publish, and that you labor particularly over the poems that you do print. So it's not at all like catching butterflies, although your poems do have an air of virtuosity about them; it's much more a matter of gestation and a near conflict to produce.

DS: Well, it changes at different times. Now that I'm an "old poet," I feel—without sentimentality—that it would be very useful to have another lifetime or two. Poetry has to be written between patients, as with a pediatrician. And one does sometime get envious of every form of contemplation, meditation, recuperation. Most of my life, I've written music and poetry. At nine I started to write every day, and I kept my poems because a madman said it would be very useful someday. They're now in bins and bins, thousands upon thousands of poems. That's not so strange; Kenneth Koch told me that he also wrote so much. He panned for a lot of false gold and then he'd get gold.

In 1963, I wrote a hundred sonnets, a hundred villanelles, and a hundred sestinas. None of them was good, but I felt that I learned a great deal by writing them. Those are exercises and arpeggios. As a violinist, you're very used to exercises, and you don't believe that sabbaticals work at all. They work against you.

But it's interesting to see when one can come up with something. For example, sometimes when I'm sick, I can write well because I'm slowed down. It used to be said of Keats that he did better when he was sick. But certain things have helped me more than others. I know that writing sonnets, for example, or pantoums, or villanelles, is very often able to cheer me up toward a certain amount of violinist discipline.

One of the things I did, by the way, was to take prose from cheap sources, like physics textbooks. A lot of my poems come out of science, and out of science museums, and out of the very aesthetics of science, you might say. And that prose is at least inflecting a lot of my poetry. I did many collage poems. I think that my Einstein poem, "Snow at Night," was a collage of footnotes of idiotic things that a biographer or two had put down. I was twisting the language to make a lyric of Einstein that I didn't feel had been done—Bob Wilson not having done his *Einstein on the Beach* yet. Also, there's a villanelle in Lateness ("I Haven't") with the repeating line "Do you have a lion in your house?" It's a collage from *See It and Say It in Italian*, some really stupid, loathsome volume that had this silly graphic thing. Then I wrote a villanelle ("An Afternoon with a Lion") with the repeating line "To the lion and away from the lion." By the way, I've decided to do one for Language poets in which "Lion" is changed to "Line." [F. W.] Dupee once asked me, because he had a bad hearing problem, whether it was "Lion" or "Line." And now I feel it's really good:

An Afternoon with a Line

Toward the line and up to the line:
First you were too dazed to gaze into the line,
Around the line and with the line

Hand over hand you were getting into the line,
Sniffing palm trees and floating upon the line
Toward the line and up to the line.

In the seventh frame you slipped above the line
Into the white sky beyond each line,
Around the line and with the line.

> Now under the line, smiling under the line
> It's a light green day edges toward the line,
> Toward the line and up to the line.
>
> But how is one to get out of the line,
> One's hat and stick sticking out of the line,
> Around the line and with the line?
>
> You ran away from the line and away from the line—
> Amazed and apart, days away from the line—
> Toward the line and up to the line,
> Around the line and with the line.

I used to wake up wondering if someone was going to be angry with me that I'd turned their physics textbook into something. The poem "The Page-Turner" was actually sent to Kilmister (the physicist-astronomer) because I was rhyming his prose and changing it in a million ways, and he said he was delighted to have a poem that was accurate.

I write in many different ways. I used to be able to put on music and simply write because the music was on. As a violinist, when I eat a madeleine, I don't remember anything but Proust, but when I put on Chopin's Mazurkas it takes me directly to 1962, when I was listening to it. Or when I put on certain quartets, it gives me my entire family vista. So one of my techniques, in terms of getting started, is simply getting to that inspired state. Kenneth Koch used to say that just to get into that state is the *real* task of poetry.

I also find that it's very useful for me to write in many different modes. I think it's useful not to wait for ten years till a voice cries out in the *Duino Elegies*, but I do take myself by surprise as much as I can—by giving myself very difficult assignments, for example.

The most difficult assignment is to summarize one's entire life in a long poem. I don't have the virtue of monotony that I think Gertrude Stein truly had. I've often wanted to make an oceanic poem the scale of Morty Feldman's late, late music—which can go one for four hours or six hours. When I was in England for two years, I constantly thought about what it would be like for a poem to be as melancholy and dense and gray as a Jasper Johns light bulb, which happened to be in the possession of one of my friends there. In those years, I kept thinking about what a long poem might be like in the condition of Rauschenberg or in the condition of Jasper Johns. I finally decided that if I wrote hundreds of poems, I could find a way to put together movements.

My chief standard was Mozart's *Divertimento in E-flat major*. I wanted something as fresh as Glenn Gould's attack—where he turns the piano into a poem of glass, almost—and I wanted to toughen up my poetry. I went with my wife to every science museum in Europe that I could manage, and I constantly collaged, put down, and transformed bits and pieces of different parts of the Europe and America that I saw were devastated by imperial problems. So I wrote "A Man Holding an Acoustic Panel" and tried to make each movement a different rhythm, a different theme, a different attack, and yet unified so that it would have to be read at one gasp. It often isn't. I remember writing it out in long lines like Whitman. I finally divided it up, so that people could explicitly see—sort of like notation.

I once asked Elliott Carter why we don't put down notation for poetry, and he said, "Ugh, it would make it even *more* difficult." But I often think that when people think that they understand rhythm, that the oral tradition is so wavering that (just as every pianist plays Bach differently) meditation is the beginning. However, I do find, for example, that I love patter in Shakespeare, I love changes in tempo in moviemakers like Preston Sturges, the constant changes and silences of Chekhov. Okay, those are my standards. So where does one begin?

Very often, when one is old—speaking of catching butterflies—one does know where the butterflies come from. You may know their migration patterns, and I'm sure that people do get better at catching them. Of course, the famous dictum is that poets have to get struck by lightning. And if you're struck by lightning more than once, it's really amazing. But if one is capable of being struck by lightning, one might become—I saw this in an *Information Please* almanac—like a man who was struck by lightning eight times ("he was unlucky in love, too," they said).

Jasper Johns was once on the floor, and I said to him, "It must be amazing to always be able to do something at the highest level." And he said, "Are you kidding?!" Inside the practitioner may be the good, self-lacerating sense that one isn't simply at the highest level by fiat. There are people—and this may even happen to me, at my age—who simply get tired from the constant wear and tear of writing.

To many people, it doesn't seem to be that exigent. My father used to be very upset by the fact that I was just going to write poetry for a particular time, when he thought that *that* could be done—*and* violin playing, *and* painting, *and* being a doctor, being a little more useful. Certainly, some in my generation have a romantic notion that not having a job except poetry meant that they were poets. That sounds good, but I also think there was a lot of bohemian rhapsody to that idea. Actually, it isn't the worst idea to think of Dante, who, when exiled from Florence, said, "Well, who will take care of Florence, now?" He was a sort of a mayor, practically. And I don't think it hurt Williams to be a doctor.

I've tried to learn from art history, because they are my sisters and brothers. (I think of the "sister arts.") One of my methods is to look at a painting, and, as Baudelaire said, to make a response. Very often, my best responses are just poems. For example, I one day saw the Mantegna *Mary with Sleeping Child*, and I wanted to make a poem as stony as Montegna sometimes is, but in this case also very touching and uneconomical and excessive. So I wrote a poem *au courant* at the Met, which doesn't seem like such a romantic place—but it *can* be and, for those of us who love art, the libraries and museums are the spooky, uncanny places for our real religion. Once I was heading down to see parts of a Giocometti, and I said to my wife, "I guess I really am an idol worshipper."

Of course, I have noticed the complexity of trying to get a linguistic object to be like an architectural object. Or, to make a house, as I tell my kids, in the condition of a sestina. But they've been able to do it. I'm very proud of my students. When I see a Jim Jarmusch film, though he's very different than the New York School, I often feel that his is one of the great dialectical achievements of a certain kind of poetics. Maybe I'm too proud of my students, but I must feel: Poetry doesn't stop.

Part of the work of poetry, I think, is reading. If you asked me how I write, I would have to say that poems come out of poems. Not to sound like Harold Bloom, but they do. They come out of painting, they come out of music, they come out of architecture, they come out of civil war and imperial war, they come out of personal catastrophes and joys, but they also come out of this pantheistic, Shelley-esque choir. I take it for granted that life would be different without my grandfather's voice, which I'm always trying to imitate in poetry. Or my grandfather Wallace Stevens.

Just to give you an idea of how I write poetry, I believe it was Richard Kostelanetz who once asked me who my favorite living poet was. I said, "Wallace Stevens." Kostelanetz said, "He's dead!" And I replied, "Not for me."

I was once taken to task by Tony Towle: "Don't think that you're the only person who loves the tradition." And that's certainly true; everybody has different forms of it. I'm right now in front of my ten thousand books. I always dreamt of having a library that would have, in a Borgesian sense, all of the analogies.

My son used to say, "Have you read all of those, Daddy?" And I said, "More than once." I try to memorize what I really love. Poetry for me is a memory machine. There are poets who would say that that's why my poetry is too simple, and it could be. The idea that a great work of art is not memorizable, is not memorable, is very strange to me.

The art critic Robert Rosenblum pointed out to me in a terrifyingly blunt way that of course one couldn't have a complete research library. What I think one can have is a library of the important books. Whitehead once joked that everything is a footnote to Plato. He also said, "There are ten important books, but what are they?" And, as I look at my favorite bookshelves, I have a lot of the things that I need, from *Don Quixote*, which one can read forever. I have Wittgenstein in my library. Kenneth Koch once said to me, "But don't we know all that, David?" I don't think we did. I'm passing T.S. Eliot next to Stevens next to Wheelwright, a very neglected poet—I love when he says:

—"What was that sound we heard
fall on the snow?

—"It was a frozen bird.
Why must you know?"

(John Wheelwright, "Why Must You Know?")

"Why must you know?" really breaks my heart. And the poem goes on....

Also in my house are a lot of paintings, and I've grown up around sculpture. It's very important for me to have "my friends" on the walls, as it were, and paintings that have really inspired me. Like the art historian Blunt, I used to think that you might as well have no paintings, because you can't get the Poussin that you want. But I've been very lucky in having friends who have given me beautiful things to look at, and I think that's important.

On the other hand, for years I've been confronted—I'm looking out my window now—by a brick wall. I've often thought about the fact that *zazen* means "sitting" or "a brick" or "a wall." And I've written a poem called "Wall" about whether I do or do not want to represent it. A critic once said to me that she only understood my work as a word connected to another word. She found it too satirical, too surrealistic, too abstract. Kenneth Koch, when he heard this, said, "What's left—rational tragedy? *Cato* by Addison?"

I want to say that still, and all, I do believe in metaphysical poetry. I'll tell you a story that reminds me of what I'm trying to do in poetry. Francis Ponge came to Columbia University. As with Borges, a lot of us respected him enormously. I asked Kenneth what he thought of him, and he said, "Well, you know, I was talking to him, and I asked him what he thought of New York. Did he like the big buildings? But that was a stupid question, and Ponge just said 'So what?' And then he said, 'But I do notice that on your martinis you place a cherry, and on the top of Riverside Cathedral you have a red light. You Americans have a mania for cherries on the tops of things.' And then I knew he was a genius." Writing poetry can be pushing forward, where your intonation gets better and your poetry has more grip. The poets who've developed in that way I brood about a lot, now that I'm 60 and not 15. I brood a lot about whether I am developing, whether I am deteriorating. That's what an old man thinks. We're tramps, Yeats said, and the young are in one another's arms.

NYQ: To follow up on the general process discussion, do you ever get blocked? How do you contend with those periods?

DS: Usually, the obstacles become part of the method. It's not that I'm a Ulithian, but I am a person who likes limits, constraints, rule systems (although I can deal with permission, too). Remember that poetry was a great comfort and utopia for me—I guess what religion is for certain people—because it brought me away from a kind of prison of interpreting other people's work on the violin to being myself. Very far from being blocked, I sometimes go through periods where I just don't want to cover up more paper.

However, I sometimes go through these periods in which everything turns into poetry, and it's actually very panic-making. For example, I think I was a poor student at Columbia—although I was almost all A's—because when I went to geology classes, it all turned into these words that I loved: "magma chamber," "incline," "anticline." I still remember those beautiful words, although I couldn't quite see it as geology. Of course, I do think it's useful to know things for themselves. (I was always sad that Allen Ginsberg seemed, I think, to be disappointed in me except as a violinist because he thought I was "too intellectual." I don't think there is a limit on what you should know or could know.)

I also sometimes go through terrible phases in which I use up every single surface in almost comical hypergraphia. I once had a dream in which my Latin teacher said to me, "If you're going to be a poet, why don't you fill up every piece of paper in the world?" And then I was blown out of this dream by a gigantic wind.

I think I was always afraid of the Wicked Witch of the West, because I had seen *The Wizard of Oz* too early, and the Wicked Witch of the West is a lot like being blocked. Not only can one not be blocked until death, but even after death. An Australian poet had a dream that Frank O'Hara was dead but still writing. He said, "What a guy!"

At any rate, as a teacher, you get to be like a sexual therapist, and it's a hard truth that one is of course always blocked. One is not, says Freud, at the highest potential. You can love and you can work and you can consistently realize that your hysterical misery should be turned into ordinary unhappiness, or what I call "ordinary happiness." I think it's very hard for anyone who's an adult not to realize that they have learned so little and that the art is so long. I am certainly beginning to feel the terrible finitude of being able to practice. A lot of musicians my age say that they've now learned how to practice—and learned how wonderful practice is. I've always wanted to write a book simply called *Practicing*. Some of the greatest experiences you can have in music are very often practicing, in which you're not playing in front of someone. Glenn Gould hated that idea that you were simply tortured by the addressee. If you want, I know a hundred different exercises. It doesn't mean that you'll go to the gym that day, but you know the exercises. Of course, the chief exercise is to be inspired.

In my classes, it sometimes seems as if people think I'm shoving something down their throats if I love something and they don't. I once asked Kenneth Koch how he thought we could get people to like our poetry. He said, "We'd have to have them since childhood." Now that I'm publishing a *Selected Poems*, I know that there will be people who will not like it. I know that I simply cannot hope to convert X or Y or Z to what they see as the horrible nature of my poetry. My wife sometimes says when I'm rejected—at least, when I was younger and was rejected; I now simply don't send out very much—she'd say, "But of course they reject you; you'd reject them!" Although I am a pluralist, I can sometimes be very monistic in matters of taste. It is hard to convince me that chocolate ice cream isn't good. (It may not be good *for* you.)

It's very hard when people don't like the comic in Kenneth Koch, where I can't imagine life without it. Once a person in 1962 responded badly to a poem in which Frank Lima describes his being seduced, or raped, really, by his mother. It's a poem called "Mom, I'm All Screwed Up." And a woman raised her hand and said that she couldn't stand the slang, the obscenity, and the horror of the poem. Kenneth Koch said, "Yes, yes, but I can't imagine English literature without this poem." That's what I loved about the great teachers: they made you feel that you were capable of a masterpiece immediately.

Empson is right that many poems simply had to be written in order to save the poets from madness, and that those are our best poems. Then, there are poems that Kenneth Koch and I used to say were merely willful. But those are very important. I'm not even so sure that people who love his poem "One Train May Hide Another" don't realize that he could do something like that almost every second with anaphora and a certain conceit. Some of the best poems Kenneth said he had ever written came out of being in love, which made him very clear.

NYQ: We've talked a great deal about certain media and their significance for you, including painting, sculpture, and of course music, but we haven't discussed cinema. I know, for example, that you teach courses in cinema. How has film been important to you?

DS: I'm lucky because I was hired by a university that wanted me to teach not only Roman art, Roman design, the history of modern art, the history of modern architecture, ideas in art, and a museum course in connoisseurship, but also three to five different courses in movies. At the time, I wasn't sure that I could do this. I suddenly felt, I guess as everyone does, like a charlatan in teaching movies, despite the fact that I've known filmmakers and have even been involved in making one or two. But teaching movies has enabled me to see masterpieces every few days. On Tuesdays and Thursdays, I would suddenly see Eisenstein, and I'd have to comment. And my eyes, I think, grew better at looking at movies, because, for the last 25 years, I've seen an Ozu or a Mizoguchi every few days.

I agree with many that it's certainly one of the great art forms that we can see the beginning though not the end of. It's finite. When you study proverbs from the Bible, there are twenty-thousand volumes on them. Now, there are probably too many volumes on movies, but the great critics, like my friend Gilberto Perez, who wrote *The Material Ghost*—great movie criticism is relatively finite, or at least that's my delusion. It's much more finite than the history of Indian sculpture and all world sculpture, for example.

I've tried to show my classes an anthropology of film in which you see film as a route toward other countries and mental traveling—that's one version. The other version of my teaching movies is to teach what

Eisenstein called the film form and the film sense; to teach movies as if they're poems, poems as if they're movies.

I'm very interested in, let's say, a movie project that gives 50 or 60 directors a Lumiere camera, a few seconds of non-synchronized sound, and a minute or two to make a movie—something that would provide cause for all the great directors, like Kiarostami, the Iranian master, to make amazing things out of a tiny, brief haiku. Haiku is obviously cinematic; I'm sure Eisenstein points this out someplace, as he does throughout his published work—he establishes the analogy between literature and painting, and theater and cinema.

I'm also very interested in the film form and the film sense as it relates to montage in language. I was able to work with Rudy Burckhardt finally; we did three movies together. Working with him fascinating. He would sometimes ask me to look at a film that was finished and give him a poem for it. But I found sometimes that it took 16 poems, and very often I collaborated with my son. Also, with some things, he would take a poem of mine and set it to images. "When a Man Loves a Woman" was a poem I gave him to illustrate, and he did amazing photographs for it. It was printed as a tiny book that I hardly have a copy of anymore. But I was very moved by how he could set my poems—illuminate them, not illustrate them.

We would joke about that. At some point, he said, during a rain scene, "Maybe you can say it's raining now." And I thought to myself, "That is exactly what I *won't* do." But it was very moving, his humility. I used to ask him how he took a certain shot, and he'd say, "Well, I'm old; I took it out the window." He turned to my father-in-law and said, "Photography is a young man's art, because you need to be very dynamic and *get there*." It upset my father-in-law, who was starting to be a photographer at age 60 or 70.

But cinema really has been one of my greatest delights, and I've learned so much from teaching movies. In Ozu, I learned what it was like to have an image that was again almost beyond meaning—what they call the "pillow shot"—where he shows something, and you really don't know why he's lingering over that vase. Is it because it's a vase of ashes? Is it because the vase is order? Is it because the vase is one of those things that, Arawaka once told me, was sort of "alive."

Godard says, "My films have a beginning, middle, and end, but not in that order." And, of course, that was one of the great lessons of my life, and a sort of non-Aristotelian moment. I said to Frank O'Hara, "Maybe even *Paterson* by Williams has some lines that don't have to be there." And he said, "So what?" And that "So what?" really resonated with me, it taught me a lot. It meant: Get away from your neoclassicism.

NYQ: You mentioned some of your collaborations with your son, Daniel. In some respects, you seem to have incorporated your parenting and your relationship with your son into your work. How did those collaborations develop?

DS: I must say that I felt blocked in a Zen sense, when I was a parent; I simply didn't have the time, it seemed to me, to write in the same way, since I had to take care of my son. When he was about one or two, I noticed that if I wanted to write poetry, but I had to parent him, or be good to him, or play with him, I wouldn't be a very good parent. What I did was put up huge pieces of paper, and I got him to paint on one side while I painted on the other. And that was really fun. Then I started to take down everything he said, and to teach him how to write poetry. We wrote many, many poems on the way to school.

I have to say that my son taught me, though, in amazing ways. He reminded me again of *kindersprache*, or child speech, which is so amazing. When he was angry at me, he said, "You're the boss of God? You're not the boss of God!" And I said to him, "Oh, wonderful, let's go upstairs." But he was still angry, and he said, "Are you more famous than angels?" I said, "We *have* to go upstairs." And by the time we got upstairs, he knew that his anger had been transformed into poetry. A psychoanalyst used to say that, yes, poetry is carved out by liberty, but it's also true that in times of catastrophe, I've found that poetry is the one thing that I can "do." Of course, it's also true that one can play chamber music—one can respond in different ways.

When my mother was dying, my father said, "Have you ever noticed that this amount of suffering is not in the books?" I felt like saying to him, "It is and it isn't." One does try to point toward moments of pathos, though I have a friend who thinks that art is exactly *not* pathos. Whenever he sees an Expressionist work, he says, "Pathos, pathos, pathos!" But you lose a lot of art that way. I think that art can be extremely humorous, and not. One of the funniest things about learning from children is that form of comedy that they have, which I think is tragic for us because it points to that moment when one didn't need comedy to laugh—that phase as a child in which one has the oceanic or the polymorphous and perverse.

You know, I was always impressed that Freud said he never experienced that oceanic feeling, because there were times in my life when I couldn't imagine not feeling it. I once turned to an Italian friend, and said, "Ah! I had a few weeks of really feeling close to some transcendental terms—feeling that I was beyond the world, or inside the world." And he said, "Two weeks! That's amazing. Some people don't have it for half an hour!"

Music and poetry both—and what is cinema, except music and poetry and painting together?—can sometimes create in me such a feeling of the oceanic. When Bresson is really doing his best in *Au Hasard Balthazar*, in which a donkey is the main character, you do feel that something has been created by the fusion of all those things.

One day after my mother died, and I have a poem about this ("Friday Night Quartet"), I said to her in a dream: "Perhaps you'll give me a new form from paradise." Sort of an Oulipian question for the transcendental. And I felt that she was going to respond, and I was terrified. I looked at a lake, and that was terrifying, because I thought that the answer would come somehow from the bottom of the lake to the top. Not to sound like a sentimental Jungian, but I found myself staring at that, really terrified that she was going to respond. But lines of color came up, like a color sestina, and I was being told that the way poetry was practiced in Paradise was in lines of color. That was a way of knowing that the *Gesamtkunstwerke* is not the last thing—there's an amateur welding together of everything, but there's also a way, skeptically, of putting things together. And those have been some of my greatest experiences.

NYQ: You've just touched on dreams. Do you dream in different languages? Many of your poems have an almost dreamlike or subconsciously infused quality. What relationship does your poetry have to your dreams?

DS: If I were going to advise someone in terms of craft, I would say, "Learn more languages, and learn them between zero and five," which is when our brains can do it. Everyone knows now, like Chomsky and others, that kids are the best linguists, and we should really teach everyone at least two other languages, I think, from zero to seven— and onward. I feel as if my best and first language was music. I didn't speak until I had already started playing the violin. They thought I was tongue-tied, and they say I've been talking ever since. For three years, I didn't speak—very funny for my friends now. Your question was dreams. Fairfield Porter asked me how I had written my poem "The Devil's Trill Sonata." I said, "Well I hate to say it, but I get a lot of lines in my dreams." He said, "Oh. That accounts for its dreamy quality." And from that moment on, I felt, "I'd better not do this, or tell people that I'm doing it." When I was young, I not only had repetitive dreams that were nightmares, but I also began to find that I was being given language. In about 1962, I heard in a dream: "The Cuban car doors smashed to bits." And I became very interested in why my Jungian friends could have ten-page dreams, and I only had one-page dreams. Bill Zavatsky made me jealous because he had a lot of Jungian dreams that were simply vast. When I was in England, reading that one gets the dream one deserves, I thought, "I never had dragons in my dreams, or snakes with strange feet." That night, I did. And the voice of God rang out, "There is nothing wrong with the architect!"

Anyway, I was interested in lucid dreams, but I found it very Californian and embarrassing, so I'll only say that I learned how to memorize about 16 lines (since I love to memorize), and a lot my poems secretly are mostly given to me in dreams. Of course, I have collage poems, like the Einstein, that are constructed, but I do sometimes get poems in dreams. But they still have to be put down. "Father Knows Best" came in a dream. My wife used to hate it when I'd wake up at

3 AM and have to type. She'd say, "Take it to the bathroom. Take the typewriter away."

Here's an anecdote: When my son would go to sleep, I would say, "Have a poem in your dream." He called me "Chief Poem-in-a-Dream." I used to say to him every morning, like a Hopi Indian, "What did you dream about? Did you get a poem in your dream?" And he'd say, "No." That might have been too mechanical of me. But one day he said, "I did have a poem come in my dream!" And I said, "Oh, what happened?" He said, "Well, an angel came down." I said, "An angel—wonderful!" And he said, "And it had this big scroll." And I said, "Fantastic!" He said, "And he opened it up!" I said, "That's great! What did it say?!" He said, "I couldn't read it! I don't read cursive." That was a very famous moment between us. I said, "Well, I think it's still a wonderful dream."

Very often, I'll get dreams that I can use as poems, but I do agree with Kenneth that you shouldn't have a poem with "indigestible dream fragments." That is, if I know that it's merely a dream, it's sometimes just useless. However, a great deal of my poetry comes to me in dreams, sometimes as pieces of paper that float down until I see the words on them. But it is embarrassing to talk about that. I'll simply say that there are many different ways to write poetry. I used to love to feel at six o'clock that I'd already worked enough. I would wake up in the morning, right after the poem or the dream, and feel that I had done my work.

A psychoanalyst's child, Larry Weider, once said to me, "Why do you want control over what should be uncontrollable?" There are so many visions of dreams. My friend Roger Kamenetz is in a dream community, and he's writing a book about dreams in which the dreams at a certain moment are sacred. One doesn't want to talk about dreams too much, but I must say that you should force your classes always to have dreams. A person I knew said that he had faked his dreams with an uncle of ours who's a psychoanalyst for a year. I said, "It doesn't matter if you make up a dream; any good psychoanalyst worth his name would still—just as if you gave him a poem—be able to say something about it." I think it's very funny to spend a year, though, faking your dreams like faking orgasms. It's a very funny and probably interesting mode of being split.

NYQ: Which poets are your favorites to read? Which poets have most influenced you?

DS: Yes, I haven't told you my favorite poets. Well, it's obvious that there are certain people I respect in the New York School. Jimmy Schuyler for his perfect nature-worship that I love so much. Fairfield Porter wrote a poem that I love, "The Wave and the Leaf," about "a pang of hope" that he felt in the particular. I love his poetry, and I've grown to love it more and more. But the poets who've really influenced me, after Shakespeare, Milton, and Blake, are the poets of the Bible. A lot of my work does come out of Hebrew poetry and Jewish prayers. Different countries have really influenced me. When I left China I said, "This is where I should be buried." It's very important to know that, from Pound to Waley, some of the most beautiful poems that we have are the T'ang poets, Li Bai and Wang Wei. And then I'm very influenced by certain visions that you get from Japanese poetry, as in *Zen and English Literature* by Bly, one of my secret favorite books. I think of the Du Fu that I know, you have to have the right translation, and my favorite translation is William Hung.

I think that for many people, being pointed to other poets is part of the craft of poetry. One of the things that Frank O'Hara did for me was not only to get my poems published before I even asked him, which was a sweet thing to do, but when I was 15, he gave me a gift of *Safe Conduct* by Pasternak. In the old New Directions edition, *Safe Conduct* has poems, stories, and a memoir, and each one is fabulously important and beautiful for its own sake. That was a very good lesson of what a poet needs, which is to be pointed toward Wallace Stevens.

But some of my favorite poets are from Italy—Montale and Dino Campana are very important to me—and France. The whole tradition of Nerval, for example, and, as I get older, Baudelaire's wisdom inside these very subversive poems, like "Le Cygne" where he's "dressing as the enemy," as a spy in the enemy camp.

Walter Benjamin is one of my favorite readers. I think of him as a poet; I think there's been a mistake made about Benjamin, where he's either treated as a Marxist or treated as a supernaturalist. There's another way, which is to treat him as a poet, where suddenly I think it's very clear why he spent so much time translating Proust, or Baudelaire. He's a poet. And his great poems are in *One Way Street*, which is just fabulous—it's one of the great books of poetry in the twentieth century, but it's not thought of that way. It's thought of as a commentary on philosophy by a philosopher.

Those are just some. Part of the craft, I think, of poetry is to learn the craft from other people. And who are those people? Very often, Auden said, they can be minor poets that you can get better than. But I do think, instead of the anxiety of influence, it should be called "the joy of influence." Keats talked about that, too. I've been joyfully influenced by Rilke, by Jewish poets such as HaNagid or, of our own time, Yeshurun.

Frank O'Hara joked that most poets alive today were "useful thorns in one's side, but not very good," I do read my contemporaries, I read my students. But, since life is short, I also try to put on AM and FM. It's not so easy to divide them, but I'm very interested in anonymous ballads and what I can learn from songs. I would love to write a book of just songs. And there are many other things I want to do.

I've only written bad novels. I wanted to write a Rauschenbergian novel which would encompass all different forms, but I wasn't brave enough to do it. I wanted to write a novel that would just be a dream diary of a man intersecting with the dream diary of a woman—just because my wife and I kept hundreds of dreams. But when I tried that, it was a little too warm, not cold enough. It would be better for a Nabokovian to do it. There are still many forms for me to deal with.

NYQ: Many of the influences you list exist outside of the English language and beyond the languages with which you're most familiar. Rilke was an example you mentioned, and I know that in your most recent book *A Burning Interior*, there is a translation, or a poem after Rilke. How do you go about translation?

DS: Everything is translation—so much so that I call it "mistranslation." Every day, for years, as one of my exercises, I would wake up, take something like Reverdy, and instead of translating him faithfully, I would make a kind of variation, cadenza, mistranslation, vowel translation of him. I remember I would take Raymond Roussel's *Locus Solus*, and, turning it into a rock opera, I would rhyme his prose. I tried to do things like that that would jar me into new imagery and new worlds. And each poet of course was like that. I've always been interested in the poetry of other worlds. Wouldn't it be great to get to another planet and find out what their music is? I love the idea of sending the *Goldberg Variations* into the air.

But yes, every day for many, many years, I would translate. I spent my junior year translating almost all of Rimbaud, sometimes very faithfully, sometimes not. I have a sort of palette of that. I love taking languages that I don't know so well—German, Italian, Romanian—and trying to translate them. In fact, one of the exercises I give to my kids is looking at a Wang Wei poem and creating a new poem from it. My poem "A Mistranslation" was made from taking a Wang Wei poem where, for example, the moss might be green, or the moss might be black, or the moss might be blue. I finally just decided to use them all—"blue green black moss."

I've learned a lot by translating. I think it's the greatest discipline. I've only been able to translate certain poems, if any, satisfactorily (to me). But from age about 15, I was very interested in learning the poems of certain languages, as Pound suggested, even if you didn't know them. I think that Pound got to be a worse and worse translator of the Chinese as he began to think that he knew it. Nothing is as good as *Cathay*, where he didn't even know Chinese. I certainly feel the pathos of someone like Akhmatova, who wanted people to rhyme her, but I also can't stand the fact that English doesn't have the greatest number of rhymes and that, therefore, there are many ways to translate Akhmatova. The best that I can find is a prose tract. In fact, I'd rather have the prose translation of the *Divine Comedy* than almost any of the twenty or thirty rhymed translations.

When I had to teach the "Great Books," by the way, I would have every single student bring in a different translation of, say, the *Iliad* or the *Odyssey*. I think that by seeing the variance of prose and poetry translations, you begin to sense the impossible perspectivism of translation. I don't like it when Robert Lowell makes Pasternak too melodramatic, but, on the other hand, there's a melodrama in Montale that *only* Lowell gets. I once told him I wished he would translate all of Montale.

I've always said to Richard Wilbur when I see him that I feel he should be locked up in prison—just to finish all the Molière plays. Although I've never felt so close to his poetry, I do love the way his Molière works on stage. It's amazing. And I think that Kenneth Koch should have been locked up a bit to have translated more of the rhymed poems, or just to have finished his translation of Ovid. He's probably the only person who could have really done Ariosto.

Kenneth Koch used to say that part of his craft was to read a little bit of Ariosto—*a little bit* of Ariosto—and then write. He would get what he said was "immortal energy" from poets like Lorca. And I can't read it now without thinking of Kenneth Koch reading it to get excited. It's the same thing as people who need erotica. The eros of poetry sometimes is getting inspired by the last poem. This is what I call the "eros of influence." And I've tried to convince Harold [Bloom]. I once asked Meyer Schapiro what he thought of the theory of anxiety. He said, "It's obviously wrong." Since I admired him, I said, "In what sense?" And he said, "You know, poets become influenced just by Rembrandt's moral example." One doesn't have one father figure in art, one has many. You may have a specific anxiety toward your father, particularly because you've had one, but Keats talked about a tuneful chime. I said that to Harold Bloom, and he said to me, "Yes, but there's always ambivalence, there's always ambivalence." But he does talk about multiplicity of responses toward influence.

I think the great poets, like Keats, have learned from Shakespeare, as an infusion of blood, not as a vampire father figure. So we have to watch out, as Joyce said, not to be too "Jung and easily Freudened." But I will say that it's been amazing to see some of the great poets develop, like John Ashbery, and sometimes it does seem to be a very daunting moment.

I think it's useful to know, as I'm publishing a *Selected Poems*, that a number of people will despise it. I can see the weakness myself. But I am a poet, only a poet. I'm not better than any other poets, and they are not better than me. That would be a terribly confident thing to say.

You know, when the Surrealists came to New York, people said that they learned from them. What did they learn from them? That they were just human beings—they were no longer "The Masters" in books. People say to me, "Become a great man, don't *know* a great man." But one of the things that helps, says Kenneth Koch, about meeting the poets that you like, you learn from them, they're noble competition. But what he didn't say is that you also realize that they're human beings with all the frailties and horrors and sadnesses that you have. That's part of the craft of poetry, meeting your masters and other apprentices.

NYQ: Auden very famously said that poetry changes nothing, and yet it seems that your involvement in the arts has certainly changed your life. Is it true that poetry changes nothing?

DS: Well, that's a famous matrix. It's a little bit like talking about whether poets are the "unacknowledged legislators of the world." At different times in my life, I've had different feelings about this—it's a political and aesthetic question. Neuronal mirroring has shown that human beings empathize in one second with other human beings. It's almost a biological invariant. There are different parts of the brain that, when you see someone smiling, give you a determination of what's happening. The lack of empathy for that is in Auden's statement, because Auden is then, I think, skeptically and darkly, and to some extent masochistically, and extraordinarily reductively saying that art produces nothing. But one actually knows that a law is simply a poem that's been instituted. As Meyer Schapiro pointed out, we know of no societies that don't treasure fine objects. Auden might have said that underscore the *d*, as in throwing the proverbial pebble down the Grand Canyon and waiting for the echo—said to be literary criticism—it's often a very good thing for people in this wreckage of a mass society to understand that very little may happen or might happen. The poet feels crushed, and so do other sorts of artists. Giacometti makes his art—almost—about what little reality he can wrest from "woman at a distance." And you can't imagine more suffering than Auden, a great poet, saying in the midst of a poem that poetry makes nothing happen.

Actually, it's interesting, because its within, let's say, a poet who could write ballads, like "Refugee Blues," that were extremely political, and that *do* make things happen. One can't imagine, let's say, the war against Hitler without the different arts—cinema by Capra. Hitler knew how powerful art was, that it made things happen. Hitler's a good counterexample, because he as a monster knew very much that monsters should be photographed as beautiful. And he was always manipulating the movie industry, not to show suffering, but to show heroism, to show himself as a hero. And he used Leni Riefenstahl and all of those people he could seduce, from Heidegger on down—or is it, Heidegger on up? Very great mountains were made to be the witnesses, the false witnesses. And I think that Nolde was rejected, though he wanted, as an anti-Semite, to be part of Nazism. He was rejected because his art made too much happen, in the direction of modernism. Poor Nolde, one of the horrible chapters in the twentieth century.

I think it's very bleak to say it makes nothing happen, and too idealistic to say we are the unacknowledged legislators of the world. Something between that, in a polarized way, making memorials matters, making the right memorial can really matter. The Vietnam War wall makes something happen. You see yourself inside that stone, right? When you see your reflection in the stone of the Maya Lin memorial, and if you touch the dead *and* see yourself, something has been set up. I think that Auden, though, as a skeptic who later needed a conversion, wants to remind poets not to be too proud. So it's a lesson in *vanitas*, to learn that we're "just entertainers."

De Kooning said, "I'm like the guy in the circus who stands on one finger. Who told *him* to do it?" On the other hand, when Guston changed his style and everyone hated him—and really, even Morty Feldman wouldn't talk to him for twenty years—Guston being very brave, de Kooning came up to him and said, "I get it: it's all about liberty."

Fairfield Porter taught me again and again to think about this libertine quality in art. He would say that it was very difficult to make a good picture. And then he would find in my doodles something he said he could put on a wall. He once placed a doodle of mine on a wall, and I felt so grateful, because he was saying there was something shameless in that that was better than my other work, where I was trying in another way.

You do have to teach people that their words count. The poet Tory Dent, when she was dying of AIDS, found nothing better than to use language as her central constellation of resistance and consolation. And I think Tory taught me a lot. We would meet and talk almost every day. For about five to ten years, we certainly talked every day. And she was a person who was about to be executed by AIDS, as it were, though she lived a long time. She was a great teacher of courage, but she also showed how much she could use poetry as a politic.

I think poets should help each other, and of course that's exactly what we do. A friend of mine once said in college, "It's hard for a leper to have a hypochondriac as a friend." I said, "That's a defense of why we need Kafka. Lepers should listen to other lepers." That is, if we're all damaged in particularly interesting ways, we need each other as compensation. I find it very hard to believe in life without Mozart, chocolate, snow, or James Joyce.

Godard said something that I want to end with. I felt that this is perhaps—part of the craft of the poet is confidence in getting over simply the fear of paralysis and failure. And Godard was asked what he would say to the people who said that his movies were not so good. And he said, "But what about your hamburgers? I eat your hamburgers and they're not very good. But I do my best." And then—that moved me a great deal—and then he says, in a film, "[I am] a man, nothing but a man, no better than any other, but no other better than he."

Graves are something that mankind does, and so anthropologists that I work with have always pointed to the skull in first sculpture, and death itself as one of the great themes. I think that gift-giving—and this sounds sentimental compared with Mauss, the anthropologist, who thought that gift-giving was always exchanging—the best way is perhaps when Louis Hyde talks a little sentimentally about the fact that the poem is a gift without getting anything in return.

And I do think that gifts are very important, make a lot of things happen, and I can't imagine life without gift-giving. I can't imagine anything more gift-giving than, let's say, de Kooning's generosity or Frank O'Hara's magnanimity. They are people who are almost famous for the idea of giving, as in Keats's letters.

A Birthday Notebook for JA: *The Vermont Notebook*

1.

I became converted to Ashbery's poetry between 1960 and 1962. Kenneth Koch said to me, You will see there are only three poets—John, Frank, and me. I said, as we climbed a little hill in Staten Island—I was fifteen—What about Martin Buber? Kenneth laughed: Why bring up Buber? He's a minor Jewish philosopher. I said, clumsily: Sometimes I would rather be a minor Jewish philosopher than …

2.

One night in August 1962, I was reading *The Tennis Court Oath*, a book given to me by Kenneth earlier that day. I read some of the fragments and thought: He uses the word "I" like any other word in the dictionary. Then, looking at a little phrase, I thought: this is like a little melody but surrounded by a fog of dissonance: "You girl / the sea in waves."

3.

Then, a bit of a conversion experience, as Elaine de Kooning said of her painter friends falling off their horses and becoming abstract painters; as if in a change of name or religion: from Saul to Paul. I thought: he is using skeins of language like the new painter (for me) Robert

---

Conjunctions: 49, edited by Bradford Morrow (2007). Part of a portfolio tribute to John Ashbery for his 80th birthday. Shapiro's contribution focuses on *The Vermont Notebook*, with art by Joe Brainard (Black Sparrow Press, 1975).

Rauschenberg. All this flat newspaper is a brilliant strategy. I remember writing to my mother that week and saying that I had found the most wonderful Cage-like music in Ashbery. I was so happy.

4.

One day, slipping into a car, John told me he agreed with me that he was "like" Jasper Johns in many ways. "We both seem to like the lazy exploration of ourselves," he said, with his canonic —is it skeptical?— smile.

5.

John once asked me, Do I have to read Jacques Derrida's work? I said: You certainly don't have to read it, since your work comprehends it exactly. Derrida, Michal Govrin, and I built a book about prayer. Jacques, whom I teased as a Jewish poet always, said he could imagine a prayer without hope. This prayer is the only one he could accept. I think that. John's work is also heartbreaking because it prays in hopelessness in a time without hope.

6.

One of the events of my life was receiving from Koch's hands a new typescript of a poem called "The Skaters." I distinctly recall waiting for a poor line or something that did not work. I read forty pages with the sensation a young violinist has listening to Heifetz play with Piatigorsky and Feuermann the late Mozart *Divertimento*. I loved each line of this poem and still feel it is the masterpiece of John's work, though I might say that of many long poems from "Europe" to "Girls on the Run," from the infinite tenderness of "Self-Portrait" to the acoherence of the dual strophes of "Litany," to "A Wave," "Fragment," "Clepsydra," and so many single lyrics, like "The Chateau Hardware," "Voyage in the Blue," and "How to Continue." Oh, it is impossible to praise Ashbery adequately. In those moments when no criticism seems to count, I recall that one of the things I love about John is how far he seemed always from dogma. I used to think the New York group would be some of the only ones without a critical corpus or a critical echo. I was wrong; but I still hope

JA will not be compulsory like potatoes in the reign of Pasternak's Catherine the Great.

7.

Kenneth Koch and I were talking about John's "The Skaters," in 1963 or '64. I had asked early on, What do you think this poem is about? He giggled and replied: It's not about anything, but it is a complete philosophy of life. John later wrote his own poem about systems and philosophies with much mirth and fecundity of irony.

8.

If I am asked to write about any Ashbery poem, I do so, but I recall that in my first volume on John I suppressed chapters on *The Double Dream*, his plays, his art criticism, his literary criticism, and his marvelous translations from the French. I usually think that the best is an endless practical critique, which would take every word and every trope, every specious simile, and every drowning elongation, and make a tonal reading inch for inch. That is not to say one cannot sum up some of John's themes, but danger lurks there.

9.

Let me say what I think has been mismanaged in Ashbery criticism, and I still think his work could be better approached than by dogmatic critics. If one only finds Emerson in him, then one will find Emerson in a grain of dust. If one only finds his sexual predilections, one will miss the eroticism of language itself. One shouldn't be so easily Freudened, but I think the ideal reader will actually see his pantheism and nature-mysticism. But that should not deny how much of a parodist he is. Don't forget the humor; don't forget the Watteau-like delicacy of his gallantries. It is a poor student of Ashbery who only turns to his most coherent pieces and remarks that *The Tennis Court Oath* should be thrown away. Everything Ashbery has done comes out of that great revolution. Like Picasso's cubism, this, say, cubo-futurism of John inflects all later poems; he cannot avoid being the poet who was once characterized as a man in a good suit with ink on his shirtfront. John is a poet who encompasses romanticism, secularism, cubo-futurism, John Cage's religion of chance, and the elegance of Pope. Allen Ginsberg once asked me: "But can you memorize him, David?" I then quoted long passages from *The Tennis Court Oath* poem "Rain." Allen demurred: "Oh I get it, it's Alexander Pope." No, it is not one thing.

10.

The multiplicity of John's work is the mastery of many perspectives. He changed his style almost before others had a chance to imitate him thoroughly. Like Picasso, of whom John says there came a time when he was used to creating beauty, John seems to have managed and mastered so many rhetorical modes that he might become lost—as in my own critiques—as a magician of devices. He is not merely that prestidigitator, but I think Helen Vendler is very close to the mark when she suggested that for a poet, self-reflexive poems of poetry are not merely self-reflexive—for a poet, poems of poetry are as visceral as any Eros.

11.

When I am asked how I think John has developed, I must say it is a startling and even dazzling path. It has the "human unity" of which Meyer Schapiro spoke, with Picasso's oeuvre in front of him. Picasso always seemed capable of making a group show a stylistic set of different, even antagonistic, ways. But to the one who has not only read "The Skaters" but heard the voice within, I don't think we see a mere literary development in John's work but increasing wisdom and even tragic late poems that are almost of the unutterable, as with Beckett and Johns. These are the poems of growth, which we feel in Yeats. They are the wisdom poems that Eliot said would be the greatest signs of a poet's growth. I think that if one can understand cubism and surrealism, which divide, O'Hara said, the world between them, one should be able to understand Ashbery's twenty volumes and the addenda. His perverse taste, so-called, has become almost canonic: He now seems, even to his enemies of many years of rivalry, an unavoidable poet. He has the daunting hijacks of a wizard of spelling bees—but he also has the soul that is not a soul, the secret that brings tears to our eyes. If one reads him from *Turandot* to the most recent lyrics—I underline "How to Continue" as the greatest poem of AIDS and private grief made public that I know of our epoch. If we look at all of this, we will find not eclecticism and not tergiversations merely. We build up a sense of his gray luminosity, of that special tone of self-laceration and Miltonic strength that is indeed his pride and his architectural and "human" unity. His plays hang with these poems delightfully. Recent volumes have become even more unnervingly dry or secco as in Montale. They are the least operatic and the most abrupt music reminding us, of course, of his continued rapport with Carter and the theme of abruptness that Carter once said was his chief desire. Like a folksinger elegantly gliding back to the spoken phrase, Ashbery has drained his poetry of false or glib euphony and has cried out sharply; this is the hot perspectivism that makes him our philosopher poet.

12.

His *Vermont Notebook* is filled with humorous positivism, like a Constable cloud traced by an engineering student. With a Joe Brainard illustration of an isolated figure in one version, the notebook starts with the comical delineation (and melancholy) of the months: October, November, December: This little "note" allows us to realize we do not know what time is and whether Ashbery in any way is trying to be "accurate." We doubt it, almost immediately. Just as the stars in "The Skaters" Chekhovian ending never rise in that order. (He told me he "liked the sound.") Taurus, Leo, Gemini. An enigmagram. The only thing really "datable" is the long hair of the male figure, seen in black from behind with enormous locks, a fashionable statement.

13.

Later, the notebook simply makes a slaughterhouse of names and places. Parking lots are close to "war memorials," and the whole is like a dump site for shifters and even shiftier nouns and common nouns. I have been most horrified by his list of crimes, which has the blank easiness of *Roget's Thesaurus*. Ashbery once asked me whether I was telling others that he worked from the dictionary. I said I didn't but that I didn't think it would have been an insult, since I loved turning to the dictionary, like tubes of paint that one might drink.

14.

There's a mighty minimalism here and very iridescent reductions. He gives us all the colors of the rainbow, as if nothing were more dead than color charts. Before crime come games. And after games comes my favorite Eros of this poem: a seemingly endless (when recited) list of friends and celebrities, poets and painters, colleagues and doppelgängers. I appear here, and I immediately felt that there was an extraordinary capture happening. Like Picasso, this poet loves to possess, and his satires are infinite. The names from Hess to Obolensky, from Benjamin to "Bricktop," from Mark Strand to Daisy Aldan to David Shapiro—one wonders if this is free association or really a very compact linguistic guide to the bachelorhood of the sign, as one used to say. Dine made a "Friends" canvas or two; on which he scrawled his proper names and proper nouns. But he allowed certain people to be bigger than others, creating a kind of loose mandala of his life. Ashbery is colder and more comfortless. The notebook becomes Kafkaesque. He has reached that hot moment, degree zero.

15.

Then he has parts of houses and material (tweed, cotton, silk). There are no predilections. In a lyrical moment, the parts of speech get entangled: "plug, dream, mope, urchin, distress, ways, many, few, found, dreaming, unclad." Koch once told me that he was even jealous of John's dreams, and certainly that is an exquisite admission. Here John turns a *catalogue raisonné* of American pure products into something as oneiric as a Joseph Cornell box. He has always taught me that poetry involved distribution and Proustian return, not an obvious content. "Sleep, reef, perfect, almost." See how this catalogue reinvents aspects of *The Tennis Court Oath*. It could never be as bumptious and agrammatical without "Europe." Let the reader beware. With Joe Brainard yielding an animal's puss, face, or mien, John writes one of his most dismal scenes.

Out of Stevens, out of Stein, out of de Chirico, out of psychoanalysis and dread, he speaks of the man of the dump, now the man in the dump, now the man who is almost telling the narratology of the dump "I will go to the dump." This is a true admission. As Kay Boyle noted years ago, "John tells great truths as if they were lies." This strophe, paragraph, prose poem, apart, gives us the tang of Schwitters and the detritus of the day, Freud's debris of dreams. And if one doesn't feel the tone of suffering, one has lost a great deal of the pathos. The analogy with the gray, severe, melancholy work of Johns cannot be avoided: "… it is printed on dump letters." No, "in" dump letters is his precision. And Ashbery comes close to a very revealing sentiment. "As I swear the dump is my sweet inner scope self …"

16.

The prose poems are not as sensuous as Rimbaud and are certainly not as moralizing as Baudelaire. They are escapades of his sweet inner unconscious dump site. Rauschenberg put it this way: "If you can't make an artwork out of a single tour around your block, you are not an artist." And from prose poems, we come close to details like food lined up in Brainard's illumination or anti-illustration. But the Menippean satire does not slow: "The high-flying clouds are eyewash." Here he reminds us of the poet who could mock Schubert and could use Constable clouds as a cover for a book. There is winsome electricity, if one can bring those together as tempi and principles and pressures. John is as breezy but elite as the Goncourt Brothers in their great notebooks and journals, sexual and anxious, descriptive, and impossibly aslant.

17.

Aug. 7. The TV is on in Joe Brainard's great untitled illumination. And the caricature of white noise is as funny, and fresh, as a Crumb cartoon. And like Crumb more than Schuyler here, he caricatures his own situation: "I think I believe this, but there is a sound in the next room." All is hilariously included. All is misunderstood, as in Freud and Koch's poem to misunderstandings. The religion is not chance but change.

18.

Nov. 3. Ashbery gives one of his most depressingly accurate and acidic lines about the whole community. He says that excretion makes him embarrassed for the whole of humanity. This is hilarious and Darwinian and mighty and mild, at once. He is a master of discretion. He has said his mother's mantra was, Never put yourself forward. How can one be, however, a poet of the scale of Stevens, without Bach-like confidence? He achieves his monument with the maximum of Lucretian materialism and the minimum of arrogance. "Something moving. Not everybody but a slice."

19.

"America is a fun country," John declares, but he also becomes suddenly obscene to mock the American socius in a special way: "This is a lot of bunk and our own President plays it right into the lap of big business and uses every opportunity he can find to fuck the consumer and the little guy." But the tone might be the parody of a political tone. He told me his animadversions about Schubert in "The Skaters" was simply a test of "how many opinions I had about everything." Everything in these poems is still put under the eraser fluid of a quotation mark. It is annoying for many that the poet seems not to be able to escape from the humor of quotation, but it is a strong tendency in Ashbery to make his brightest colors still go gray with pain or iridescent gray. He is not putting himself forward. John Ashbery, at least, is one thing: he is not an infantile leftist. But he reserves the right to a peaceful Chaplinesque plume of a protest (see Michaux's poems about Plume; the adjusted one, the crushed one).

20.

This is not a poem that ends, it includes. Lyric poems are suddenly stuck in, as if photographs on a valise or memorial. The prose tries a thousand angles of nature description, but usually, as the poet says, he sees his own face. Is it solipsism, as Bloom once suggested out of Wittgenstein: is it not solipsism that at least has the right tone? The horror of liberation, as he says elsewhere. Not a poet of happiness but of a realism of the stunted potential, he is willing to admit to a grave darkness at the center of his "lazy," actually severe, self-exploration. This is the soul's notebook, where jottings, dates, and dilemmas ("little nuts big nuts) are all included.

21.

Porter praised Cornell, as I would praise Ashbery, for including the highest and, I would add, lowest reaches of the human spirit. In Cornell, there is a toy glass, there is a marvelous sun and moon and the exotic escape in dreams and in all those childlike "toys for adults." Cornell once exhibited his work at "child" level. Let us say that in John the longing for an escape from the self is as uncertain as any solipsist could hope for, but all painted and parsed by a very fastidious assembler. He does not carve, he does not mold, he doesn't even let be—he assembles, and this is his analogy with Picasso, Rauschenberg, and Johns, a man who could make a memorial out of a target, a biography out of numbers, and a masquerade out of the letters of the alphabet.

22.

Let us remember that the poem is not always best approached without love and receptivity itself. The poems of Ashbery may seem so open that they become, like Hamlet, that rare inexhaustible thing, the irreducible fact of great art. For this reason, some exclude *The Tennis Court Oath*, and some exclude *Self Portrait* as too Eliotic. But just as Picasso gave birth to the art of Mondrian and Tatlin, to Braque, who gave birth to much of Picasso, and to Juan Gris, whom he did and did not understand or admire, so Ashbery has been one of the forces that gives birth to many other poems, and this may be the critical statement. Ashbery makes one want to read and to write, and, as someone said of Meyer Schapiro, to be slashed by reality. His eclecticism was once brilliantly compared by John Ash to the New York motley of midtown and the whole incoherent city. For all of his ecology now noted, what could be more urbane than his particular pastoral?

23.

Jan. 2. Multiple Choice(s): Ashbery uses the notebook as a form, to be almost as attentive to the particular as that mature poet Jimmy Schuyler. But he doesn't need the telescope or microscope to render his lascivious fictive voyage into the blue suburbia of America. Koch said to me of "The Skaters" and we may say it of the *Notebook*: "Isn't this the loneliest poem you have ever read?" (August 1964).

24.

To understand the wit of *The Vermont Notebook*, and much else in Ashbery, use Meyer Schapiro's infinitely witty remarks about cubism and collage. First, the master art historian reminded us that collage is an old story—think of the textures in medieval uses of gold and other jewels and media. To reach the multiplicity of levels in the *Chair Caning* collage of Picasso (1912, very mixed media), Meyer lectured about linguistic analogues. Listen, to these levels, as it were. I am Meyer Schapiro, I is or am a pronoun; I is a straight line. Thus, Picasso and Ashbery and Joe Brainard's non-illustration drawings show us the chair, the profile of the chair, and the raw slippage or passage of the medium itself. The critics of Ashbery have made a mistake. They have attached themselves to one part of this axis of the multiple aesthetic. They have concentrated on John the I, the man, the sexual; they have concentrated only on the lonely slippage; they have, as I often have, delighted in the abstract musicality of the textures Dante too extolled. But the density of John's *Vermont Notebook*, "Wave," "Litany," "Fragment," *Three Poems* (which is really one poem), or even the smallest, "The Chateau Hardware," is the way he combines these "stages" of the semiotic, and without theory, a young poet might fall in love with the sexuality, the melody, the noise, and the aesthetic innovation given at once. Like Constable, he does not just yield a cloud on a bus ride or any state; he is elated like Meyer Schapiro, and his aesthetic elation makes him a rare poet of happiness. Even when he utters his terrifying line "I am still completely happy," we laugh at this Chekhovian momentum. Even when he hates himself and calls himself early on "a chair-sized man," we know his Chaplinesque strength and the wilderness of his quest.

25.

The Vermont Notebook is a long poem, or is it a play, or is it a meditation aesthetique? And it is a Menippean satire of many styles. It is, of course, a sequence, and not least, not quite a "notebook." The dates are fudged, the places are dislocated. Shoptaw has documented that this poem is not of Vermont. It is not of any Vermont you and I will see. It is a mental, symbolist Vermont. It is a pragmatist's universe. July 6, Cambridge.

26.

In Ashbery there is no Platonic heaven, no uninflected affirmation, except the shameless shame of the human body. His so-called distortions or difficulties are that of the lived nobody, the internality of the body, as Paul Schilder put it. Ashbery's broken notebook is the bright book of life for those who, like Kundera, are searching for the "dump site of Europe." Intricate and almost infinite, his mazes lock us into pleasure, if we read correctly. Like William James, inside the multiplicity of Wallace Stevens, here we have a notebook toward a poem. And those of us reveling in ideas understand also the great farewell here to all violating dogmas and too simple ideals. He is proud of those fat Poulenc notes that to some are minor phases. A dictionary of clichés is not a cliché. Parataxis is the guide.

27.

For those who have underlined landscape in his work, I would say he is a critical regionalist if one remembers his ecstatic region is the mind. And perhaps, to change the philosopher the best model of the human mind is the internality of the body. Cezanne's doubt and Morandi's faith here come together in our inescapable comedy of the American sublime. Brainard's collages and sketches remind us of the reiteration of the child. Ashbery once told Cavett on television that his parents didn't know "what to do with me." He remains a whiz kid but of wisdom, and like Henry Green, a constant violator of authoritarianism, a poet on the run, and a poet who knows that standing still is also wise. Music by Busoni swells.

The Painting that Took the Place of a Mountain: Letters to Tsibi

There it was, word for word,
The poem that took the place of a mountain.
—Wallace Stevens

To Tsibi Geva from D. Shapiro
Riverdale, New York, January 2, 2008

Dear Painter,
Or should we say architect, or sculptor, or video-artist, or thinker, teacher? Or should we say dear brother, father, colleague? I write to you from Exile on a little computer that I disdain, but it brings us closer, or does it stretch us further away? You grew up on a kibbutz, and we should never forget that. But your real address is Israel, and I would like to say my own, before someone in the States accuses me of being an ambiguous American. I often describe myself as a Russian poet, and this is partly how I see you. It is true that when you filled a wall with automobile tires, I was probably less aware that these had other and secret meanings. Your displacements of space honor conflict by awareness and attention and tensions that cannot be merely from the American world of business and late capital. We might think of you, as Walter Benjamin did Baudelaire, as a secret agent in the enemy camp, but we also agree with the man who said: the only enemy is the

---

Tsibi Geva: Mound of Things, Works and Projects 1982–2008 (Tel Aviv Museum of Art, 2008).

word "enemy." In your lattices, adorned and pierced and laden, we are given a special form of Eastern calligraphy. Your work, like the great Jewish poets of ancient Spain, is written in Hebrew and Arabic. This bilingual communication makes your work very close to a sacrifice of idols. Both of us know how our tradition is iconoclastic; we are the ones who should menace the world of mere images. But this is also a relative proposition, because we know from students of Israeli art, like Meyer Schapiro, how synthetic, how syncretistic Israeli mosaics are. And who could look at your terrazzo work without being filled with the joy of the mosaic?

We may raise the specter of [Walter] Benjamin once again, a man of Galut and of the tragedies of Homecoming, the man of no luck, who is always with us, nevertheless. Benjamin said of the essay and the mosaic that they were peculiarly the modern form—the peculiar gaps, the idiolects of discontinuities, and the sharp edge, like sudden low words in the poetry Benjamin traced, from Proust through Kafka. And we may add, if this work of yours does not contain Proust's rage for decoration and horror of all snobbisms, then we do not have a foundation-stone to lie upon. Our God must include in the new prayer book Proust and Kafka, or we cannot pray. We pray in the dark light of your darkest birds, trees, and flowers, because we are aware of the starless heaven above and the starry disorder within. In this sense, your work may look like Basquiat's but cries for other interpretations and is not unraveled until those multiple doubts emerge. Your badge of courage is to unite this method of revealment and concealment, as Bialik had it.

Now I want to praise you in the highest form of my pluralism and the purity that Meyer Schapiro told me cannot be forgotten, because no pluralism can contain such purity. Your great work of black and gold mountains is for me a leap beyond the painting and poetry of our time and scene. Your work in the mountains reveals, like Rothko, a lack of complaint or even ejaculatory demonism. Your mountains are also not the literal, though we know they are also the landscape of your life in Israel, mountains of Justice and Injustice, to adapt a poetic title. Your mountains emerge also as allegories of a surrealist summit and depth. But we also can only expect to glimpse in them their maximalist force and demand by understanding the Maimonidean levels of interpretation and suspicion. As the Zohar says, if it says anything, the stories cannot be mere stories, or we could have thousands of entrancing stories. Jewish art is not Scheherazade. The art that you propose in each mountain is an art splashed by a mystical intuition that makes it sacred when we are immersed with the profane. I cannot forget that it is Gershom Scholem who proposed in one speech the antinomian habit of finding God, as in Whitman, in a blade of grass. The more we read the tormented early diaries of Scholem, the more we see how entirely turned to revelation and mystical Zionism he was. Your work, for me, cannot be understood as realist, socialist, symbolist, or allegorical. It combines in a syncretistic fashion to launch images that are indeed clear darkness.

Riverdale, New York, February 13, 2008

Dear Tsibi,
I look at your flowers and trees and am struck by what a colorist you are. The critics have had a problem with Jasper Johns' *grays*, which are not *gray*. For you and for Jasper, as Schapiro described cubist analytic tones, these are the colors of thought. Your way is nobly to find out then the rhymes between brown, white, and a variety of passages between. Thus, a hundred rainbows of modulations can be seen in your least aggressive forms. And as Picasso told William Rubin, it is not always an object that one finds, but it is perhaps more like the flavor or "fragrance of an object." Your long skinny blossoms are thus uniquely your own, even less symbolist than Mondrian, but also, at the same time, those flowers that could be described as "beyond" flowers, as they achieve a density that is not always naturalistic. Your elongated flowers also often have the "glamour" of Pollock's *The Deep*, which staggered the poet Frank O'Hara with its Melvillian strength. Somehow, your birds, trees, and flowers always demonstrate your fine draftsmanship, so that the clear edges of these "figures" fight with any tonal diffidence. You have broken here with the quarrel between line and color. Your white—something true of Robert Ryman—is

filled with a palimpsest and *pentimenti* of color. These figures must be understood, I would assert, before your mountains to have an adequate sense of your mastery. I observe, for example, how a liquidity of sepia and brown and foggy grey can make the flower echo within itself and be falling upward rather than in scientific grammar like so many Mondrians.

A bird perches on a branch. You have reminded me of how often these are your true country kibbutz branches and birds and blossoms. Still, it is impossible for me not to remember Poe's ravens often and other portents rather than country particulars. Perhaps the best way to meditate on these is again to use the four-rung ladder of interpretation, from literal and symbolic, to allegorical and anagogical. Isn't there a way in which we must remember that the very word "surrealist" was invented by the poet Apollinaire, who risks misunderstanding by inventing the name for a whole century of works that are irreal, unreal, or relatively more-than-real, uncanny? "Uncanny" is the word for those things that Freud says we are frightened by, not because we know them—country birds, symbols of lament—but, because we cannot know them, except as codes and more than codes of an accelerated grimace. Each mountain is as terrifying as Rilke's angels. Your birds are so thin and filled with lamentation that we remember them as if a special *niggun*, a wordless hymn, were given for the sadness or melancholy studied by Benjamin in *The Origin of German Tragic Drama*.

As I look at the desperate flowers, whose petals may resemble, after all, the spiders of Louise Bourgeois, we recall her uncanny way of saying what her art was about: "The spider is my mother." Your work is never bland or desiccated as a mere dream-world, because you are insistent on a kind of erotic uncanniness. We are at home, and we are not at home; we are frightened, because of the paradox of primary antitheticals. *Shalom*: hello and goodbye and peace, but as if war were already trying to be comprehended inside our greetings. One way to see these monstrously beautiful blossoms is to note that they come forward as Mannerist giant hands floating in a Parmigianino. The blossom is bigger than the sky. The petals are more damaging than the scythe. The whole is calligraphic and speedy as Chinese ink.

What do the Chinese call the perfections? Painting, poetry and calligraphy. Your work is always an accompaniment of the sacred texts. This is what keeps them from being decorative. Whereas Mondrian fights with the vagaries of Theosophy, I find a direct Hebrew in your motifs. That is what must disturb those who find in your barbed wire and in your *keffiyeh* too much timeliness for comfort. Kafka's cold comfort is underlined with every line: "There is comfort, infinite hope—but not for us." These are indeed prayers without hope, as Derrida and I once formulated, with Michal Govrin suggesting another formulation: "Prayer in a time of hopelessness" or "The Body of Prayer." We cannot be comforted with anything less than this utter refusal, in Kant's terms, to grovel.

Your flowers are as filled with movement as a Calder mobile. Whereas we might have suspected the painting without hope to give us stable scientific specimens, we get in you the surrealist slice of impossible libido. There are chrysanthemums which I have seen grow to forbidding heights of ten feet. Then there are strategies to make ten of these flowers burst into bloom at the same moment, like an ecstasy of birth. That is perhaps the best way to see your series paintings. Not to see the flowers, trees and birds as happening in a narrative of Monet-like change and flux. To understand these blackened buds and uproar of ground and quasi-collage—to comprehend all this—is to understand the niggun of painting itself, painting which creates simultaneously a cinema of itself. They are dancers; they are prayers; they are everything multiple and exposed. They have the most doubt and the least unity. There is no difference between the impact of a bird's concave eye and the openings of the Hebrew language and the alphabet of the body. This eroticism has been noted in Francesco Clemente's work, and you accomplish it wisely without recourse to pastiche or parody. Your birds are vascular and bleed. They are part of the vast world of Israeli mosaic with clear discontinuities. In profile often, your birds are what Meyer Schapiro subscribed to in the semiotics of profile: they refuse mere frontality and become the shifting shifter seen in a poet's favorite words: it, he and she.

The foundation of the sacred texts of Judaism is the mountain. It is where the voice of God can be heard, and it is also the place for prophets and extremity and starvation and vision and law. There is every reason to suspect that this is the great example of the Hebrew sublime. The terror of mountains in the Western tradition actually supports this rhetoric of the mountain-God. It is not for nothing that we learn that the first walk in the mountains for pleasure, not vision, was with Petrarch, a paradox and permission. When we see the blue mountains of the Renaissance, all stippled and soft, we know that indeed we have come a long way toward the landscape of pleasure. But in the work of the mountain, we see something that Barnett Newman was raging toward in his tall sculpture, tall zips, so-called, and the mountainous sense of his "Stations." The false messiahs, all of them, must be tilted toward the mountain. Art history has many profane mountains, many attempts at the mountain: the mountains of Georgia O'Keeffe, the mountains of Caspar David Friedrich, the mountains of Brueghel, the mountains of the Southern Song masters, the fantastic mountains of the Chinese including the sacred Yellow Mountain with its disappearing mists, the mountain of Fuji climbed slowly by Matsuo Basho's snail, the rivers and mountains of the American Hudson River school, and the blue poles of Pollock, and the sacred mountains of the American Tribes, Sinai, Horev, Carmel, Mt. Eval, Mt. Nevo, Mt. Ararat, the Mt. of Olives, Mt. Zion. Mount Analogue, I call your gold impossible landscape.

What do we find in a mountain but the antonym of the mosaic? The floor we lie on like a flickering essay is perhaps the lowest, the humblest of aesthetic attempts. The personal essay may later be the Romantic crossing of the Alps. But in our tradition the mountain is the place of the irreducibly holy and the place of refuge. When the Chinese place a rock as a Buddhist brother, and the mountain as the scale of the Tao, they are closer to the Mosaic tradition. The rock is alive: bones of the earth they are called, kernels. We find our volcano-God the terrifying true beginning of *the* Sublime we are never able to bear. These are the mountains that Rilke tried to limn and could not, at the last, transform into something labile as lamentations. These are Rilke's petrified rocks and rage. But there is your further range.

Riverdale, New York, April 13, 2008

Dear Tsibi,

You may begin with the essay, but you end with the achieved mountain. In your mountains we find what all the branches, birds and blossoms have been tending. We find something stronger than barbed wire and prisons of the mind, something stronger than a single bewitching tree. In your mountains you have created finally a wall without windows, the place where the dove returns, the ship rests, and the wild God speaks, if we would hear. And Minimalism gave birth to this....

 We might start with the Sublime, according to Quintilian: "And God said, let there be light; and there was light." The intense immediacy that Newman desired and that Rothko achieved and that you have lent your hand to—this is the "one-ment" of the mountain according to our most severe rhetoricians, who are inside and behind and within you. So the blossoms predict this in their anguish, like a bush that is never consumed, in incandescent fury and obligation and law. And so all the fury of a blossom. Remember: the mountain is not a motif; it is the mode. The mountain is never beautiful; it is the terror of being one who cannot cross over or hear the future. The mountain is the macroscopic cosmos unadorned. The mountain of the lawgiver is a boundary and an architecture indeed without license. The mountain *disappears* us, like so many deaths. The flower is almost decorative; the mountain is the sublime face transformed into adamantine. The mountain is a Remembrance movement.

 As we approach the Mountain, some are aware that we are approaching the Analogue of René Daumal. The mountain is another way of beholding the Voice, whereas a flower is a part, the mountain is the anti-metonymic whole. There is the tradition of taking the part for the part. There is the nominalist path of taking nothing but that: Johns, Duchamp. But the mountain of Cézanne is the analogous distance that we will never cross except in ritual and disaster and hopelessness. Cézanne not only makes the apple his gift, but he returns to the giving Mountain, as if to say, one hundred times is not enough for me to understand the motif of majesty. Mount Sainte-Victoire is well-named, because it always defeats us. One inch, says Cézanne, and there is a new motif.

The bloom is alive in the blackness. A kind of monochrome predicts the worst nights on the valley side. Tsibi, your blossoms in the caliginous night are preparations for the magisterial darkness. Johns once told me that he was not involved in the eclipse of form; he was hoping for his own hand to signify that the presence of his body was his only guide: "My hand was there." Your work indicates that such heights are extravagant temptations, as in the architect of Ibsen, always ready to fall. Too much excess, even for the mountain, which was created in number, weights and measure.

I have observed in the poetry of a young Venezuelan, the call of the heights, the song of the mountain. This youthful poetry was always singing of the Fall from the mountain. This is the "falling upward" of Ludwig Binswanger, where the sick human in trouble has not yet learned to balance the things of the world, the world of relations and the world of the relations with ourselves.

Flowers are instances of our body and are not beyond the body. The mountain is an indication of where the body is in extremis and perhaps finally transcended. Kant was perched against, he wrote, the groveling religions. Mountains do not make us grovel, but they do lead by Joyce's "commodious vicus of recirculation" toward our recognition of frailty. The weak poet is also part of the contraction or zimzum of the tradition toward and including Barnett Newman's inverted, thus weak, Obelisk. Our mountains grow with difficulty, and we return because, like Cézanne, these changing inches give us entirely new homes.

Riverdale, New York, May 1, 2008

Tsibi,
Your flowers are black and are indeed sacrifices to the tradition of Van Gogh, who said he wanted to paint religious paintings but then went out and painted the night sky. You have decided, it appears to me, to go beyond your essays in your *terrazzos* of the floor, in your lattice patterns, toward a world that has the absolute minimum of adornment. The mountain is like a problem for the conceptual child. We know that the mountain is larger than us, but how do we make it larger than the canvas itself? You have solved this problem. You have

created, after a long preparation as the architect's son, an immanence of the mountain, a solitary home in the poet's phrase. You have gotten beyond the clichés of height, to what Pablo Neruda was trying for in his epic *The Heights of Machu Picchu*. Neruda was only marred by the clichés of Stalinism. You have gotten away from the too-facile poles of our politics today, a politics which might have seemed to be the ultimate barrier toward a large and enlarging art. You could have rested with your fundamental lament. Instead, you moved from the crippled symmetries of the flowers and terrazzos and the allusion to the seemingly never-ending wars surrounding and within—toward a mountain of reconciliations.

Riverdale, New York, June 1, 2008

Dear Tsibi,
There is always the danger of too much esotericism. You avoid it. Now I will. At my class at Cooper Union, you spoke of yourself being a *collection of pressures*. In each of your mountains, I feel this collection of pressures. You have said to me that the series of mountains may have begun years ago with a panoramic landscape series onto which you projected place names in different languages. Your accomplishment is not one of piety, but of the international fabric of art and history. Thus, Cézanne is inside these mountains as much as they are also the mountains of Moses. There is a certain pathos in realizing that we live in a world that is threatened by this learned aggregation.

The paintings are so large that they continue to allude to the gigantic, mural-like space of the Mexican painters and their students, the Abstract Expressionists. Your accidental touches may remind one of the intimate suggestions in Pollock's gigantic landscapes. Or are they universes? In your case, the mountains, with lattices sometimes added as delicate as shadows, traces or cobwebs, are shrouded in a snowy pallor. The gigantic scale is the scale that we find successfully held in only a few artists. One thinks of the verticals of Rothko and his Chapel; one knows the landscapes too big for the eye in Newman and Pollock, and one thinks of the narratives of Philip Guston and even of the new scale of German photographers and Jeff Wall, seemingly named for scale.

But your gigantic anti-landscapes are never infantile or illustrations. They are bounded by black, and they have the grave flatness of Cézanne, who wanted an art as durable as the art of the museums. The Poussinist in you makes these also works of geometry and drastic diagonals that balance through disequilibria. You have never given up the hand, and your most colorful collage-like terrazzos show this. There is a kitsch of reproducibility today, and there are artists who have worked to deny hand and gesture all their lives—our own grave salon of smoothness. But these mountains are wet and alive. Shadowed and present with an aura that can never be deleted, they are not in love with preordained geometry. They have an illogical fire about them. The accomplishment of Pollock, it is often suggested, is his combination of the mural size and the inclusion of intimate caress and touch. The philosopher Derrida concluded a long history of skeptical close readings with a series of volumes on radical refuge: the city of refuge, the forgiving of the unforgivable, the religion of paradoxical despair, and the eccentric relations of touch and sight. In your work, touch is once again a dominant theme and crisis. Your work is not for the color-blind, but it is tactile to the last inch of its largesse. It will accept the readings that might include it as narrative art. (I have been led by my own misreadings to see parts as sacred as a prayer-shawl, but this may be the ultimate misreading.)

The mountain suddenly stained with blue is an unforgettable nocturnal glimpse. There is the man who goes away, and the man who stays, says the unlucky Benjamin about storytelling. Are you the man who went away or the man who stays, with a collection of pressures, or both? These binary codes, these eruptive anti-semiotics, must be seen not as possible worlds, as the philosophers have it (describe a language without body words, for example), but impossible worlds like the impossible loves in *Hiroshima, Mon Amour*, in the shadow of catastrophes. Derrida stunned some of us by his late-in-life conversion, one might say, to love that is never buried if what we love is radical singularity. Painting is such radical singularity, with your touch and your seeing, and the mountain that is a place perhaps of awakening, not the place of danger and law. Here, the mountain, painted with mortal care, is the place of desire and concern. The painting, as Wallace Stevens almost has it, that took the place of a mountain. Thank you, dear Tsibi.

Shapiro at Columbia University, November 2006. Courtesy of Columbia University. Photo by Michael Dames.

Shapiro was by all accounts a born teacher. His interviews abound with gratitude to his own mentors and teachers—and with great enthusiasm for being "part of the relay." As a kid he taught poetry to his sisters, and in the last stages of Parkinson's disease, to his caregivers. He taught poetry-writing to schoolchildren in Bedford Stuyvesant, taught literature at Columbia University and Princeton University, Art History at William Patterson University, and for many years also taught an interdisciplinary course in aesthetics at the Irwin S. Chanin School of Architecture at the Cooper Union. "The Joy of Influence," (next page), is a madcap riff, not only on the wonders of reading, but on Shapiro's indefatigable passion for teaching.

The Joy of Influence

1.

My whole life has been haunted by the great pleasure of reading. I can remember no greater joy than seeing, for the first time, the refulgent poetry room of the Newark Public Library. Before that, I had read many books from the children's library near a Newark supermarket, drab and tarnished compared to the seeming infinity of the Newark Public Library—where when I was eleven, one librarian even knew which book of Roethke's to suggest. Rexroth, Patchen—I remember them as I met them in the adult wing. In the little rooms at Newark's big library—where Joe Ceravolo and Philip Roth both worked at different times—what I loved was the open stacks. I decided at around eleven or so to try to read every book of poetry in the library. All of this was a snare, a dream, and a delusion. But every day I would take home ten or more volumes—however many I could carry and was permitted—of poetry. It was in those stacks that I first read Koch's review that mentioned Ashbery's new techniques in "Europe." I can still quote from the review.

Libraries are referenced pejoratively by Kenneth in his poem "Fresh Air," even as he writes a poem that is a reading list: Supervielle, Jouve, Lorca—the names that are mentioned are part of the great poem he is preaching—the fresh poem that does not yield to "the myth, the Missus, and the midterms."

Cambridge Library I loved because it had a special section for new books, and one was permitted to eat there in some small way. I liked to

---

Bookshelf II: Contemporary Poets on Books that Shaped Their Art, edited by Peter Davis and Ted Koontz (Barnwood Press, 2008).

think of going in the morning and coming out as the last bell sounded.

When a communard burns down the library in a Hugo poem, there is a vexed stichomythia: "I don't read," says the communard.

It's easy to be seduced by a library like Harvard, which possesses such a treasure as Jacobson's recording of Mayakovsky's "intimate yell." What follows after hearing this hardly matters.

In my current neighborhood, there are few libraries that match the resources of my own. But my wife is an architect and does not want 10,000 books, or my dream of 20,000. Robert Rosenblum agreed with my dream of the complete research library—then added, "But we know this isn't possible, David, since every new subject implies a whole new shelf." That is true.

But I dreamed of a Borgesian library that would, on most occasions, be comparable to Meyer Schapiro's mind, say—of which Koch cackled: "They say that if Western Civilization is destroyed, Meyer could reconstruct it from his head in ten days." Meyer had a custom with his library that I continue in mine. He would say: "Take anything you want." I insisted that a signed Adorno not be given to me. One day he left me a mound of books and magazines including about 10 volumes by Origen. When I told a Greek scholar of this magnanimity, he said, "He has given me many of his Greek volumes, too."

Reading, reading lists! When [Robert] Motherwell asked Meyer for a reading list of Marx and Marxism, Meyer is said to have remonstrated: "Marxism is not a reading list, it is a way of life." An important truth to be kept in mind while assembling anthologies and encyclopedias.

One of the ways I feel I am being a decent teacher is to give a student the book *Safe Conduct*, which was Frank O'Hara's first present to me. I gave it back after it changed my life. He made no request. I kept, for almost 40 years, a French Theatre anthology that his roommate Joe Le Sueur had lent me. I gave it back at a poetry reading after Frank's death. "Aha," said Joe, "now I know where it was." Arthur A. Cohen got very upset if someone (not me) didn't return a library book from his private collection. After his death, his wife Elaine suggested I might like a collection of 2,000 or more poetry books. I knew my wife would disembowel me, so I gave the collection to Teachers and Writers

Collaborative where you can still see it. Arthur's library of 230,000 volumes, which included many rare copies of the Talmud and Hebraic pamphlets, was overwhelming. He gave me a Valéry from the Bollingen when I visited. There were poets who, when given these gifts, sold the book the next day. I was shocked, seriously shocked. I couldn't imagine back then that money might be more important than a book. A book seemed in those days like a Constable cloud study, for which one would gladly become homeless.

In my youth, I was denied comic books. I lived on Milton and Blake. My neighbors' kids seemed in heaven, because they could read about Scrooge and Donald and his nephews. But, but. My father's ideal was the serious reading of Lenin by 10, of Rhone history through early adolescence, gone over in endless walks around Weequahic Park, the place where I also told Allen Ginsberg to read more Ashbery. "But can you memorize it?" challenged Allen in regard to the poem "Rain" in *The Tennis Court Oath*. But before long he whispered: "Oh, it's like Alexander Pope. I get it."

He didn't.

Allen also loved reading lists.

Less agoraphobic than I used to be, I love the laughter of a cab driver at seeing a friend's library: "I notice," said the cabbie, "that you read all in one language?"

Francesco Pellizzi's father, a great translator of English sociology, never kept an encyclopedia in the house. But my father kept buying copy after copy of the 1911 edition of the *Encyclopedia Britannica*, for its Tovey on music and a little slice of Swinburne and Whitehead. I gave some of my copies to artists who loved the snake plate and other masterpieces of Victorian illustration.

2.

Whitehead formulated the joke well: There are 10 all-important books. The question is: What are they?

Here is a list I love: I tell my students to read everything Pound advises in *ABC of Reading*: Sappho, Corbiere, Rimbaud, Laforgue, etc. Then read everything he leaves out: the Romantics, Pindar at his bombastic best, etc., etc., etc. Eliot waffles on Milton many times, therefore it is useful to read the Metaphysicals Eliot loved and the Shelley he despised. This is an entire career. By 1964 I had read the masters Pound designated, but I believed by then in also doing something else: I learned to imitate each of these poets and translators. I have never believed in passive reading. Reading to me was a form of human sexuality and joy, as well as a science.

I would say the same thing of reading the Great Books, which I taught for something like a decade at Columbia. I believe in the lists from Plato to Cervantes to Dostoevsky and Virginia Woolf—but I always taught these things somewhat askew. (When I taught Rilke, Pasternak, and Mayakovsky at Columbia for architecture students I'd say, "Make a sestina by Bishop or Pound, Auden or Ashbery into the condition of a house ...") Any book in translation must be read in 10 to 20 different translations, if possible, and usually it is possible. Compare and contrast the original, if possible, with the questionable translations, mistranslations, fidelities, betrayals. I always taught Dante with 10 translations. I also taught *The Iliad* with 10 translations, and none left triumphant.

I hate those lists of the last 20 years that delete the Eastern philosophical classics. A very fine reading list is the evolving canon of the Columbia East Asian Studies program. I was depressed however when Burton Watson told me there were probably 100 great books left unpublished for every Chinese book (even of the *T'ang*) published.

Of course, one's reading list seems to languish with the linguistic palette. I feared that nothing better could come of my memorizing *The Waste Land* than to follow it linguistically toward Latin, Greek, German, etc. But Pound's advice is cruelly nice: It's not important to read Chinese, but it is important to WANT to read Chinese.

As Pound's Chinese get better, as we say, his translations lose almost everything. He translated *Cathay* as a man who knew not a single word of Chinese. But no translation has surpassed the perfection of that book, which I got published with Korean cuttings of Clemente's art. Sadly, the printers and editors left out the Anglo-Saxon poem that made this book replete.

My son would say while entering the Metropolitan, "What country are we going to today?" That was a useful momentum in my agoraphobic youth. My father disdained travel after the horrors of the Second World War. He said, "The streets there are not colored differently, David."

But they are.

When I am with someone I care about, I ask them by country and language: Do they have the best Tu Fu (William Hung) translation? Do they know Montale and Dina Campana and Leopardi's prose? Do they know all of Stein and all her circle? Do they know all the painting and sculpture of any given period so that books of poetry can be placed within art history? Then, as a musician: Do they know medieval music? Do they know the music that Shakespeare would have heard? Do they know Gould's version of "Sellinger's Round"? And the science and philosophy of the day? Do they know Islamic contributions?

In every country there are a variety of competing traditions. But do they also judge the art, music, and philosophy of a period with skepticism? With the sense of overlap that Meyer Schapiro points out in the work of the 7th and 8th centuries? And so the admonition must be: Find out the dogmas and contexts of every part of the list. Trilling said of the Humanities—one must read as if very, very near to the work, and one might read also as if very distant from the work. Therefore, he illuminates a truth (even in what might seem a mere fudging of directions): Formal and social analysis should be combined, even if at different times.

Teach Baudelaire to those who know no French.
Teach it to those who are French, indeed.
Teach Baudelaire in relation to the first Romantics.
Teach the prose poem and the Alexandrine tradition in Racine, say.
Teach architects Baudelaire and to draw in that condition.
Teach Baudelaire through a bad biography, such as the polemic Sartre.
Teach Baudelaire through Benjamin.
Teach Baudelaire through his own journal.
Teach Baudelaire through imitation, always.
Teach Baudelaire through Rimbaud's letter of the *Voyant*, May 15, 1871.

Teach Baudelaire with Housman and 1848.
Teach Baudelaire in relation to Marx, 1870, the Commune, 1968, the Global Year.
Teach Baudelaire through Meyer Schapiro's sense of Paris and the 19th century.
Teach Baudelaire through his own art criticism.
Teach Baudelaire in relation to Manet, and to Wagner, and to Daumier and caricature.
Teach Paris, the city, as a social fate.
Teach Rimbaud in Africa but also Baudelaire's desire to leave.
Teach the 20th century and its fateful re-readings of Rimbaud and Baudelaire.
Teach Eliot and Freud through Baudelaire and Paris of the pleasures.
Teach Baudelaire's reception in London, in Africa, in America.
Do the same for Whitman and his vistas: Eakins, pantheism, the East, The Brooklyn Museum, Egypt, operas, Lincoln, the Civil War, Allen Ginsberg, sexuality, empire, egoism, etc.

Thus does a single author becomes a lifetime of worldly pleasure, a radiant crystal at the no-center of an ever-increasing form of reading.

3.
I have some books that are my secret favorites. I don't like to tell too many people what these secrets are, but I might here.
—I love Blyth's *Zen in English Literature and Oriental Classics*. I love every page of its courtly, plain, philosophical subtleties and its wild if straightforward commentaries. Zen and Don Quixote. I was also inspired by the way an unexpected illustration ravishes the book.
—Yes, at age 12 to 13, I loved *The Lost Son* by Roethke, and not till August 6, 1962 did *The Tennis Court Oath* seem dry but better, noisier and killingly flat.
—I love John Cage's stories, which he tells better perhaps than anyone on an old Folkways record. Indeterminacies.
—My whole life has been spent going from one mystical text to another.

I have special relations with The Angel of Selesia, hardly ever translated without sentimentality.
—I love, as is said, every dot of Pasternak.
—I notice in my library, more than twenty volumes in many languages of these masters: Kafka and Proust—the two who dominate me. I have the sense that there is nothing else but Proust outside and Kafka inside—Proust's dissolute heavens and Kafka's starless interior and exteriors. And within Kafka I love Milena and her statements in Buber-Neumann's biography. Also, Benjamin and Scholem using Kafka in a last intimacy. They can't talk of much, but the poets in both are severe and radiant. And, yes, I think of Proust as Jewish and have not yet found that book about him. I love many others, from Celeste to Moss to Kristeva—funny company. But where is that book? Must I write it? *Proust the Jew* or *Proust and Judaism*.
—Secret books: Buson, Issa, Basho, of course, but where are the decent translations?
—All of Waley lures me, and like my friend, Larry Weider, I am obsessed by Lady Murasaki.
—I have read Hölderlin as the peak of Western civilization and its madness. I still love the white look of the Hamburger translations, even more than the so-called better translations.
—I like Mallarmé's *Recueil de "Nursery Rhymes"* in the French edition. I have learned so much from that book. Ashbery recently translated it, and I felt its secrecy passing.
—I spent many years opening the day by mistranslating Reverdy.
—My favorite songs: Shakespeare's madrigals. Sung by the countertenor—a poet told me countertenors make him giggle—but the great Deller doesn't make me giggle.
—And so I love the blues as steely poems: Sometimes I feel like a motherless child.
—When others were studying their Latin, I was entranced by Lucretius, and a possible Lucretian epic stole upon my dreams from age 15.
—How is the Tanakh to be read? And the New Testament? And the Gnostics? Slowly, with commentators like Rashi. With historians like

Pagels. With true mystics like Rav Kook. *The Sacred Books of the East* to coordinate this vast achievement.

—And next to that, my love of Darwin and the medical prose that influenced Flaubert.

4.

Well, if our reading list looks too normal and normative, what about this: All the neglected poets summarized in his Norton Lectures by Ashbery, from Roussel to David Schubert? I have been planning this as an anthology for years.

I feel proud that almost all the New York poets were published together for the first time in Padgett's and my anthology, *An Anthology of New York Poets*. Of course, I tried to get Barbara Guest into it, and Ron has taken complete responsibility, but I am sad that there are those who despise us for that deletion. They say: "But Frank Lima was in, and Clark Coolidge, and Ceravolo, and O'Hara in new ratios, and Ed Sanders is hardly even a NY School poet ..." I think we did a decent hole in their holy prison. For those who only say what was left out, I wince and go on. Of course, we left out hundreds, even thousands. Even Esenin in NY, and Mayakovsky!

Anyway, my reading list has no end.

Lionel Trilling didn't know Borges in 1968. He said: "Who is this Borges?" He did not know Vallejo. He did not know South African writers. I was appalled, but I am pleased that now Columbia is teaching a much more, as they say, diverse reading list.

It's not that any single author will save you. But it is on the other hand true that a single author at the right time may save you. That is why one must read Chekhov many times, and hear him presented many times, in many different countries. England taught me how great Chekhov was. Nothing else had done this.

Just as one Palladian or Corbusier tour may convince one, one has to see—no matter how limited—each Shakespeare play done a hundred different ways in many languages. I am not against reading Shakespeare; I've done so since birth. But one must also see him as producer, director, and lightning of the theatre. O, for a stage of fire!

So reading lists must be balanced by Beethoven quartets, by the philosophers of logical positivism my uncle forced upon me when he thought I was reading, at 13, too much Nietzsche! He said: "Nietzsche is not philosophy. Read Quine, Carnap, Ayer." I did. That was perhaps the slap in my face that I needed, but most of all it led me to Wittgenstein of whom I now own more books than any other author except for Pasternak and Stevens. The writing of poetry for me has been through Mozart, Bach, Stevens, Pasternak, and a few others. Of course, there is Tolstoy, and I have had to read everything twice in different translations.

I have learned from Isaiah Berlin, whom I used to think was merely a Tory. Have I become more Tory than the Tory in Berlin? No, I simply still love Herzen and where he leads.

For some years Hegel's *Phenomenology* built up in me a lust for German idealism. Also, I kept Kant nearby, as illuminating as I could wish. The same for Schopenhauer. And the great aphorists, Joubert and Chamfort.

All the surrealists have passed through me. Man Ray's film *The Starfish*. But after all, I learned from meeting Max Ernst and wondering what his reading was.

I have also learned from Jasper Johns, an exigent reader, who taught me to pursue Kawabata's black and white. He dedicated a painting to Kawabata's translator, Seidensticker, who did not seem to understand it. Imagine. I learned from Kawabata and read, again and again, every syllable of him I could find. I give his work to certain students. Kenneth Koch told me he learned from me about Schklovsky, Benjamin, Braudel, and Kawabata.

I recall two girls in a bookstore. One said she had taken Greek to learn the quotations in *The Waste Land*, and now that she knew what they meant, it was all so simple. I could not avoid repeating: "But isn't it wonderful that a poem led you to a whole language, to a country, to an empire, to a world?"

Then again, it may be that the best thing an old poet can do is to point to the so-called best without calling it that. At a certain moment, Koch gave a friend the strange Raymond Roussel, after asking a bookseller which book an erudite friend wouldn't already know. Koch steered many people to Supervielle. And furthermore, there may be one wonderful Supervielle translation in the works. If one has read only the poor Desnos translations, all may seem lost. When Ron Padgett translated Cendrars, Koch told me: "He's made it a little better than Cendrars."

Among all the books in my library, I keep a few since my thirteenth year on my desk: A dictionary (the *OED*), the print now too small for my eyes; a Shakespeare complete, which has become more of a sculpture than my many other Shakespeares. I keep a small dictionary from which many poems have profited. And sometimes a practical item: a *Chicago Manual* I don't believe in and the Hebrew Bible my grandmother gave me.

5.

You may now Google a hundred reading lists. Rarely are they utterly wrong. It's usual to say, "Don't believe in a canon but follow the dispute." I see no reason why one can't study Cézanne and Duchamp, even when they seem part of a great divorce. And the art criticism of Frank O'Hara rests uneasily with the criticism of, say, Michael Fried. But that's fine. I expect anyone who is a reader will read aesthetic enemies and love it. One can read early and late de Chirico, and Tolstoy early and late. One might want to know the libretti of Wagner, and a hundred versions, but one also wants to study German anti-Semitism in a few books including Arendt, and then the controversy on Arendt.

Among anthropologists, there is an entirely interesting list that extends from the *Popol Vuh* to Octavio Paz on Mexican art, to the codices of the Aztecs. All of this must be read, along with the anthology of masks, here and abroad. This illuminates Lévi-Strauss and is illuminated by him. What would we do without the anthropologists who are also, among other things filmmakers (Mead), thinkers, and translators?

In reading, I agree in part with Jacobson, but I believe books, great books, are inexhaustible, because they are dominated at different times by addresser/addressee, context, contact and code, and the axes of the aesthetic are so shifting and tectonic that most of our arguments are not fair even in the Aristotelian sense. One man loves the Freudian interpretation; another is more interested in Marxist analysis of reception. My pluralist spin is that all of these axes function like notes in an octave and are, of course, inexhaustible, almost by definition.

Remember the student who was told that music can't be heard the first time? And so reading must after all, become re-reading. Dupee told me he was going to write one day a great book in homage to reading. Isn't this what great criticism—Auerbach, Curtius, Spitzer, Schapiro, Tovey, Alfred Einstein in music—is? Isn't rereading an ode to reading the substance of so many books? And so I conclude that no one should conclude, and it becomes obvious over the years that we do not know exactly where to begin or end our reading,

"Memorize many poems," said my mother, "they will be useful to you in prison." Even the bad anthologies I have tried to memorize. Poetry may sometimes be memorized easily because it is a machine for memorizing. It is harder to memorize Turgenev. But it is not only useful to go back to touchstones and memorize but also to memorize the patterns and shifting structures, the fields and frames that Schapiro spoke of in relation to the ingressions (from Whitehead). The musical: restless ingressions that make form's fate.

The writing reader.

The reader writing.

Writing in bed.

Reading in the dark.

The great pleasure of finding a poem of mine translated by an architect, a composer, another composer. A poem that then went to Prague, where the brother of the suicide Jan Palach—of whom I wrote in tears in February 1969—hugged me and thanked me from his whole family. But I was only one part of the relay.

PS:

—Read everything Meyer Schapiro ever wrote on art—medieval, Romanesque, modern, and theory, and then read everything he alludes to in citations and generous footnotes.

—Koch memorized Borges, he was so in love with his work. Borges seemed to change toward me when he realized I had memorized his prose.

—You can't learn enough. Meyer: "When you use your brain, you do not use it up."

—Don't tell people what they can't read. "Do what thou wilt"—Rabelais.

—One poet may hide another.

—"If the little stars go out," said a wise old poet to me when I was 12, "then all will be dark."

—The so-called minor poets are wonderful. Without them, no Cavafy, for example.

—Don't banish any poets, or country. Watch out for racist theories of excellence. Even Ruskin said Asia had no art. Beware!

—Don't make the Renaissance your center, or even Western art.

—Western art is imbricated with the East. Think of Van Gogh without Japan.

—Think of Japan without Fenellosa.

—Learn languages through songs: German through Piaf. And through poetry and/or The Bible. The children in the garden learn the language playfully through songs while the ambassador learns nothing and doesn't mind.

—Kill no one whose language and poetry you do not know thoroughly and backward.

—The index of a great country is the translations and homage it bestows upon other nations' arts.

—The only reason to believe in heaven and other planets: so much more reading to do!

—In love with reading, one tries writing. Dazzled by the difficulties, one goes back to reading.

—But at a certain moment, these readings and writings marry each other in a faithful faithless climax.

—"The Song of Songs" was accorded sacred strength in a strange canon—Be that strange.

—Literal, allegorical, symbolical, anagogical—learn to read and remain perplexed.

PPS:

Of course, we can always think of those poets who have particularly influenced us, the reading list that is simply or not so simply the practitioner's code. A kind of list by Pound or Zukofsky, and the history of writing shares this sense of tradition. The Chinese painter told me he was influenced by Nature, Tradition and Heart. He was not going to list one master; one tree, say, or one author's mere originality. I have learned to imitate the voices of Pound, Stevens, Thomas, Cummings, Gielgud's Shakespeare, Auden, Ashbery, Koch, O'Hara: all these are voices I could "do," for a while. I would like to say that among the moments in my life I'll never forget are those when I recited works by heart to my family—or recited, say, Kenneth's poem "Permanently" at his memorial. My students know I love "The Burial of the Dead" when I recite it and teach it without a book. One thinks of the Talmud scholars who pass their "pin" test; that is, they know the whole passage from being touched by a pin anywhere. The violinist proves that he knows better than the composer what the notes are. To change a voice is to change a world. I remember when a poem I thought was loud was recited quietly by Koch and suddenly I under stood qualities in grey I had not understood before. Jasper Johns changed my poetry more than almost any poet. I wanted my poems to be as melancholy as his objects, and his critical voice changed my sense of poetry. So our reading list must include *The Letters of van Gogh*, *The Old Masters of Belgium and Holland* by Fromentin, *The Journals of Delacroix*, the aphorisms of Braque, the statements, so rare, of Jasper Johns. We must transpose him. Take a reading list. Do something to it. Do something else to it. Memorize something every day, and then even when you are waiting for a bus, you will be able to play "Silence" by Cage or recite the poem you love. Like Buson's "The sound of the bell / as it leaves the bell." Or: "One candle lights another candle / evening twilight." Thousands of memorized poems, and you will endure all the glut and exile of the world.

You Are The You

You are the you in this poem,
Mon amour.
Harrisburg mon amour.
Boats break.

So-and-so asked me,
To whom does the you in your poem
Refer.
I said, Are you feeling well, So-and-so.

I can't believe I said
It. So sue me.
I said, It's the beloved, So-and-so.
Oh is that all.

Well, I said, she wouldn't think
It was so little.
To look up into your face
Is like looking into the devastated stars.

Lights of all kinds I traced,
You and you and you and you.
You are the you of this poem, mon amour.
Boats break.

—David Shapiro, *After a Lost Original* (The Overlook Press, 1994).

Acknowledgments

David Shapiro died of complications from Parkinson's Disease on May 4, 2024, soon after the completion of *You Are The You*. David had been thrilled about the book's forthcoming publication and, needless to say, he was as grateful as I am to all those who helped bring it about. Thanks go, first and foremost, to David Lehman, who talked me into this project seven years ago and has helped out with advice and encouragement ever since. David and I were also immensely grateful to Don Share for his astute literary and editorial assistance as the book took shape. His meticulous perusal of the manuscript and subsequent insights and suggestions have been invaluable. Crucial too was a lengthy email correspondence with Eugene Richie about various publication issues. Thanks to Joanna Fuhrman for bringing our attention to Robert Archambeau's superb prose series at MadHat Press and for other help and advice. Robert Archambeau gave this project vital support early on and offered kind editorial guidance as I transcribed the book to a digital format. It has also been a pleasure to work with Marc Vincenz, MadHat's founder and executive editor. He and his team were wonderfully helpful, going out of their way to find creative solutions to a variety of thorny issues.

As the book progressed, David and I were especially grateful to his wife Lindsay, an icon of patience and thoughtful intelligence throughout. Lindsay joined David and me on numerous telephone calls, talking through possibilities and offering practical ideas and endless support and wisdom. Thanks also to my husband Bob Blumberg, a stalwart help; ever-judicious, kind and encouraging.

David and I took great pleasure in dedicating *You Are The You* to Kenneth Koch. David Shapiro, David Lehman and I all studied with Kenneth at Columbia and gained tremendously from his extraordinary teaching and friendship. Kenneth was an early and unstinting admirer of Shapiro's work, poetry and prose, and he would be delighted to see this book come out. We are also grateful to the editors of the publications where the works in this volume originally appeared, sometimes in slightly different versions and/or with different titles. Publication details are given on the bottom of the first page of each piece.

Biographies

DAVID SHAPIRO grew up in New Jersey, a violin and literary prodigy in an artistic family. At 10, he decided to become a poet. He left high school after his junior year and studied at Columbia University with the poet Kenneth Koch and the art critic Meyer Schapiro. He published *January* (Holt, Rinehart & Winston, 1965), the first of his eleven books of poetry, as an 18-year-old Columbia undergraduate. Awarded a Kellett Fellowship upon graduation, he earned an MA from Clare College, Cambridge University, before returning to Columbia for his PhD. His other books of poetry include *A Man Holding an Acoustic Panel* (Overlook Press, 1971), nominated for a National Book Award; *New and Selected Poems* (Overlook Press, 2013), and *In Memory of an Angel* (City Lights, 2017). He also coedited with Ron Padgett *An Anthology of New York Poets* (Random House, 1970).

In addition, Shapiro was a prolific prose writer and a respected art historian and critic. Associated early on with the New York School of Poets, he wrote the first monograph on the poet John Ashbery (Columbia University Press, 1979). His other books include *Jim Dine: Painting What One Is* (Harry N. Abrams, 1981); *Jasper Johns: Drawings,1954–1984* (Harry N. Abrams, 1984); and *Mondrian: Flowers* (Harry N. Abrams, 1991).

Shapiro taught literature at Columbia University, Princeton University and Brooklyn College and was a tenured art historian at William Paterson University. For twenty years, he also taught an interdisciplinary course in aesthetics at the Irwin S. Chanin School of Architecture at the Cooper Union. He translated extensively and collaborated with Rudy Burckhardt on three films. His honors include a poetry grant from the Foundation for Contemporary Arts; the 1977 Morton Dauwen Zabel Award from the American Academy of Arts and Letters; fellowships from the Bread Loaf Writers' Conference, the Graham Foundation, the Ingram Merrill Foundation, the NEA and the NEH, as well as the 2018 'T' Space Poetry Award. Shapiro died of complications from from Parkinson's disease on May 4, 2024.

KATE FARRELL, a poet, grew up in Southern Pines, NC. She graduated from Columbia University Phi Beta Kappa with a degree in English and Comparative Literature. Farrell was Kenneth Koch's co-teacher in the American Nursing Home poetry workshops that led to Koch's book *I Never Told Anybody*. Her seven books include two coauthored by Koch: *Sleeping on the Wing, An Anthology of Modern Poetry with Essays on Reading and Writing*

(Random House), a poetry handbook widely used in high school and college classrooms, and *Talking to the Sun, An Illustrated Anthology of Poetry for Young People* (Henry Holt), a teaching anthology illustrated by artworks from the Metropolitan Museum. She was also Koch's writing assistant for a dozen years. Farrell has taught at Columbia University and in the New York State Poets in the Schools Program, and she acted for a decade with the literature-oriented New York Art Theatre, playing lead roles in such venues as Joe Papp's Public Theater and the Minor Latham Playhouse at Barnard College. Her work has appeared in numerous journals, including *Poetry*, *Harvard Review*, the *Manhattan Review*, and several editions of *Best Spiritual Writing*, and a collection of her poetry, *Visiting Night at the Academy of Longing*, was published by Lavender Ink. Her essay on the work of the environmental sculptor Patrick Dougherty accompanies James Florio's photographs in *Sticks*, forthcoming from Radius Books in 2025.

DAVID LEHMAN was born in New York City. A graduate of Stuyvesant High School and Columbia University, he spent two years at Clare College, Cambridge, as a Kellett Fellow. Upon his return to New York, he worked as Lionel Trilling's research assistant and earned his PhD at Columbia with a thesis on prose poems. Lehman launched *The Best American Poetry* series in 1988. He edited *The Oxford Book of American Poetry*. *The Morning Line* is the most recent of his poetry collections; his prose books include *One Hundred Autobiographies: A Memoir* and *Signs of the Times: Deconstruction and thebFall of Paul de Man*. In 2010 he received the Deems Taylor Award from the American Society of Composers, Authors, and Publishers (ASCAP) for *A Fine Romance: Jewish Songwriters, American Songs*. Lehman lives in New York City and in Ithaca, New York.

www.ingramcontent.com/pod-product-compliance
Lightning Source LLC
Chambersburg PA
CBHW031313160426
43196CB00007B/510